SCANDINAVIA

I COPENHAGEN: The Baroque Church of Our Saviour still dominates the east of the town

From a lithograph by Heinz Hansen (c. 1850)

SCANDINAVIA

SWEDEN, DENMARK
AND NORWAY

By

ERIC DE MARÉ

LONDON
B. T. BATSFORD LTD.

First published, 1952

MADE AND PRINTED IN GREAT BRITAIN BY
WILLIAM CLOWES AND SONS, LIMITED, LONDON AND BECCLES, FOR THE PUBLISHERS
B. T. BATSFORD, LTD.
LONDON : 15 NORTH AUDLEY STREET, W.I AND MALVERN WELLS, WORCESTERSHIRE
NEW YORK : 122 EAST 55TH STREET   103 TORONTO : ST. CLAIR AVENUE WEST
SYDNEY : 156 CASTLEREAGH STREET

CONTENTS

ACKNOWLEDGMENT

THE Author thanks the Swedish Institute for Cultural Relations in London for help in obtaining photographs and for reading the manuscript on Sweden to check matters of fact; also Arkitekt Preben Hansen of Copenhagen for reading and checking the manuscript on Denmark; and Herr Fredrik Wulfsberg, Cultural Attaché to the Norwegian Embassy, for doing the same to the manuscript on Norway. He also wishes to thank the Architectural Press for permission to use extracts from his articles which have appeared, or will be appearing, in *The Architectural Review* and *The Architects' Journal*. He acknowledges the great amount of information obtained from *Sveriges Konsthistoria* (History of Swedish Art), by Andreas Lindblom, 1944.

The Publishers thank the following photographers and institutions whose work appears in these pages :

Akademisk Arkitektförening, for fig. 62; Almquist and Cöster, Hälsingborg, for fig. 32; J. Anderson, for fig. 5; Eric de Maré, A.R.I.B.A., for figs. 2, 12, 16–19, 23–26, 28–31, 36–38, 42, 43, 46–51, 56, 59, 61, 63–66, 69–76, 78, 88, 90–95, 97–99; A. Granqvist and Co., Skara, for fig. 13; Carlo Harboe, Hillerødgade, for fig. 53; K. Harstad, Oslo, for fig. 84; A. F. Kersting, F.R.P.S., for figs. 79, 82, 96 and 100; N. Lagergren, for fig. 15; Landslaget for Reiselivet i Norge, for figs. 85–87 and 101; Sam. Lindskog, Örebro, for figs. 4 and 8; Mittet and Co., Oslo, for fig. 81; Nordiska Museet, for figs. 21, 22, 34, 35 and 45; Nordisk Rotogravyr, Stockholm, for fig. 39; Normanns Kunstførlag, for figs. 86 and 89; C. G. Rosenberg, for fig. 20; R.I.B.A. Library, for fig. 10; G. Svaknström, for fig. 6; the Swedish Institute, for figs. 11 and 41; the Swedish Tourist Traffic Association, for figs. 3, 14, 33, 40 and 44; Turist-føreningen for Danmark, for figs. 54, 55, 57, 58, 60, 67, 68 and 77.

The Publishers thank Abr. Lundquist & Co., Stockholm, for permission to reproduce the music on pages 54 and 55; Arkitekts Olaf Platou, Arne Pedersen and Reidar Lund for permission to reproduce illustrations appearing in *Norwegian Architecture*; Arthur Reader & Co., for loaning the original from which the jacket is reproduced; W. T. Spencer & Co., for loaning the originals from which the frontispiece and fig. 9 are reproduced; and Kartografiska Institutet, Stockholm, for permission to reproduce fig. 27. Thanks are also due to Aalborg Domsogns Menighedsråd for the drawing on page 194; to John Murray & Co. for that on page 64; to the National Gallery, Oslo, for that on page 208; to Hasse W. Tullbergs Förlag, for that on page 255; and to Wahlström and Widstrands Förlag, for that on page 80.

NOTES ON PRONUNCIATION

The following sounds will help the reader to pronounce the names in this book more or less correctly :

a as in *hut*
ar and *ah* as in arch
e as in *hell*
i as in *eel*
o as in *fool* (e.g. *stor*)
o also as in *stock*

u as in *cur*
ä as in *heaven*
å as in *awe*
ö as in *earn*
ø is like *ö*
g as in *yes*

LIST OF ILLUSTRATIONS

LIST OF ILLUSTRATIONS

LIST OF ILLUSTRATIONS

LINE DRAWINGS IN THE TEXT

THE TOWN HALL, LIDKÖPING,
IN ITS ORIGINAL STATE
(*See page* 98)

I

Introduction

"ANY traveller who wishes to write a book about foreign parts should decide, before even he embarks upon his voyage, on the purpose which his work will serve and the type of reader for whom it is intended." So wrote Mr. Harold Nicolson when reviewing a travel book. This sound advice has been followed in preparing this work. The purpose has been to convey in one volume as clear and detailed a picture as possible of Sweden, Denmark and Norway, both past and present. The reader is presumed to be one of normal intelligence, who is interested in everything and wishes to obtain a broad knowledge of these three countries before and during a pleasure journey to them—one who desires guidance on what to seek there of beauty or interest in landscape, architecture, general culture and national character. Perhaps in time, too, this volume will serve to bring back memories, now and then, of an enjoyable voyage to the North.

The days of old Baedeker are over, and the reader will not expect or receive here such practical knowledge as the traveller of the 1880's could obtain—that the Grand Hotel at Molde, for example, is "finely situated at the E. end of the town, R. $1\frac{1}{2}$–$2\frac{1}{2}$ kr., L. 25 ø., B. $1\frac{1}{4}$, D. 2, S. $1\frac{1}{2}$, 'pens', incl. L. and baths, 6 kr.; English spoken", or that Ystad is a "busy seaport with 7800 inhab." and has an English vice-consul called Mr. H. Nilsson. Yet this book will try to give as much information as possible.

What information should be given? It would be impossible to tell all about one country, let alone three, in some 80,000 words. Selection is necessary, and selection implies personal choice. History has been wisely described as being nothing but anecdotes, or a fable agreed upon, and so, in a way, must be the description of a country, created as it is by all the infinitely complex interlacings of geography, climate, history, economics and all the irrational deeds and vagrant ideas of men. Only an impression, through personal selection, of the Scandinavian countries can therefore be evoked here.

The stress will be on architecture, not merely because that is the author's special subject, but because through the mistress art we can most clearly discern a country's culture, history and *Weltanschauung*. Architecture, indeed, reveals a nation more clearly than any other art, especially if the word is used in its widest sense to encompass such things as structural engineering, man-made landscape in town and country, and street furniture from lamp-posts to litter bins. It is, after all, the visible environment, whether consciously created or not, which provides the most accurate and detailed source of information about a nation and its outlook on life. Its will-to-form, so to speak, is the outward realization of its desire to shape life in a particular way. Culture in its widest, deepest sense, spelt with a small *c* and not with a capital *K*, is a vague thing and hard to define, but a good working definition might be that culture is the conferment of specific forms on a civilization—especially visual, architectonic forms.

In these jaded days of easy travel and of camera journalism the travel writer cannot hope to impress the reader as did Marco Polo or Hakluyt with wonderful tales of discovery. We now travel rather to re-discover in three dimensions what we have already seen in two and to find new beauties which others have been unable to perceive. We travel also to compare one country with another and so perhaps, through widened personal horizons, to learn how to enrich our own ways of living.

The Scandinavian countries have much to teach the world in the art of living. This writer is in a fairly fortunate position to reveal why this is so. Though born and bred in England, his blood is almost entirely Swedish—almost, because several drops come from one of those Scottish families who have settled and prospered in Gothenburg, and several drops, too, from the French Huguenots who fled to Sweden in the seventeenth century. Mixed blood like this has the advantage that it is likely to produce a cosmopolitan, objective outlook. Apart from this, the writer knows the countries well by direct experience—in particular Sweden, whither he first travelled at the impressionable age of seven. Then he enjoyed a brief spell at a Swedish state school and a barefooted riot under the eye of a tolerant grandmother in a small country town set among the lakes and pinewoods of West Gotland. Later came many holiday visits to Sweden (often reached through Denmark), a long cycle tour as a student across the three countries, a spell in a Stockholm architect's office, a canoe trip from Gothenburg to Stockholm and a journey by more orthodox methods of travel over large tracts of Denmark and Norway.

Your guide's whole youth was spent in a Swedish atmosphere—in a London household run with Swedish customs and associating closely with the social life of London's Swedish colony of merchants, tailors, journalists, masseurs, diplomats. Highlights of this life were such ceremonial events as the annual Goose Feast

2 STOCKHOLM: One of the pair of lions which guard the Royal Palace

3 SWEDISH LANDSCAPE : Forestland and floating pine logs in Norrland

4

held by a kind of esoteric mutual-aid society called the *Berserks and Vikings*, when winged Norse helmets adorned the polished pates of modern burghers, an anachronism which seemed to grow less absurd as the fumes of snaps and punsch lifted off the mental accretions of eleven centuries. There was the annual church bazaar in aid of the Swedish Sailors' Home when pretty girls dressed in their grandmothers' bright peasant costumes sold you gingerbread goats or a piece of shining Orrefors glass. There was the charming ceremony of Christmas Eve when the blinds were drawn on the grey, suburban scene and the candle-lit Christmas tree began to stir deep pagan memories of the mysterious northern forests. Memories come back, too, of a small figure, writhing in an agony of self-consciousness and dressed in the yellow leather breeches, white stockings and red tassels of Dalecarlia, being dragged through the London fog towards the horrors of an organized folk dance. Memories of people—old Baker Anna who would call with a great basket on her arm to sell sweet, exotic breads to the epicurean London Swedes. There was old Stina, strong as a horse, who came to scrub the floors and to tell in her queer, husky, lilting voice (surely from the shores of Lake Siljan) tales of the trolls and princesses, bears and wolves of Nordic folklore. Another memorable being was a tall, dignified cook from Bohuslän, skilful in her art, whom one learned very soon, as Proust would say, to treat with those marks of respect necessary to her moral well-being. At no time was she more stately than when she entered the bedroom at a surprisingly early hour of one winter morning in flowing white gown, vine-leaves in her hair and crowned with a ring of lighted candles, to proffer cakes and coffee—*Santa Lucia Rediviva*, personification of returning light.

They were simple, kindly folk these London Swedes of childhood and typical of their countrymen as a whole. Dumb Swede, the Americans say, meaning presumably *dum* (Swedish for stupid). But he is never that. Naïve perhaps, but he (the Dane and Norwegian also) is shrewd enough; when he emigrates he always falls on his feet, adapting himself by hard work, honesty and good sense, whether he settles in a capital city of the Continent or on the wide spaces of that other Sweden known as Minnesota, U.S.A.

Let us now visit the Scandinavian on his home ground. How shall we proceed? *Scandinavia* this book is called and should therefore rightly include Finland and Iceland, but some elimination in an already over-crowded canvas is necessary. Finland and Iceland are farther away from Europe than the other three countries and are less frequently visited. They will therefore be entirely eliminated here. Nor will the Lapps be considered, for they, too, are far away and perhaps more romantic when kept at a hazy distance than when seen in close reality. The Lapps are, nevertheless, an interesting people to the ethnologist. The ways of the Scolt Lapps are especially so—that gentle, telepathic tribe which is believed to have come from Tibet. In *The Enchanted Forest* Mr. Robert Crottel has told some of their delightful folk tales which bear none of that sense of darkness and fear which characterize most of the legends of the North. To the Scolts all nature is loving and lovable; even the wolf, so deep and terrifying an ideogram of the unconscious to other people, is to them an "interpreter of the forest" who through the night, filled with the breathing of snow, "sings for those who cannot give voice to their longings . . . the saddest and the hungriest of them all."

We of the industrial west, who have been so drastically severed from the old intimacy with nature and who try with pathetic yearning to re-establish that old contact in our suburban gardens or with rod and line by some sullied stream, find the Lapps a peculiarly attractive people—until a closer view reveals that perhaps something can be said for hot water on tap. Even so the bowels stir to hear the old Lapp song:

> Reindeer wander; so must all Lapp folk.
> Farther wander stars in Heaven's yoke.
> Wand'ring, wand'ring; I shall not repine,
> But go stoutly; so free life be mine.

Sweden, Denmark and Norway will here be treated separately both for clarity's sake and because, in spite of their ties, they are remarkable rather for their differences than their similarities. First a solid framework of general facts will be constructed to which we can later add the covering of direct experience. Then we shall depart on a tour through each country following the course of the author's own travels in the past. In Sweden the journey will be unorthodox but thereby the more revealing, for it will bring us into that close contact with the intimate lives of the people which cannot easily be made in daily wanderings from an international hotel or from the seat of a speeding luxury coach. In Sweden we shall travel from coast to coast most of the way by canoe across the lake-spattered midlands—a journey which will provide a typical cross-section through the heart of the country. In Denmark we shall move in no planned travel agent's way but stop when and where we will. In Norway we shall do the same, though there we shall be largely restricted by nature to the limited transport routes of the valleys and the fjords.

We shall, of course, spend some time exploring the three capitals —Stockholm, Copenhagen, Oslo—the nodes of culture, commerce and administration. Typical provincial towns will be visited and also the three lively ports which look towards the western world— Esbjerg, Gothenburg and Bergen.

Finally we shall sort out our impressions in an attempt to create some kind of significant pattern from what we have seen—to discover what these three small, clean democracies have to offer, both by commission and omission, in the struggle towards the Good Life—what, in fact, they *mean* to humanity in these violently changing years, so full of despair, so full of hope, years that would have been unbelievable only three-quarters of a century ago when the American explorer Paul Du Chaillu toured the North.

In his "Land of the Midnight Sun", Du Chaillu then wrote: "I tarried awhile in the city (of Falun), in order to present my letter of introduction to Herr de Maré, the Governor of the province (of Dalecarlia), who received me with the unpretending but none the less earnest Swedish manner, and expressed much pleasure at meeting me before his departure, on a vacation, for the southern part of the country. . . . 'When do you intend to start?' inquired he. 'Immediately after my visit to you,' said I. 'We cannot let you go without taking a quiet Sunday dinner with us tomorrow,' he said, adding, 'it will give me time to write some letters of introduction for you; and then we can talk quietly together, and I may perhaps give you some good advice.'"

In the way of his worthy grandfather but in a different world, this writer now talks quietly to you in the unpretending but none the less earnest Swedish manner, and so presents his own letters of introduction to Scandinavia.

SWEDEN

S/ EDEN.

II

Land and Livelihood

THE most curious thing about Sweden in a geographical sense
is its shape. If you place a pin on its most southerly point and
then with a great heave swivel it right round, its northern tip
will reach for 978 miles right down to Naples. Yet at its widest
from the Skagerak to the Baltic it is only 310 miles. Sweden is, in
fact, the longest and nearly the narrowest country in Europe, so
that Turkey is nearer to Malmö than is the North Cape. The head
of the country stretches nearly 200 miles above the Arctic Circle
lining up with Alaska and the south of Greenland. Its south lines
up with Newcastle and is not far above Hamburg (p. 16).

In spite of this long strip of some 173,000 square miles (nearly
twice the size of England), the climatic differences between north
and south, though considerable, are less extreme than one would
suppose. No doubt the relative nearness of the coast at every point,
the large forests and the prevailing westerly winds off the Gulf
Stream have much to do with this and make life tolerable in parts
which might otherwise be almost uninhabitable on account of the
cold.

In this area live some 7,000,000 people very unevenly dispersed
at an average of 40 per square mile to make it one of the most
sparsely populated in Europe. Stockholm alone contains a tenth of
the population. Southern Sweden holds 290 people a square mile,
in sharp contrast to Lapland where each inhabitant has a space of
about a square mile to himself. About 40 per cent of the population
now lives in the 125 towns, of which only 33 hold more than
20,000. A few minorities live peacefully and without problems—
10,000 Lapps up north, 30,000 Finns, 6,500 Jews and about 700
gipsies. (Some of these last the writer has been surprised to meet
strolling arrogantly through the streets of Vänersborg, well dressed,
the women in bright flowing clothes like saris, and apparently of
exceptionally pure blood, for one of the women at least had the
clean-cut features and small beak nose of a Hindu temple goddess.)

Purity of race has been shown of recent years to be something of a
myth, but so far as the term has any meaning the Scandinavians,
especially the Swedes and Norwegians, are an old, pure race, the
fair hair, blue eyes and tall stature being those of the original
Stone Age settlers who followed the retreating glaciers northwards

some 4,000 years ago. Their origin is uncertain, but they may have been descended from the so-called Iberians of the Mediterranean. This fair-haired type (28) is by no means ubiquitous and one meets many people with brown hair and dark eyes in Sweden. Since the Middle Ages Germans, Dutchmen and Walloons have settled in the country, especially in the mining districts. Many Finns have trickled in from the north and in the seventeenth century migrated to the central provinces. Some Jews came, particularly in the eighteenth century, and in the south, when Gothenburg was founded in the seventeenth century, Scotsmen arrived and more Dutchmen and Walloons. French Huguenots, too, have added their quota, while in the last fifteen years has come perhaps the greatest immigration of all, refugees seeking asylum from the tyrannies —mostly Balts, Finns, Danes and Norwegians. Of these some 87,000 had settled permanently by 1950.

A large part of the surface of Sweden is older than any other in the world—the primeval granite and gneiss which so often reveals itself with that characteristic smoothness and rotundity produced by the action of the Ice Age glaciers and the weathering of un-countable years. Because of this rock the land does not generally make for good farming except where the post-glacial deposits have formed, as in the loamy plains of the south and in the moraine lands which lie between the rocky outcrops farther north and on the littoral of the Gulf of Bothnia. There exists some sandstone and limestone, as the old buildings of central Sweden and of the islands of Gotland and Öland show, and some marble also, notably the lovely green variety which can often be seen as decorative slabs in many modern buildings. The primeval granite itself, especially the black kind, is a useful building and paving material valued both in Sweden and abroad. We shall find strange evidence on our cross-country journey of the great age of the land, for it shows that during the melting of the ice cap between 15,000 and 5,000 years ago, large parts of Sweden, and indeed most of Finland, were under water. Then the Baltic flowed into the North Sea right across the country.

In prehistoric times the country was roughly divided into three main regions: Götaland in the south, the land of the Goths, or *Goutoi* as Ptolemy, the Greek geographer, named them in A.D. 150; Svealand in the centre, the land of the Svear, Swedes, or *Suiones* as Tacitus called them in A.D. 98; Norrland in the north, which takes up 60 per cent of the whole area of the country. Later on the twenty-three provinces were formed. Though these are still cultural entities whose names are used in everyday speech, administration

4   TIMBER CLASSICISM: The church of Bo, in Närke

5 The apsidal East End of
Lund Cathedral

6 The Font of Löderup Church, Skåne

has now divided the country into twenty-four districts called *Län*, whose boundaries do not necessarily coincide with those of the historical provinces. As most Swedes do, we shall use the old provincial names here.

Let us now, like the boy from Skåne in Selma Lagerlöf's delightful children's book, *The Wonderful Adventures of Nils*, who flew over the whole country on the back of a gander, ourselves take a bird's-eye view of Sweden, travelling from south to north. How does the country look?

Both north and south, east and west are strikingly different. From north to south the country can be divided into four characteristic parts. The south, mainly contained in the provinces of Skåne and Blekinge, is an extension of the Central European Plain. Thus it is unlike the rest of Sweden and more like Denmark, to which it is indeed closely related in history. Being a flat, fertile area of rich Silurian soil of great economic and strategic value, Skåne has caused frequent conflict between Swedes and Danes in the past. The Skanian people themselves are perhaps more like the Danes than the Swedes—forthright, jovial, self-confident, with a distinct throaty dialect—the Yorkshiremen, one might say, of Sweden. Skåne is the granary of the country, mostly undulating farmland broken by beechwoods and studded with many old manors and castles of Danish style. Great white half-timbered barns, whitewashed brick churches with stepped gables and long avenues of willow trees add to the charm of its landscape.

Skåne's two main towns are Malmö and Lund. Malmö, the largest town in Sweden after Stockholm and Gothenburg, is a busy port and industrial centre facing across the Öresund to Copenhagen so conveniently that it is far easier for those in search of a spree in a capital city who live in Malmö and the south to pop over to the Danish capital than to make the long journey up to Stockholm. Lund is a university city, standing in relation to Uppsala in Uppland rather as Oxford does to Cambridge, for both universities have ancient foundations. At Lund rise the twin towers of a twelfth-century Romanesque limestone cathedral, the finest cathedral in the country, which though largely restored has an original apsidal east end of outstanding beauty (5). From Skåne, or, to anglicize the word, Skania, is derived the word Scandinavia, the suffix being *awi*, meaning coast, which suggests how strategically important this part of the country has been since early times through its command of the narrow strait of the Öresund, the link between the North Sea and the Baltic.

North of the southern plain lies the wide area of Sweden's lake

SWEDEN

district, comprising such provinces as fishermen's Bohuslän, Östergötland, Värmland, proud Dalarna, historic Västergötland and Södermanland, often called Sweden's most typical province. This area is still fairly flat but less open than the southern plain. It reaches as far north as the Elv River in Dalarna. Here stretch the two great lakes—treacherous Vänern, over 2,000 square miles in extent, and the long, mysterious Vättern. Lovely Lake Mälaren is here too, at whose western end lies the ancient iron district of Bergslagen, where mining began as far back as the thirteenth century and later closely affected Sweden's history and economy. As long ago as the end of the sixteenth and the beginning of the seventeenth century, for example, the Bergslagen district was virtually a large industrial centre almost in a modern sense, for it then produced 40 per cent of the world's iron. These midlands of Sweden contain not only Stockholm and Gothenburg but most of the industrial towns as well—Jönköping for matches, Norrköping for textiles, Örebro for shoes, Bofors for armaments, Huskvarna for shotguns and sewing machines. This is the heart of Sweden which we shall most closely explore, typically composed of farmland broken frequently by pine and birch woods, by lakes and by outcrops of granite—a unique and lovely countryside improved by man where the red timber farms, as bright focal points, form perfect foils to the dark green of the conifers, the black and white of the birch trees, the grey of the rocks and the blue of the lakes and sky (33).

Roughly above the line formed by the Göta Canal, which links Gothenburg and Stockholm, and below the Elv River, the land was adaptable in the past to the formation of self-contained communities which though joined by communications were not closely enough joined to allow powerful centralized government. This geographical feature has had a strong influence in shaping Swedish character which has throughout history shown a strongly democratic, anti-tyrannical attitude and has found its usual source of inspiration among the freemen of Dalarna.

Between the south and the midlands lies the hilly No Man's Land of Småland and Halland, a past military buffer between Danes and Swedes—a rather poor, stony land, not easy to penetrate in the old days. Here the crofters have cultivated every possible patch of lean soil. It is so lean that Selma Lagerlöf has told the story of how God left the creation of Småland to Saint Peter while He Himself was at work on Skåne. Here the people have become hard and strong as a result of their unfertile environment—the Scotsmen of Sweden.

The east and west coasts of the south and midlands are similar to the extent that they both contain numberless small rocky islands. Gothenburg and Stockholm, for instance, each have their extensive and labyrinthine archipelagos. But there the similarity ends. On the west most of the indentations are less deep than on the east, and therefore the west provides few points for military assembly. The result on history, especially in Viking days, has been that the Swedes have tended to expand east across the Baltic rather than west and south. The east has many useful inlets where protected towns and harbours could be built. Stockholm itself was founded for military reasons as a protection against Teutonic marauders, while Karlskrona was built as a naval base in the seventeenth century. The west coast has a distinct character with its volcanic, often treeless, rocks. It is more austere and less friendly than the east, but in the clear light of a summer evening when the red fishermen's cottages glow magically and the lingering sun catches a white sail far off among the smooth, grey skerries, the effect is beautiful indeed, and to be seen nowhere else in the world. The east coast is softer and more verdant. This also has its special charm, and to voyage in one's own small boat among the thousands of small, and for the most part uninhabited, islands of the Stockholm archipelago through the tideless water of the Baltic is one of the most delightful and romantic experiences that life can offer. So numerous are these islands that though Charles X, some 300 years ago, offered 1,000 kroner to anyone who would count them accurately, no one claimed the prize. Modern surveyors number them at 7,000.

From about the centre of Dalarna, or Dalecarlia as we say, the endless forests of spruce and pine begin, fed by the lean soil which has been formed by the disintegration of primary rock. These forests, monotonous but impressive in their vastness, stretch for 200 miles and more right up to the bleak tundras and high, bare ranges of Lappland, where the wandering herds of reindeer, the chief source of livelihood of the Lapps, search for moss among the juniper bushes and the stunted birch trees—where a night may last for two months and a day for as long—where mosquitoes swarm in summer as thick as smoke—where vegetation is meagre, the winter cold is intense and life is tough. Up here in Norrland the mountains, which have hitherto kept fairly close to the Norwegian border, encroach well into the country as the great massif of the north-west. This massif contains the highest peaks of the country, including Mount Kabnekajse towering to 6,966 feet. It also has the grandest waterfalls, like Stora Sjöfället tumbling 131 feet and Stora Luleålo roaring down in a series of falls and cataracts for 243 feet.

8 Glanshammar Church, in Närke : a Gothic church with elaborate wall painting and baroque decoration

9   Vadstena Castle (1545), one the Vasa type of the Renaissance
From a nineteenth-century lithograph

10   The old Royal Palace, Stockholm, destroyed by fire in 1697
From an engraving in Erik Dahlbergh's "Suecia Antiqua et Hodierna"

Formerly inhabited only by the nomadic Lapps and a few pioneers, this cold, bleak country has in the past half-century been colonized from the south to become a source of great wealth. At Kiruna and Malmberget rise two great mountains composed almost entirely of iron ore, much of it as rich in pure iron as 68 per cent, the richest known deposit in the world. The quick transport of this ore by rail to the ports of Narvik in Norway and Luleå on the Gulf of Bothnia, combined with the ease with which it can be obtained merely by blasting it out of the mountainside, has greatly helped Sweden's prosperity in this Second Iron Age.

Apart from the mountains of the north, Sweden is fairly flat. Except in Skåne, however, the landscape does not appear as a plain, for it undulates slightly, is frequently clad with forests, and is broken up into small separate areas by rocky knolls and ridges, dells and valleys. It lacks the grandeur of Norway and yet it is unique. Though tending towards monotony and being often sombre, at its typical best it has a lyrical beauty of which the inhabitants are deeply aware. This typical best can be seen round Lake Siljan in Dalarna, where the landscape is as moving as the sad, sweet folksongs of the people.

Sweden has two main sources of great natural wealth—its iron ore now mainly mined in Norrland (copper and gold are also found there) and the vast forests which cover more than half the area of the country. These forests are now under severe laws and their systematic replanting ensures a perpetual growth which provides not only raw deal but a growing number of processed goods— factory-made houses, newsprint, motor spirit, silk stockings and, before long, possibly food as well. Scientific research supported by the State plays an important part in Sweden's timber economy and, though little older than a fully grown pine, has already greatly improved cultivation and discovered new ways of using wood.

Nature has helped the distribution of both iron ore and timber. Kiruna lies fairly near two seaports, while the forests are amply supplied with many rivers which run from the western slopes south-eastwards to the sawmills, paper-mills and ports situated all the way up the Baltic coast. About a tenth part of the country is covered by the water both of these rivers and of the 96,000 lakes, large and small. Owing to their direction the rivers melt in the spring first at their mouths and later at their sources and so provide a magnificent natural system along which the logs from the forests can be floated (3). Moreover, the abundance of snow in the forests during the winter is a boon to logging operations.

Besides acting as carriers of timber logs the waters provide valuable electric power at their falls—the White Coal of Sweden which compensates for the lack of oil and the lack of coal itself, which is complete except for a few scanty deposits in north-west Skåne. The harnessed power is so great that Sweden has become the most electrified country in the world both in home and factory. The grid is widespread and extends even to Denmark, so that electric power is actually exported. Two great advantages accrue from this White Coal—decentralized industry and unpolluted air which keeps all things indefinitely clean and bright and halves the housewife's toil. As a result Sweden has no black and blighted places; nature is never unduly disturbed and is always close at hand for the enjoyment of the townsman and industrial worker.

This wealth of forest, iron and water power, combined with the high technical skill and sense of order of the people has turned Sweden in little more than half a century from a poor agrarian country into a rich and pre-eminently industrial one. In 1800 the rural population was 85 per cent of the whole. Today the number earning a living from the soil is only 20 per cent, a good deal less than the 37 per cent engaged in industry. Whereas our industrial revolution began about 1770, Sweden's did not arrive for another century. In 1849 the first steam sawmill was built in Sweden, but not until another twenty years had passed was much progress made; then came a development with the railways, a development which was greatly speeded up after 1890, when the first waterfalls were fully harnessed and the phosphoric iron ore of the north could be exploited by the new Thomas process.

Even today Sweden manages to produce 90 per cent of her own food from fishing and from that 9 per cent of the surface of her land (about the same in area as that covered by water) which is under cultivation. By comparison the British Isles have about 20 per cent under cultivation and Denmark has 60 per cent. This high food production has been attained by scientific methods based on outstanding research, by rationalization, by electrification, by Government aid and by co-operative marketing. Most of the farms are small. Over three-quarters of them are less than 25 acres and are owned by peasants and smallholders today as they have been throughout Sweden's history. Roughly the proportion of area tenure of farmland is 35 per cent smallholdings, 45 per cent peasant holdings, 20 per cent large estates. Often the smallholders mix their occupations. Up north, for example, they may give half their time to tree-felling, they may hunt and fish a little, they may apply some building skill or lend a hand at stevedoring or factory work when extra labour is needed. In the forest country most of the small farmers spend the whole winter in lumbering, using their own horses to haul the logs to the rivers over the snow.

A realization of how many Swedes live in the countryside came to the writer one summer when camping at the end of the beautiful Gulmarsfjord which penetrates the west coast in Bohuslän. Here lived during the summer months in a quiet, healthy way a small, scattered, mixed community. There was a smallholder, a simple, gentle man who loved to pay a call in the evening at the tent to enjoy a Gold Flake, bringing with him his single cow to graze. His income must have been low and he augmented it by taking such odd jobs as unloading small coaling vessels which sometimes called at a rail head about a mile across the fjord. His neighbour was a fisherman and hunter. In summer he caught salmon in the fjord while keeping an eye open for a profitable shoal of herring. In winter during the short open season he hunted elks in the woods. The salmon he sold to another neighbour, a colonel's widow, who organized its marketing in Gothenburg and also kept bees. Other local folk included a young couple on holiday who had here built their own timber shack among the pines and an engineer who had retired to these parts on a small fortune he had made in South America and was himself now building his own house and developing a smallholding. One gained from the environment an invigorating sense of freedom not to be acquired in our crowded island— the primitive sense that Nature will always provide one with a direct living where men have not congregated too closely. One could in fact survive in these parts with very little money, living free on fresh fish and mussels from the fjord, on rabbit and game from the woods, on the bilberries and cranberries which grow profusely all around.

Timber, metal mining, farming, shipbuilding, matches, heavy engineering, ball-bearings, textiles and a hundred and one light industries from glass and pottery to clothes hangers and mousetraps bring a good standard of life to the Swedish people, a standard which has been enhanced by unbroken peace since 1814 (and that was no serious war) together with a flourishing export trade. The organization of this economy of an industrial democracy has shown a sensible, *ad hoc* compromise between state, private and co-operative enterprise—the Swedish Middle Way as it has been called. The State confines itself mainly to controlling public utilities such as railways, post office and telephones, but it also owns one-third of the electric supply plant, some mines, some iron and steel plant and the largest area of forest in the country. It also has monopolies in tobacco and alcoholic drinks, these being run by companies in which the State owns practically all of the shares. As a branch of the drink monopoly there now exists a nation-wide chain of restaurants known as SARA which are inexpensive and well run. The State also has the sense to run public lotteries, the profits from which go to finance various cultural projects. Even football pools are under government direction and profits go to finance athletics. Broadcasting is under a semi-official company in which the Press and radio industry hold shares.

State manufacturing, however, amounts to no more than 1 per cent of the whole, and private enterprise still runs 95 per cent of all production. Mostly the private business concerns are small, and of a total of 22,000 only 10 per cent employ more than fifty people. The remaining 4 per cent of industry is run by co-operative bodies, of which the most important are the HSB and the famous KF. HSB is concerned mainly with house building and furnishing; it has greatly improved housing standards. KF is the consumers' co-operative and was founded as far back as 1899. These co-operatives have been remarkably successful and have set a standard in co-operative enterprise for the whole world, especially in their excellent building projects and general design. They express the best side of the Swedish character which relates a realistic, business-like practicality to an idealistic humanitarianism and manages at the same time to symbolize these attributes visually with elegance and a developed sense of aesthetic order. The KF alone has 900,000 members, a third of the country's households, and turns over about 14 per cent of the country's retail trade.

Municipalities also go in for business, mostly in public transport and utilities, and town councils occasionally run the main hotel, which at Ludvika and Karlskoga-Bofors is linked with the town hall (26). An interesting case of municipal enterprise is the company of the Krångede hydro-electric works in Norrland, one of the largest in the country, which is jointly owned by the City of Stockholm and several large industrial concerns.

This compromise, which permits private initiative and individualism while holding control for the common good, is, of course, an outcome of industrialization. It is a modern development. Yet the present grows inevitably out of the past. By examining Sweden's history now, we may be better able to understand her as she appears today.

III

History and Heritage

SWEDISH HISTORY can be conveniently divided for clear under-standing into these periods: Prehistoric (about 5000 B.C. to A.D. 800), the Viking Age (A.D. 800–1050), Medieval Times (1050–1521), Reformation and Vasa Epoch (1521–1611), Age of Greatness and the Baltic Empire (1611–1718), Age of Liberty and Gustavian Epoch (1718–1809), Age of Democracy and the Industrial Revolution (1809 to modern times).

Prehistory (about 5000 B.C. to A.D. 800). The south of Sweden began to emerge from the ice about 12000 B.C. and by about 3000 B.C. settlements had been formed and farming had begun. Wanderers came up from the south to people the country as the ice cap receded, but who exactly these wanderers were is not clearly known, though we call them Germans. Eventually can be distin-guished Lapps and Finns in the north, the Suiones or Swedes centred round Lake Mälaren, south of these the Goutoi or Goths (hence Götaland and Gotland) and in Skåne the Danes. Between them the Goths and the Danes drove out a remarkable tribe called the Herules, who migrated southwards to the Danube to form a wedge between the Slavs and to establish themselves as the Magyars. In time the Svear became dominant with their chief centre at Uppsala. At the decay of the Roman Empire between A.D. 400 and 800 the Folk Wanderings had their effects and brought civilizing currents. At the same time emigrations took place from Scandinavia to the Continent, especially to Eastern Germany.

Round about A.D. 600 the Svear and the Goths were united under a Swedish king, and as one of the medieval Provincial Laws founded on ancient oral tradition declares: "Through the union of the land of the Suiones and the land of the Goths in heathen times, the kingdom of Sweden was founded." This shows that Sweden is the earliest united nation in Europe.

*　　*　　*　　*　　*

Relics of the Stone Age (down to about 1500 B.C.) can be seen in the great number of grave chambers in the south and west of Sweden. In the following Bronze Age (down to 500 B.C.) sporadic cultural effects were brought from the Mediterranean by the trade routes over Germania. The arms, jewellery and other bronze objects

25

of this period which have been unearthed show a high, if barbaric, skill in craftsmanship and design often distinctly reflecting the influence of the Roman Asiatic provinces. From the first period of the Bronze Age have survived the rock engravings frequently found in Bohuslän—engravings portraying dramatically the life of those times, the warfare, the hunting and fishing, the seafaring adventures and the religious ceremonies (p. 64). Later on, contact with the Graeco-Roman civilization brought, among other things, the runic script.

*　*　*　*　*

The Viking Age (A.D. 800–1050). This was the time, following the Folk Wanderings, when the planned raids and commercial expeditions of a more or less united people took place, the time when the Scandinavians dominated the European seas in their long-ships and plundered distant lands. Probably over-population and monopoly of land by ruling families were the main causes of these expeditions. The Swedish or Eastern Vikings (Viking meaning originally a man from a bay or *vik*) thrust east, though many individual Swedes also joined Danish and Norwegian expeditions to the west, for the three peoples had a common basic tongue and a common pagan faith. The predatory expeditions were carried out with ruthless ferocity, but these Vikings were, to their credit, well disciplined, and did infuse a certain vigour into the people of Normandy and England. Moreover, they were traders as well as marauders and in that capacity the Eastern Vikings reached as far south as the Byzantine Empire by way of the Dnieper, as far south, indeed, as Piraeus. A pointer to the amount of southern trade at that time is the discovery of as many as 40,000 Byzantine coins in Sweden. The Swedish Vikings also reached as far to the south-east as the Caspian Sea and as far due east as the heart of Russia, where they founded a state which was to develop into a great realm. The *Rus* people, from whom Russia takes its name, were indeed the conquerors who came from the district around what is now Roslagen, north of Stockholm.

*　*　*　*　*

The decorative arts of the Vikings were a somewhat decadent development from those of the Bronze Age, but the Vikings were highly skilled in timber construction, not least in their ships. The simple timber stave churches which still survive from the Middle Ages in Sweden and the more elaborate ones of their kind found in Norway must be very like the temples which the Vikings built for their heathen gods Thor, Odin and Frey. It is known that carved wooden effigies of these gods stood in the gilded temple at Uppsala, where a great festival was held every nine years at which the outstanding events were blood sacrifices and sexual orgies in honour of Frey, the god of fertility. The symbol of the great god Thor was the battle axe, for to the Viking warriors courage in battle was the supreme virtue. Then gradually the symbol of the Cross, looking much like a sword, usurped its power.

* * * * *

Medieval Times (1050–1521). Christianity came slowly and with much bloodshed to Sweden, largely through the exertions of two English missionaries. Not until the twelfth century did Christianity gain a permanent hold on the country, a hold which was consolidated by Cistercians sent by Saint Bernard, who founded monasteries at Alvastra, Nydala and Varnhem. Sweden remained virtually pagan for two centuries longer than Denmark and about a century longer than Norway. By 1200, except for the remotest districts, Sweden had become Christian and an archbishopric had been established at Uppsala. By now the fighting between pagans and Christian converts had impoverished the country, and Swedish power in the Baltic had so declined that the sea had become infested with pirates. Stockholm was therefore founded to guard the entrance to Lake Mälar, and in the reign of Birger Jarl replaced Uppsala as a seat of government, for it was more convenient.

In the twelfth century closer contacts with Rome and Western Europe brought a desire for more culture. Migrations southwards into fertile Danish Skåne took place and missionary crusades into Finland were organized, with the result that Finland was subjugated by King Erik the Holy to become part of the Swedish kingdom for more than six centuries. The Hanseatic League was now threatening Swedish power in the Baltic, had stretched a tentacle to Bergen and had virtually captured the island of Gotland in the Baltic, where it had set up a strong trading centre in the town of Visby.

Elected kings were trying to increase their power and the prestige they had lost when they ceased to be High Priests of the pagan cult. At the same time nobles were gaining authority over the peasants and feudalism was being slowly introduced. The peasants, as they often did in future years, turned to the king for protection. From 1250 to 1389 the Folkunga dynasty of Jarls (or Earls, as we would say, who were next in hierarchic importance to the king) reigned, among whom was the outstanding Birger Jarl, who built Stockholm and brought a unity to the country on which the foundations of the Swedish constitution were laid.

The time between 1389 and 1521 is known as the Union Period, because then repeated attempts were made to unite the three Scandinavian countries under Danish rule, the most serious attempt being the Union of Kalmar of 1397. Sweden, however, reacted with strong national spirit, the first rising against the Danish oppression being organized by the yeomen of Dalecarlia, who were least dominated by feudalism and most oppressed by the Danes. Under the great Engelbrekt Engelbrektsson, a lesser nobleman and a mine owner, the brutal Danish bailiffs were purged, and in 1435 the first Riksdag, the Swedish Parliament, was convoked with representatives of the Four Estates—nobility, clergy, burghers and peasants (who included the miners). This was the second oldest Parliament in the world and was not radically altered until the middle of the nineteenth century (40).

Sweden now regained control of Gotland, and the powerful League was forced to bide its time and to make capital by balancing power between Denmark and Sweden. The Church grew in strength, sought too much power and privilege, behaved with treachery and thus precipitated the fall of Catholicism, so helping to bring the Reformation and the age of modern nationalism which went with it. During this period the University of Uppsala was founded in 1477.

In 1497 the Danish King Hans entered Stockholm and was formally elected king. Thanks partly to trouble in Holstein, the Danes were soon driven out by a nationalist party. In 1517 Sten Sture the Younger deposed Gustav Trolle, Archbishop of Uppsala, and so directly challenged Papal authority. Christian II of Denmark, nephew of Charles V, then interfered in the name of the Holy Roman Church and having defeated Sture's peasant army was proclaimed hereditary king of Stockholm. Following a splendid ceremony and feast, the new king indicted eighteen people— bishops, burghers and noblemen who had attacked the Church— and had these men executed in the appalling Blood Bath of Stockholm's market place. These massacres were extended to the provinces, but by chance a relative of Sten Sture, escaping from prison, survived. This man wandered about Dalarna and then, on hearing that Christian was approaching to punish the peasants of that province for harbouring him, started out for Norway. The rumour was false and he was called back to be elected the peasant leader. His name was Gustav Vasa and his journey is today honoured by an annual ski race along the route he is presumed to have taken

11 VADSTENA: The Brigittine Monastery Church in the simple
Cistercian style (1303–73)

12 The Parish Church of Skäfthammar in Uppland
(twelfth century)

13 The Cistercian Monastery Church of Varnhem (medieval with
baroque additions)

called the Vasa Run. In 1521 Gustav, not yet twenty-five years old, began the final War of Liberation as Lord of the Dales and of Sweden. Having gained a splendid victory at Västerås, he was elected Regent by the Riksdag at Vadstena and in 1523 accepted the crown. So was founded a dynasty which was to hold sway for three centuries. On June 6th, 1523, Stockholm, held by the Danes under siege, fell to the Swedes and a new epoch began.

★   ★   ★   ★   ★

What happened to the arts in this turbulent medieval period? In general they expressed the typical international character of the times in somewhat simplified form. Stone began to replace timber in church building. At Lund, for example, a cathedral of stone was begun about 1080 and grew into a fine edifice in the Romanesque style, with its round arches and cross vaults, which in England we term the Norman (5). Oriental and Germanic in its origins, Lund is a Danish rather than a Swedish creation. It was unfortunately disastrously restored in the nineteenth century, but some of the original remains, notably the east end, the large crypt and some carved details.

The greatest cultural influence during the early Middle Ages in Sweden was that of the Cistercian monks from France, who brought the pointed arch and the true Gothic. Most of their foundations are today in ruins, but we shall at least be able to see on our journey the abbey church of Varnhem, one of the finest Gothic buildings in Scandinavia (13, 37) (p. 80). Uppsala Cathedral, built in the second half of the thirteenth century, is very French, almost a small Amiens, with its short transepts, high interior, apsidal chapels and its *flèche* over the crossing. The cathedral suffered a severe collapse during a storm in 1402 and was damaged by fire in 1702. It has been altered considerably at various times, in particular during the restoration of 1885. The north transept, however, remains complete in its original form on the outside, while the rose window in the west, the general ground plan and the grand unity of the interior are original at least in effect. Much of the carving of the capitals, too, remains—the work of French, German and Swedish craftsmen.

Linköping Cathedral is the least restored Gothic building in Sweden both within and without, if one ignores the nineteenth-century tower. It is a magnificent example of the fourteenth century, the choir interior being especially fine, Perpendicular, very high, with tall refined pilasters peeling away into the vaulting without caps.

Of special beauty and character are the simple yet sophisticated,

31

well-preserved stone churches of the island of Gotland, built between 1260 and 1360. The highest expression of medieval architecture in Sweden, these churches are the outcome of the marriage between the traditions of the mainland and the international modernism of Visby. This local style is typified in Gotland's Hablingbo Church with its sturdy, circular columns, its caps of curiously carved decoration, its plain stone walls and vaulting whose junctions are without ribs and have given rise to the term tent vaulting. The power and drama of these churches, particularly of the interiors, comes from the contrast between the plain grey wall surfaces and the isolated details of intricate stone carving, and the crucifixes, altars and choir stalls of brightly painted carved wood. Bold towers are a feature of this Gotland style, as in the tallest example at Rone, with its square tower surmounted by a broach spire.

Another Gothic speciality in Sweden is the ecclesiastical architecture initiated by the holy Bridget (1303–73), one of the Folkung family and a remarkable and energetic personality—politician, visionary, saint and unofficial envoy of Sweden in Rome for twenty-five years—one of the great medieval figures. She founded a monastic Order composed of both monks and nuns and established its first monastery at Vadstena (11). Other foundations of Brigittines followed not only in Sweden but throughout Europe. Saint Bridget laid down definite rules for the buildings of her Order, such as the curious one that the choir should be built at the west end of the nave. The style is Cistercian in feeling with light, high interiors, simple rhythmical vaulting, austere, undecorated, geometrical monumentality of form. Most of the Blue Church at Vadstena is still intact, though the quarters for monks and nuns are mainly in ruins. Part of them have been reconstructed to serve as a Youth Hostel.

In Gothic times brick was often used in Swedish churches and cathedrals. For the sake of economy Uppsala Cathedral was built partly in brick. Strängnäs Cathedral on Lake Mälar, built in the first half of the fourteenth century, is almost entirely of brick with heavy, circular brick piers. The material was originally introduced from Denmark, and in Skåne many brick churches were built in the Middle Ages. At Gumlösa, for instance, you can see a small church with Romanesque round arches which is Sweden's oldest existing brick structure, having been built in 1191.

Finally the carved stone fonts of early medieval Sweden, for they are of outstanding beauty and are unsurpassed anywhere in the world. Superb examples can be seen at Löderup (6) and Valleberga in Skåne, and at Barlingbo in Gotland. The names of some of the artists are known to this day.

* * * * *

Reformation and Vasa Epoch (1521–1611). Gustav Vasa took the difficult situation in hand with resourcefulness, courage, single-mindedness, immense energy and, when occasion demanded, with ruthlessness. In that the king needed funds, which he could most easily find in the Catholic possessions, the Swedish Reformation was similar to our own. It was, however, even more nationalistic in temper, for Rome was associated with Denmark and Denmark was the nation's great enemy. The religious aspect was less important than the political and the new creed was not at once forced on the people. From 1529 the Church of Sweden was gradually and peacefully evangelized.

By the end of his forty-year reign Gustav Vasa had settled most of the problems and created a strong and united country. Sweden's King Hal was a great man in an age of great men—of Luther, Charles V, Francis I, Henry VIII. When he came to the throne, though Denmark had at last been defeated, the treasury was empty, the nobles were divided, the peasants and miners were eager for rebellion, the Church was in a state of schizophrenia. With the help of Luther's disciple, Olaus Petri, Gustav set about reforming the Church, confiscating the Catholic wealth, building up a navy and a new, disciplined army organized on revolutionary military principles. Soon he had gained power over the Hanseatic League, broken the monopoly of the German merchants in Sweden and established a flourishing trade. He improved mining, established royal farms as models of agriculture, cleared forests, drained marshes, organized hunts to kill off the wolves and bears which preyed on the cattle, and created an administration free from corruption. A truly benevolent despot.

On the death in 1560 of Old King Gösta, as he became affectionately called, his three sons followed in succession to the throne. There was strife between them and they lived through a period of struggles with Russia, Poland and Denmark. Until 1568 Erik XIV reigned, and then Johan and Carl united to depose him. Erik, though passionate and cruel almost to madness, was at least a good soldier, encouraged the Renaissance arts and dreamed of greatness for his country. At one enterprising moment he sought marriage with Queen Elizabeth and it is said that to gain his end he was prepared to assassinate Leicester, whom he took to be his rival.

The Queen, however, courteously informed him that she preferred the virgin state. Johan III followed Erik. He had leanings towards Catholicism and the Counter Reformation and was an ardent patron of architecture. He had more practical success than his brother and managed to increase power over Russia in the Baltic and to secure the election of his son Sigismund to the throne of Poland. Before a severe religious crisis could arise, Johan died and his son was crowned at Uppsala Cathedral under an oath that he would not interfere with Protestantism. Papal power, however, began to re-assert itself, Sigismund returned to Poland and his strongly Protestant uncle, Duke Carl, was nominated Regent. Carl at once began to prosecute the Catholics and ordered all Catholic priests to leave the country. In this he had general support, for Catholicism and foreign domination were still linked in people's minds. Sigismund led an army against his uncle, which, after gaining a brief victory in 1598, was annihilated two months later and Carl was acclaimed king. Though an unlovable character, Carl IX brought economic benefits to the country, notably by currency reform, but his best act was to produce a remarkable son, the great Gustav Adolph.

* * * * *

The Vasa period found its chief architectural expression in castles and manor houses, rather than in ecclesiastical buildings— naturally enough under the new nationalism which had dispossessed the Church. Portrait painting and handicrafts, influenced by European trends, reached a high level during these times. The sixteenth century brought from Italy, *via* the Lowlands and Germany, the transition from Gothic style to Renaissance. Whereas the castle at Gripsholm built in 1537 retains many Gothic features (14), Vadstena of 1545 is definitely Renaissance in that early, naïve and unscholarly type which occurred before the pure Vitruvian classical orders had been introduced (9)—the type which we call Jacobean. Much of the new Renaissance work was the creation of immigrant craftsmen from Europe, especially from Germany and the Lowlands and even Italy. Master builders like Påvel Schütz from Leipzig and Jakob Richter from Freiburg are remembered. Only one Swedish name stands out—Anders Larsson, who began as a painter and later, in typical Renaissance manner, became an architect, especially of royal fortifications. No existing building, however, is known to be his.

The castles are the outstanding monuments of the Vasa period and differ fundamentally from the medieval type. The new army

14 GRIPSHOLM CASTLE (1537): A Renaissance castle of the Vasa type; built before Vadstena, it retains many Gothic features

15 DROTTNINGHOLM PALACE : Sweden's Versailles; begun in 1662, it is the elder Tessin's major work
From the painting by B. A. Säfvenbom

was stationed at certain strategic points, usually at castles which were at one and the same time fortresses, garrison depots and royal residences. The defensive moat remained from the past, but with the development of artillery the old high tower with projecting castellations from which projectiles could be hurled or dropped disappeared and was replaced by low, circular bastions where cannon could be placed to face in all directions. The three outstanding examples of the Vasa-type castle are Gripsholm (14), Kalmar and Vadstena—the last standing as a curious contrast to the nearby Brigittine monastery. Externally these castles have bold, simple forms which are decorated with skilfully executed carving and sculpture at a few telling points. In this they are quite different from the splendid, elaborate affairs of the same period which we shall see in Denmark. Internally, by contrast, the royal rooms are lavishly decorated with carved panelling, decorative plasterwork and painted ceilings created by European craftsmen. Vadstena is undoubtedly the finest and the least altered of the three—one of the most splendid monuments Sweden possesses. Begun in Gustav's time, it was improved by Johan III, who added the fine portals and the decorations of the gables (9).

The noblemen's houses of the Middle Ages consisted of a collection of small buildings of solid, axed timbers. At their centre often stood a defensive tower of stone, the whole place being surrounded by a stockade as a protection against wild animals and, perhaps, wild men. In the sixteenth century stone and brick began to take the place of timber and the houses became rather like the royal castles but on a smaller scale, with moats and possibly a pair of towers for cannon. A good typical example can be seen at Ekenäs in Östergötland and another at Vittskövle in Skåne with its central courtyard. Planning was still asymmetrical.

Sixteenth-century church building, unlike the military and lay building of the same period, did not, as it did in other countries, change greatly. Indeed, the Gothic continued in Sweden right into the seventeenth century. This was no doubt due to the very gradual acceptance of the Lutheran dogma by the people, an unslavish acceptance, for the Swedish reformed church retained for a long while much of the Catholic colour and ceremonial. As we have seen, the Reformation in Sweden was political rather than religious, and the attitude of the Protestant rulers towards purely religious matters of worship was tolerant. Only in details such as carved stalls, pulpits and monuments was design clearly Renaissance in character. The pointed arch and vaulting continued, though sometimes with a curious half-way adaptation to the new classical style.

4*   37

In Sweden is found no such great technical development as fan vaulting.

★   ★   ★   ★   ★

The Age of Greatness and the Baltic Empire (1611–1718). Gustavus Adolphus, or Gustav II Adolph, is one of the great figures of world history. When he ascended the throne as a youth of seventeen he inherited three wars—those against Poland, Russia and Denmark. Within six years, thanks partly to the help of his brilliant and loyal Chancellor, Oxenstierna, thanks partly to his own vitality and military ability, the Lion of the North, as he came to be called, had made Sweden secure against her three most dangerous enemies. By the end of his reign of twenty-one years he had staggered Europe by his successes, and by joining the Thirty Years' War and defeating the Catholic armies of Tilly he had saved Protestant Europe for ever from Catholic domination. His was Sweden's most vigorous, scintillating and spacious age. A new generation of educated, cultured Swedes had arisen and Gustav Adolph was not compelled, as Gustav Vasa had been, to call in foreigners as administrators. The seventeenth century was particularly a great age of building in Sweden. Then many castles and fine public buildings sprang up, of which the finest example is the Riddarhus, or House of the Nobles, in Stockholm—a place for social and political meetings of the nobles, though not one where laws could be made (44). This nobility was a mixed and not always harmonious kind, for the king had added to the old landed lords a new administrative aristocracy chosen for ability rather than blood, to whom the king gave gifts of land as rewards for services to the State. In spite of the jealousy of the old aristocrats, the king was universally respected and managed to create a remarkably efficient, balanced and democratic government.

This was a period also of industrial expansion, especially in the copper and iron mines—an expansion initiated largely by the industrial genius Louis de Geer, a Dutchman who became a naturalized Swede and is known as the Father of Swedish Industry. Attempts were made at this time to found trading companies like the English East India Company, to which, however, they were never serious rivals. A trading colony was founded in Delaware in 1638 called New Sweden, and though it was soon absorbed into the Dutch New Netherlands even today the Swedish language can be heard in parts of Delaware.

In 1632 Gustav was killed at his last victory, the Battle of Lützen. The tricky situation was saved by the steadfast Oxenstierna, who became Regent for Gustav's daughter, the romantic Christina, then only eight years old. In 1648 the Treaty of Westphalia was signed by the Swedes and the Hapsburg Emperor, and an uneasy peace prevailed in Sweden until Christina's abdication in 1654. Christina's distinctions are that, besides providing incomes for future novelists and film producers, she held the peace and encouraged learning and the arts. Unfortunately she was extravagant and showered expensive gifts on her favourites, especially on the prodigal Magnus Gabriel de la Gardie, the greatest patron of the arts of the times, who was at one time building at forty or fifty different places. Restless in mind and body, Christina became at last a Catholic convert, retired to a convent and handed the crown over to her warrior cousin, Carl X, one of her many rejected suitors.

Carl managed to save the financial situation and then went to war with the ostensible object of compelling the Polish king to renounce his claim to the Swedish throne but with the real one of subjugating the country while it was in a state of disintegration of which Russia might take advantage. Carl was a brilliant general. Within five weeks Poland was conquered. Now Denmark seized her chance and declared war on Sweden, but again Carl was victorious and in his immediate campaign against the Danes made his famous surprise march across the frozen water of the Little Belt. The Danes sued for peace and a major war was averted. At the Peace of Roskilde, at which Cromwell acted as mediator, Sweden at last established her natural boundaries by taking over Halland, Skåne, Blekinge and Bohuslän from the old Danish rule. Now Sweden was all-powerful in the Baltic, with control of Finland and with possessions along the Baltic coast and at the mouths of the German rivers—an even greater and more influential European state than she had become under Gustav Adolph (p. 73).

In 1660 the sudden death of the king again left the government in the hands of a Regency. This was composed of the Queen Mother, Carl's brother Adolph Johan and a cabal of leading heads of State including the extravagant Francophil, Magnus de la Gardie. It was a weak regime and much of the ground that had been gained was lost. Sweden suffered a serious defeat by Denmark in a war in Skåne among other misfortunes. When Carl XI, son of Carl X, came to the throne in 1672 he at once denounced and punished the responsible ministers for treachery and incompetence, confiscating many of the estates of the nobles, who had come to own two-thirds of the land. By 1682 the king had gained absolute power and had established a despotism which, though out of key with the Swedish temperament, lasted until the end of Carl XII's reign. As his father had done before him, Carl XI set to work to save the desperate financial situation. He organized severe retrenchment, strengthened the administration, re-established the peasantry, radically reorganized the forces, formed a territorial army and founded a naval base at Karlskrona. The cultural brilliance of the times was dimmed and life became drab. But the situation was saved, and by the end of the reign Sweden had regained much of her lost prestige and enjoyed peace for the rest of the century.

When in 1697 the fabulous ascetic and warrior Carl XII ascended the throne while still in his 'teens, he inherited a stable and solvent regime. Twenty years later powerful Sweden was reduced to poverty and impotence mainly as a result of the tragedy of the Great Northern War. At first Charles was dramatically successful. In his war against the Russia of Peter the Great at the start of the eighteenth century he took the enemy by surprise at Narva and captured prisoners three times as numerous as his own army. Next he triumphantly occupied Warsaw and then invaded Saxony. There followed the disastrous march on Moscow during the terrible winter of 1708, the worst known for three centuries. Defeated by General Winter and the traditional Russian scorched earth technique, the king, severely wounded, reorganized the remains of his army and set off with two hundred followers to Turkey to raise the support of the Sultan. His army, however, dispirited at last, laid down its arms and was marched off to Siberia. Meanwhile in Turkey Charles became virtually a prisoner. In time he managed to escape and, disguised as a horse dealer, galloped home through hostile territory to arrive safely after an absence abroad of fifteen years. During this time Denmark had attacked Skåne but had been repulsed by a stout army. In 1718 in the general international turmoil Charles, still undefeated in spirit, tried to take advantage of the dissensions by invading Norway. He was killed at the Siege of Frederiksten by a stray bullet, the last of the European kings to fall in battle. Sweden was left without a direct heir to the throne. Though she retained the south, she had lost most of her empire and was now poor and demoralized. So ended the Carolinian Saga.

*   *   *   *   *

The seventeenth century in Sweden was a golden age for architecture—the age of the Baroque. Round about 1650 came the transition from the classicism, chiefly influenced by Holland, to the Baroque (15), chiefly influenced by Italy and France, from the impersonal harmony of the classical Renaissance to the explosive reaction of grand, despotic vistas, rigid axes, rich and restless detailing and dramatic contrast between light and shade—the design of pomp and power intended to impress the observer with the owner's prestige. Broadly speaking, exteriors were stimulated by Italian manners, while interiors and arts and crafts imitated those of France. The century was one of almost continual, but successful, warfare, a flamboyant, exciting time when the fighting landed noblemen returned home with cartloads of booty from foreign lands with which to embellish their new palaces and manor houses. An incentive for their building was that up to the retrenchment imposed by Carl XI these domains had been free of tax—a privilege which had first been granted by Erik XIV. This was an age, then, of aristocratic castles and palaces, not only in the countryside, where there was space to lay out grand formal gardens as part of the whole conception, but in the capital too, where the nobles were often compelled to reside in order to execute their official duties incurred by the constitutional reforms of 1634. Many of these Stockholm palaces still stand.

The finest example of the earlier Dutch classicism, a kind of Germanized Palladianism, is the beautiful Riddarhuset in Stockholm built of red brick and sandstone with copper roof, Corinthian pilasters and small circular top windows decorated with carved swags (a feeling there of Wren, who did, after all, work for Dutch William) (44). The initial designer was in fact a Dutchman, the gifted Joost Vingboons who was commissioned to do the job in 1656. It was completed by Jean de la Vallée by about 1672, the beautiful roof being his work, a type of roof which became popular and is an architectural mark of the century exclusive to Sweden, being distinguished by a bold ogee section surmounted by a smaller recessed roof of ordinary low pitch. This double roof, called *säteri tak*, persisted well into the eighteenth century and stamps the Swedish manor house style, *säteri* meaning a small manor.

An earlier example of the Renaissance than the Riddarhus is the palace in Götgatan, Stockholm, designed by a Dutchman in 1646 for Louis de Geer in a very Roman and restrained manner.

Four architects stand out in this period—Jean de la Vallée, the two Nicodemus Tessins, the Older and Younger, and Eric Dahlbergh. De la Vallée's father, Simon, who died in 1642, was himself a distinguished architect, a Frenchman who had worked in Holland and had spent the last five years of his life actively in Sweden where he prepared a project for the Riddarhus and carried out several magnificent mansions, notably those at Tidö and Fiholm for Axel Oxenstierna. These are in unequivocal Dutch style while possessing that boldness of conception which is characteristically French.

41

His son Jean (1620–96), who became naturalized, was patronized largely by de la Gardie, for whom he carried out at least four palaces, notably Karlberg near Stockholm (16, 46). His most charming work, which is still in perfect preservation, is his small palace at Runsa built about 1670 for de la Gardie's old mother, Ebba Brahe, who had been a youthful flame of Gustav Adolph. It has symmetrical side wings joined to the central main block by single-storey links, the typical de la Vallée *säteri* roofs, simple pilasters and careful proportioning—a unified and highly original work, quite indigenous and delightfully situated above Lake Mälar.

The elder Tessin (1615–81) was a Frenchman by birth but settled in Sweden at an early age to spend his working life there. His designs are powerful and dignified but less audacious and fanciful than those of de la Vallée. Perhaps that is why he became the Royal Architect. In that capacity he built his major work, Drottningholm Castle, begun in 1662 for the widow of Carl X (15). Situated on Lake Mälar to the west of Stockholm, it is called Sweden's Versailles, being an imposing Frenchified pile in white stucco and stone planned with rigid symmetry among grand formal gardens, in the style of Le Nôtre, which stretch away below a wide terrace. It is typically Baroque and quite different in plan and conception from such a royal domain as Gripsholm (14), lying some miles farther west, which had been built only a century before. How much more picturesque and less boring is Gripsholm's asymmetrical, *ad hoc*, working plan. The palace is like many of the grand, artificial, unfunctional structures which were built all over Europe at this time. Their main object was to impress rather than to serve any useful domestic purpose, and it is significant that of the two domes at the extremities of Drottningholm one covers a chapel and the other a kitchen.

Of more charm than Drottningholm, and in strange contrast to it, is Tessin's country house at Sjöö, on the wooded shore of Mälar, which was built for a nobleman of limited means. It is very simple, has no trimmings and is finished in pale yellow stucco—almost a piece of Swedish cubistic functionalism of the twentieth century, for it has grace and simplicity without crudity.

In 1661 Tessin became City Architect for Stockholm and carried out a considerable amount of work there, the most important being the old State Bank in Järntorget, which was begun in 1676 and is still standing in a good condition. Both Tessin and de la Vallée became highly honoured men and both eventually took their seats on the State Council.

Tessin's son (1654–1728) has been called Sweden's Christopher Wren. He was named Nicodemus after his father and was carried to his christening by an exalted lady, none other than Queen Maria Eleonora, widow of Gustav II Adolph. He succeeded his father as Royal Architect and lived to become not only Sweden's most famous, and favoured, architect but also university chancellor, State Councellor, Lord High Chamberlain and earl. He was a doctrinaire classicist and turned always to Italy or France for inspiration. He was for a while a pupil of Bernini in Rome. His greatest work was the famous Royal Palace at Stockholm, the construction of which came about in the following way (2, 43). The old palace, which was partly medieval, had become dilapidated and unsafe in Christina's time (10). Christina decided to rebuild it, but it was left to her cousin Charles X to give the order to Jean de la Vallée to prepare drawings. These were ready in 1656, and the work had been started when the king died and the work stopped. Later the elder Tessin prepared a design in a Palladian style, but it was not until 1688 that his son began to develop the scheme which was to be finally realized. Under Carl XI the job made headway and the whole north block was finished by 1694, the side wings being added three years later. A terrible fire in 1697 gutted the whole of the remaining old palace but happily did not destroy the new north block. Tessin began at once to extend the new palace and building proceeded until the Russian debacle of 1708, when all work ceased for twenty years. In 1728 Tessin died and his son Carl Gustav took over superintendence of the uncompleted palace. Carl was a cultured man who loved all things French, an aesthete, an art collector and as great a patron of the arts as de la Gardie had been. He became a politician of importance during the so-called Age of Liberty. The work on the palace began again, but progress was slow and the whole as we now see it was not finished until 1760.

The palace began as the residence of an absolute king ruling a powerful state. It was completed for a constitutional monarch of a small country which had lost an empire. Yet the building itself remains one of the grandest and most dignified monuments in the world. Perfectly sited on the Stockholm water with its noble approach on the axis across the bridge, its simple, bold massing, its strong stone base supporting long façades of buff stucco (originally yellow), its stone dressings, its rhythmical windows, its entrances like triumphal arches decorated with sudden, vigorous Baroque carving, it represents classicism at its most splendid and serene. Grand without being grandiose, its inspiration was Bernini's remarkable design for the Louvre project, a project for which the younger Tessin himself prepared a design at one stage in his career.

Tessin was an internationalist with his heart in Rome, but his work somehow takes on a Swedish character willy-nilly—even his Royal Palace. It is difficult to accept Strindberg's remark that in the palace can be found nothing that is either original or Swedish. When the lights come on in the winter evening to send their reflections dancing on the icy water and the snow begins to cover the manes of the two great bronze lions which protect the northern entrance (2) and to line the mouldings which were originally conceived for the sunshine of a southern climate, the great geometrical block takes on a mysterious, romantic character which is pure Scandinavian.

Tessin the Younger carried out much other work which has tended to become overshadowed by his palace—notably a house for himself in Stockholm, the Södra Town Hall in Stockholm, an uninspired Roman villa at Steninge in Uppland and the lovely country mansion at Sturefors in Östergötland built about 1700 for a favourite of Carl XII, Carl Piper, who indeed never lived to see his fine house completed, for he went campaigning with his king and died in a Russian prison in 1716. Sturefors, however classical its creator intended it to be, is Swedish in its graceful effect, an effect greatly enhanced by the elegant clock tower (21).

Unlike the younger Tessin, his contemporary Eric Dahlbergh (1625–1703), a Swede of peasant stock, was an out-and-out individualist in his expression, romantic and nationalistic. Eventually he became a field-marshal and spent a large part of his life designing fortifications and military buildings. So expert was he in this that both Charles II of England and Frederick III of Denmark made offers for his services, both of which he patriotically refused. As well as being a military engineer, Dahlbergh was a skilled topographical draughtsman and produced the famous and monumental work of engravings called " Suecia Antiqua et Hodierna ", in which are recorded both Sweden's ancient towns and buildings and the new noblemen's palaces and formal gardens of his time (10). The number of buildings he designed is therefore, not surprisingly, limited, but the few which still stand, mostly ecclesiastical, show genius, especially so the lovely church at Karlshamn.

Of the Swedish Baroque three other remarks remain to be made in this brief summary. First, on the interiors : These were highly ornate in the palaces. Walls and ceilings were decorated either with painted wood panelling, as at Läckö, or where cost was less material with Italianate plasterwork, as at Karlberg, though walls were often

44

16 KARLBERG PALACE, Stockholm: the North Side (1670) designed by
Jean de la Vallée (see fig. 46)

17 DROTTNINGHOLM: The Chinese rococo Pavilion (1760's)
designed by C. F. Adelcrantz

18, 19 *Left :* Painted sawn work of the eighteenth-century Delsbo farmstead, Skansen
Right: The early solid untreated axed work at the seventeenth-century Mora
farmstead, Skansen

20 Modern panel work in the Gustavsberg Industrial Village
THE TIMBER HOUSE TRADITION

covered with tapestries or with oil paintings. Staircases in the larger buildings were grand and formal, as for example the masterpiece at Drottningholm by both Tessins, father and son.

Secondly, on the church building: Here the Greek cross tended to replace the Latin on plan and the Roman round arch to replace the Gothic pointed arch. An example of this is Stockholm's Katarina Church by Jean de la Vallée (altered by G. J. Adelcrantz), with its tall octagonal central tower surmounted by a dome. Detailing of altars, organ lofts, church monuments and pulpits was highly ornate in the European Baroque manner and was mostly the work of foreign craftsmen. A magnificent example of the time is the pulpit of Uppsala Cathedral designed by the younger Tessin in collaboration with the Hamburg sculptor Burchard Precht (22).

Thirdly, on the vernacular timber building: This is exemplified in the country houses of the wealthier peasants, in many village churches and in that fascinating tradition of bell tower construction which is unique to Sweden (49). Towards the end of the Baroque period, the old, solid, untreated, axed timber construction was giving way to the lighter construction of sawn planks which needed the protection of paint (18). Thus we see the continuation of the solid, untreated work in much peasant building and at the same time the erection of a new type of country house for wealthier folk, painted in white or yellow and occasionally in the new and startling red ochre from the Falu copper mines. Features of the charming small manor houses of these times are the double-tiered, *säteri* roofs initiated by de la Vallée in his Riddarhus and the symmetrical composition round a courtyard of the main house and detached wings in one, two or sometimes three pairs—a homely application of the grand Baroque vista. No doubt fear of fire had something to do with these wings being detached. This type of small country house continued well into the eighteenth century. Typical examples can be seen on Värmdön near Stockholm and at Västsura in Västmanland.

*   *   *   *   *

The Age of Liberty and Gustavian Epoch (1718–1809). The first half of the century was a period of political confusion, though culturally it was far from sterile, in spite of the losses the nobles had sustained under Carl XI and in spite of the stifling of initiative through the dictatorship of Carl XII. On the death of Carl XII there were two claimants to the throne—Charles Frederick of Holstein, grandson of Carl XI, and Ulrica Eleonora, sister of Carl XII. Frederick, Prince of Hesse, Ulrica's husband, who was strongly suspected of having arranged the direction of that stray bullet which killed Carl XII, secured his wife's coronation but only on the condition that all royal prerogatives were signed away. In 1720 the queen abdicated in favour of her husband, a colourless individual, who remained little more than a figurehead. In 1751 Adolf Frederick, cousin of Charles Frederick of Holstein, took the Crown under another stringent oath which renounced any royal authority. Until his son, the great Gustav III, became king in 1771, the affairs of state were in the hands of quarrelsome and corrupt factions and reached their climax of discord in the bitter struggle between the Hats and Caps. Two badly mismanaged wars disturbed these years, one in connection with the War of the Austrian Succession, when in 1741 Sweden attacked Russia in support of her ally France, the other in connection with the Seven Years' War of 1756-63, when again Sweden went to France's aid against Frederick the Great of Prussia. In spite of these wars, art, science and trade flourished during these times which were enriched by the work of such men as Emanuel Swedenborg (1688–1772) who personified the best of his age. He is known mostly for his religious mysticism, but he was in fact far more important as an inventor of genius and a scientific pioneer. One could almost call him Sweden's Leonardo. During this period Gothenburg, which Gustav Adolph had founded in 1619, came into her own as a great maritime trading centre and was of such value to the country that during the 1720's Sweden's shipping tonnage rose by 50 per cent. It is possible that if it had not been for the Enclosures Acts of the 1750's which consolidated the smaller farms, ensured that large tracts of forest came into the hands of the State and drove many country people to seek livings in the capital city, Gothenburg might have come to rival Stockholm in size and importance.

In 1771, when Gustavus III hastened home from France to assume the throne, the incompetence and chicanery of party rule had brought the country to financial ruin. The following year Gustavus achieved what he had been planning for a long time—a daring and bloodless *coup d'état*. This ended the Age of Liberty, a title that had by then come to be regarded with irony. The reign which followed was a brilliant one, not least on account of the king's personality, for he loved drama both on the stage and in life, held a scintillating court in an unadulterated French style and acted always with boldness and initiative, often at the risk of losing his throne. For one thing, he broke the constitution that the king could not declare war without the consent of the Riksdag when he attacked Russia under Catherine the Great in 1787. The Riksdag was greatly annoyed by this, but, luckily for the king, Denmark suddenly attacked Sweden. Gustav at once returned from Russia, ignored the government and with a theatrical gesture appealed in person, dressed as a peasant, to the Dalecarlians, who saw in him another Gustav Vasa. With bubbling zeal they flocked to his army, which marched towards Gothenburg, whither the Danes and Norwegians were converging. The enemy received a shock on discovering a nation in arms and hastily signed a peace. Returning to Stockholm, the king took over for a time a power even greater than that wielded by Gustav Vasa. He immediately resumed the war against Russia which was almost lost until, on the day in 1790 when the Russians had decided to hold victory celebrations, Gustav brought his new fleet into action at Svensund and once again accomplished a dramatic coup in the Grand Manner by winning the greatest naval victory in Swedish history. The king was advised in naval matters on that occasion by one Sydney Smith, an Englishman who had served under Rodney and had been sent on this assignment possibly because England was not keen on Russia's dominating the Baltic.

Sweden was in a bad financial way once more, but she had at least regained her prestige, self-respect and independence. Now the nobles, especially the younger members of the aristocracy, were becoming restless under the new despotism and, perhaps inspired by the mood engendered by the French Revolution, hatched a plot against the king. On March 16th, 1792, at a masked ball held in the Opera House in Stockholm, Gustav III was assassinated. He lingered for some days, during which time he nominated his brother Duke Carl as Regent to act for his thirteen-year-old son, who was to become Gustav IV Adolph.

Apart from succeeding dramatically in politics and war, Gustav III patronized the arts with enthusiasm, spent lavishly on a hedonistic court life in the extravagant style of Versailles, befriended all talented painters, poets and writers of his day, founded the Swedish Academy and the Royal Opera and eulogized all things French. He was himself a not incompetent writer of plays. A vain man, but a great king—perhaps not Sweden's greatest but certainly a gifted, colourful and humane personality who re-established the prestige of the country he loved with a romantic fervour.

The king's death was a blow to Sweden, for once again no capable hand was available to direct the state. The Regent, Duke Charles, was well-intentioned but muddle-headed. Against European opinion, he recognized the new French republic. However, when Gustav IV came to the throne in 1796 the pendulum swung the other way. Napoleon had by now turned Europe into a battlefield, and against him the new king showed an implacable opposition. Following the treaty between the Czar and Napoleon, Russia opposed Sweden, with the result that in the war of 1808 Sweden lost the remnants of her Baltic Empire, when Finland, which had been linked to Sweden for 650 years, was captured by Russia. In 1809 the king was deposed and a new era began.

*   *   *   *   *

The eighteenth century in Sweden was the age first of the Rococo and then of the Classical Revival. It was not an age so much of great building as of flowery, refined ornamentation of interiors—ornamentation based on wildly curling rock and fantastic plant formation—which formed a suitable background for gracious living. The influence, encouraged by royalty, especially Gustav III, and by such courtly figures as Carl Tessin, was essentially French. The France of Boucher and Watteau set every standard and so brought an elegant, light-hearted gaiety to the austere North as a playful reaction against the heavy pomp of the Baroque and the rigid conventions of the classical. Its object was to entertain rather than to impress, to sing rather than to shout. Chinese decorative influences were strong, stimulated by the import of beautiful Chinese wares by the Swedish East India Company which had established its headquarters in Gothenburg in 1731—lacquer goods, embroidery, wall papers and, above all, porcelain. The cult of the time was one of educated pleasure to which Rousseau brought the influence of Naturalism, an influence which was in fact not in the least natural but as sophisticated as an actress posing as a shepherdess. Later in the century England brought influences also, especially in landscape gardening of Capability Brown's informal type—one of England's greatest gifts to the world. Other influences from England were those of Chippendale and of our Swedish-born William Chambers* who laid out Kew Gardens. In Swedish Rococo's swirling, restless decorations, plant and flower forms predominated, perhaps as a gesture to a famous man of the time, the lovable naturalist Carl Linné, one of the initiators and the first president of the Swedish Academy of Sciences, founded in 1739.

* Sir William Chambers (1726–96) had close connections with Sweden. He was grandson of a rich merchant who had financed the armies of Charles XII and had been repaid in base money. His son stayed in Sweden for many years trying to obtain redress, and so William was born in Stockholm. At sixteen William became supercargo to the Swedish East India Company and, voyaging to Canton, made there his famous drawings of Chinese architecture.

The pleasure-seeking cult of the period was in Sweden not confined to the luxury-loving ruling classes but permeated the whole community. A social conscience was developing and the peasantry grew relatively prosperous, with the result that for about a century, that is between 1750 and 1850, the folk art of Sweden entered its most brilliant phase—a phase most vividly expressed in the so-called Dala paintings of the peasant artists, which have the Rococo touch while possessing at the same time a naïve and charming style all their own (48).

The outstanding architect of the age was Carl Hårleman (1700–53), renowned for his homely country houses, the "Cits' Country Boxes" of the period. Symmetry remains from the Baroque, but the grandeur and impracticability have been replaced by a gracious and friendly intimacy. French influence is seen in the mansard roofs and in rusticated angles, while the first intimations of the Classic Revival are apparent in Hårleman's restful house at Åkerö in Södermanland, one of his last works, for it was not begun until 1752. Here those elements of Swedish simplicity and grace, which recur through the centuries, from the Gothic of Linköping Cathedral to the *Funkis* of Stockholm's 1930 exhibition, are apparent. As Architect Royal, a post which he took over from his friend Carl Tessin, Hårleman accomplished a great amount of official work in his short life, such as improvements to Drottningholm, the university building and the royal residence at Uppsala, the Observatory at Stockholm and the East India Company's offices at Gothenburg.

Two other important contemporaries were Carl Frederick Adelcrantz (1716–96) and Jean Eric Rehn (1717–93), who was for a time Adelcrantz's chief assistant. "The kind and genial" Rehn, as a writer of the time called him, was apprenticed to Hårleman as a youth and then went to Paris with the main object of training as an engraver. Later he carried out much work for the royal family, mainly as an interior decorator. He was gifted in several ways and as a draughtsman alone can be set among the European masters of the century. During the latter half of the century, after a European tour, he became the chief exponent of the Classical Revival, which he adapted to that particularly Swedish manner called the *Gustavian* style, in which for the third time in three centuries the logical Mediterranean influence calmed the restless romanticism of northern Europe. This came about partly as a result of the archaeological researches of the Comte de Caylus of France, but mainly as an inevitable swing of the pendulum of taste. In his Rococo manner Rehn designed, among other houses, Stora Väsby in

Uppland, as well as much brilliant interior work in the Stockholm Palace, in the delightful China Palace at Drottningholm and in the Katarina Church in Stockholm in the form of a splendid organ façade executed in collaboration with one J. Clerck. As a reaction to the gilt and fol-de-rols of the Rococo, Rehn produced only a few years later such calm and austerely simple designs as the functional Forsmark house in Uppland with its English park. Many of the later houses of the period, such as Rehn's, were built for the rising mercantile class, especially for the wealthy iron masters who were now producing the best iron in the world and were responsible for no less than a third of the country's exports. A typical merchant's house of the period can be seen at Gunnebo near Gothenburg, built in 1786 to designs by C. W. Carlberg. With its white-painted wooden walls and generous classical portico it is almost American Colonial in feeling.

C. F. Adelcrantz, the son of G. J. Adelcrantz, who had worked with Jean de la Vallée and had been an apprentice to the younger Tessin, was less imaginative and daring than his pupil Rehn, but as an official architect he had a considerable influence. His most significant work, which epitomizes the Rococo, is his China Palace in the grounds of Drottningholm, built in the 1760's (17). With its central pavilion and side wings decorated with Chinamen's heads, dragons, temple bells and curling copper roofs, it is possibly the most charming example of Chinoiserie in Europe and, of course, like nothing you would ever see in the East. This architectural folly, as it might almost be called, was the permanent result in brightly painted stucco of a temporary Chinese palace of timber, a typical conceit of the times, which in 1753 had been transported by water from Stockholm in sections (an early prefab!) and erected in Drottningholm's park as a surprise birthday present from King Adolf Frederick to his wife, Louise Ulrica, sister of Frederick the Great of Prussia. The occasion was a festive one and the whole court dressed up in Chinese costumes, among them the seven-year-old Crown Prince, who became Gustav III, resplendent in mandarin silks. Near the China Palace is the charming village of Kanton built at the same period. There Queen Louise set up her handicraft workshops for the weaving of silks and other wares. Close by Drottningholm Palace itself is the wonderful little theatre which Adelcrantz designed in 1764 and where Gustav III loved to play at amateur theatricals. It can still be seen in its original and fully working state.

Like Rehn, Adelcrantz went over to the new classicism during the later part of the century and carried out much official work in that style for Gustav III. He laid out Gustav Adolph's Place in Stockholm, which lies across the water to the north of the Palace, and designed the old Opera House which stood there and wherein Gustav II was assassinated. He also designed the north part of the bridge which links the square with the Palace. The Opera House was pulled down in 1891, but the fine granite bridge with its elliptical arches and strong simple detailing is still there.

Another architect who worked in the Classical Revival manner was Fredrik Henrik Chapman (1721–1808), a man born in Gothenburg of English immigrants. His most important work can be seen in the buildings at the naval port of Karlskrona, where he was harbour master for many years.

Two other names stand out which, though not architectural, are of great importance to the eighteenth century. The first is Johan Tobias Sergel (1740–1814). He is Sweden's greatest sculptor, the only one, apart from Carl Milles, who has gained an international reputation. Born of a German immigrant, he was the pupil of the Frenchman L'archevêque. France and the antique world were otherwise his teachers. Yet his work, with its clear, vigorous classical lines, rises above eclecticism to a powerful individuality. Some of the best of his pieces can be seen in the Stockholm National Museum, while a fine statue of Gustav III executed by him stands on the Logården Steps of the Royal Palace, Stockholm.

His contemporary, Carl Michael Bellman (1740–95), whose head was carved on a medallion by Sergel and can be seen on Bellman's tomb in the Klara Churchyard, Stockholm, was a typical Rococo type, a man greatly honoured in his country for his delightful ballads, alternately gay and melancholy and always vivid and sparkling—"sorrow clad in rose colour" as a poet has described them. One might almost say that he produced a musical cult which has survived to this day, for at the famous cellar restaurant called *Den Gyllene Freden* in Old Stockholm, formerly a haunt of the pleasure-loving and bibulous Bellman, you may still hear his music played when some enthusiastic customer suddenly rises from his meal to the astonishment and frequent embarrassment of the foreigners present, to regale the company with a Bellman song accompanied by a lute, just as Bellman himself did here nearly two centuries ago. The profits from this restaurant, incidentally, now go to benefit indigent Swedish poets. Bellman's most famous piece is "Fjäriln Vingad Syns på Haga" ("The Butterfly on Wing is seen at Haga"), but for neatness of composition and melodic charm this writer's favourite is "Lik Som En Herdinna" ("Like a Shepherdess"). Its refrain goes thus:

Pastorale.

29.

Lik - som en her-din - na, hög - tids-klädd, Vi ro - si - ga bädd Sin pryd - nad och små be - hag strimman-de sken In - om den krans, i blom-mors va

* * * * *

Age of Democracy and the Industrial Revolution (1809 to modern times). For nine years after Gustav IV was deposed, his uncle Carl XIII was king. The dangers of absolute monarchy had been realized and were, in any case, out of harmony with the times. A new constitution was therefore adopted in 1809 by which a reasonable balance of power between King and Riksdag was established. The king was an old, enfeebled and childless man, the young Crown Prince had died suddenly at a military review in 1810, and a crisis arose as to who should next ascend the throne. It was decided to sound the all-powerful Napoleon and so a young lieutenant called Mörner was sent to Paris with a message to the Swedish Ambassador there. One of the strangest episodes in Swedish history followed. On his way to Paris, Mörner fell in with the Emperor's marshal, Bernadotte, and the bright idea occurred to him that Bernadotte would make a better candidate for the throne than any who had so far been proposed. Mörner returned to Stockholm and placed his bright idea before the Council, whose members, staggered by his impudence, thereupon placed him under arrest for insubordination. However, it was slowly conceded that the young lieutenant's idea

-lan en Ju-ni-dag___ Hop-le-tar ur grä-sets

h ej bland väp-ling, hägg och sy-ren In-blan-dar per-lors

(8)

flä-tar med le-kan-de qval,

might be a good one. Napoleon's consent was obtained and so the French General became the Swedish King, Karl XIV Johan. His extremely popular line has continued to the present day.

Bernadotte was not crowned until 1818, although he had acted as Regent for a number of years. He died in 1844 and during his twenty-six year reign he took his job seriously, in spite of the disadvantage that he never really understood the Swedish traditions and temperament, nor even learned to speak the language of his adopted country. Nevertheless he was a great success and died an honoured man. His first move was to declare war on England in order to satisfy Napoleon, but, realizing that trade between the two countries was essential to Sweden, he made it known by diplomatic means that trade would continue. This was a strange war for not a shot was fired on either side. Happily Bernadotte was a realist. In 1812 France invaded Swedish Pomerania, which had been restored to Sweden in 1810, and relations between the king and his former master became strained. Bernadotte then made a pact with Russia and, realizing that Finland was lost to Sweden for ever but could act as a useful buffer state, he bargained for the acquisition of Norway in return for military help at the moment when Napoleon's Grand Army was about to invade Russia. The outcome was the Retreat from Moscow and the Battle of Leipzig at which Bernadotte, by a cunning ruse, kept his Swedes out of action without losing face. After the victory, his army still fresh, Bernadotte marched into Denmark, which was powerless to resist. By the Treaty of Kiel, Denmark agreed to the cession of Norway, and the whole European war ended with the Treaty of Paris of 1814.

Following a history of almost ceaseless warfare since early times, Sweden at last entered a fruitful period of uninterrupted peace which has been maintained to the present day. Norway was restless under the new Crown, in spite of her retention by treaty of considerable independence. She possessed a strong independence movement and at last through its influence a friendly dissolution was arranged in 1905.

After Bernadotte, kings ceased to dominate Swedish affairs. The Government became more democratic under a constitutional monarch, and in 1866 the bi-cameral system superseded the old structure of the Four Estates in the Riksdag. As industrialism developed the political situation altered radically. Groups, movements, writers rather than powerful individuals dominated events and Liberalism became the new political creed. In 1909 general male suffrage and proportional representation were introduced, to be followed in 1918 by universal suffrage. During the twentieth century a high standard of general education had been established together with other social advances such as the state medical service. Their development has produced what G. B. Shaw described as the most civilized country in the world.

*   *   *   *   *

The period from about 1810 until the death of Bernadotte (King Karl Johan) in 1844 was the period of the Empire style of design called in Sweden the *Karl Johan* style—a development and simplification of the formal new-classicism. In England we would call it Regency for it was the period of Nash in England and of Schinkel in Germany. The character of the period in Sweden, as throughout Europe, was one of refined and restful dignity in the design of everyday things from fireplaces to coffee-pots, design which represented the beautiful swan-song of the age of handicrafts and educated patronage which was vanishing. In England architecture and engineering enjoyed a brief and happy honeymoon and produced the finest functional edifices in her history. In Sweden little of great note was built apart from a few utilitarian structures of power and unaffected simplicity such as the impressive outer fortifications at Karlsborg with their two squat round towers of stone at the ends of a long rampart (39). These were built in the 1840's to designs by Major C. F. Meijer who thus developed the fine tradition of military architecture which had begun in the Vasa period and had been continued by Eric Dahlbergh in the seventeenth century.

After about 1840 a new phase of design began which we would call Victorian—the romantic, eclectic design which borrowed ideas from every conceivable culture of the past from Gothic to Saracenic. Its foundations were literary, built by the Beckfords, Scotts, Hugos of the day, and later supported by the rising class of individualistic industrialists and tradesmen who had little time to develop their taste. Most of its architectural products we despise today though we are beginning to see that much of it had considerable character and fantasy. Sweden luckily escaped the squalor of slums and uncontrolled industrialism which went with this middle-class escapism and from which Britain still suffers. Modern industrialism, as we have seen, came to Sweden late in the century by which time good general education of all the classes had begun, industry had grown up in a decentralized way, population was limited, society was on a human scale, the country possessed no Black Gold to cast its blight of fog and dirt, *laissez-faire* was controlled but not frustrated by the State and the innate traditions of the old peasant culture helped to keep the scene tolerable to the sensitive eye. Looking at Sweden today we must always remember the history and traditions which have created the present. The country appears to be quite modern and well-regulated in all things, so that one receives the impression that it is all quite new, whereas in fact this modernism is a growth from the past—in government the democratic tradition of the Four Estates, in the arts and crafts the old, refined culture of the kings and nobles and the more homely, cruder but no less vigorous culture of the peasants.

An interesting example of this tradition of orderliness, which has retained visual comeliness, is that brought about by the founder of modern Sweden, the great Gustav Vasa. He took a personal interest in scientific farming and saw to it that the industrialism of the day in the mines did no harm to agriculture. The land above the mines, for instance, then had to be cultivated by law and even today farm bailiffs are attached to the mines. A result has been that the landscape has nowhere been disfigured, as it has in England, by grim and sterile slag heaps.

A typical piece of nineteenth-century romance is the curious spire of 1838 on the tower of Riddarholms Church in Old Stockholm—the ancient mausoleum of Sweden's kings and the Mecca of national romanticism. The tower, designed by the sculptor Eric Gustaf Göthe (1779–1838), was built in cast iron and has been described by Ragnar Östberg, who designed the Stockholm City Hall, as "a veil of black mourning crêpe thrown over Sweden's sepulchre". For other examples one has merely to glance round any of the larger towns like Stockholm or Gothenburg to see the strange chaos created by the Battle of the Styles during this century— breweries like medieval castles, schools and banks like Roman temples, office blocks like French châteaux. Finally, the reaction came at the turn of the century in the form of a curly, novel style called *Jugendstile* or *L'Art Nouveau*, of which the Dramatic Theatre in Stockholm is a sugary example.

One of the best of Sweden's stylistic architects, who flourished during the last half of the century, was Isak Gustav Clason, Sweden's Norman Shaw, who designed the Nordiska Museum in Stockholm in the Danish Renaissance style as an echo from Elsinore mixed with Swedish Vasa and German Baroque. Another of his works is the impressive town mansion of a wealthy tycoon called Count Hallwyl in Hamngatan, Stockholm, which is in a Spanish-Moorish-Gothic style. It is now an interesting period museum which reveals how a millionaire's family lived in Stockholm some fifty years ago. In spite of his stylism, Clason was an innovator to the extent that he did believe that the façade should not be merely a superficial and romantic screen but an honest expression of the functional plan behind.

In literature an anti-romantic movement of social realism developed in Europe, of which Balzac and Dickens were the chief exponents. They were followed in Scandinavia by Ibsen and Strindberg. This movement did not greatly affect architecture until the twentieth century, but it no doubt indirectly helped to bring about the Functionalism of the 1930's. In the latter part of the nineteenth century, however, this realism produced a group of painters in Sweden who are still greatly honoured. Examples of their work can be seen in the art galleries of Gothenburg and Stockholm. The greatest and the most individualistic of them all was Ernst Josephson, a member of an old and distinguished Swedish-Jewish family. He went over to a form of impressionism and his last canvases produced during a state of mental illness are perhaps his finest works and have only recently been re-assessed. Others were the eccentrics, Carl Frederik Hill and Ivar Arosenius, the vigorous and colourful Anders Zorn, born of a peasant woman, who might be termed the Augustus John of Sweden; also the inter-preters of Swedish nature and everyday life, Bruno Lillefors, the

21 STUREFORS MANOR: An early eighteenth-century country house in Östergötland designed by Tessin the Younger

22 UPPSALA CATHEDRAL : The baroque pulpit designed by Tessin the Younger and B. Precht, the Hamburg sculptor (1707–09)

painter of wild animals, and Carl Larsson, the painter of homely, family scenes. Two important landscapists are Carl Wilhelmson and Prince Eugène, brother of the late King Gustav and last, but not least, is the humorous Albert Engström, Sweden's Phil May, also well known as a writer, who loved to caricature the ordinary folk of his country in an affectionate, if sometimes cynical, way (p. 255).

A good deal deserves to be said about modern Swedish architecture and craftsmanship, for these have been greeted with respect throughout the world under the slogan Swedish Modern and have had a definite world influence. The new design began in Sweden at the beginning of this century as a revolt against foreign eclecticism at a time when Sweden was becoming a proud and wealthy industrial nation. It was romantic still but now strongly nationalistic, though it owed a great deal to that handicraft movement of William Morris which had protested against the machine and its cheap imitation of handicraft design. In literature this nationalism was reflected by such famous writers as Selma Lagerlöf and Verner von Heidenstam, and in sculpture by Carl Milles.

The leaders of the new nationalism in architecture were Clason's pupil Ragnar Östberg, Carl Westman, Cyrillus Johansson and Sigfrid Ericson. The Golden Age of Swedish architecture had begun with the start of Sweden's full industrial development. Trappings were romantic and eclectic still, but now home-grown and imaginatively adapted. Rich red brick, copper-covered turrets, high-pitched roofs of tiles and carefully proportioned fenestration characterized the style, expressed, for example, in its first example, the Läkaresällskapets House, Stockholm (1904, Carl Westman), and its last example, the Centrum office block, Stockholm (1927, C. Johansson). In between there was the most famous of all, the Stockholm City Hall, the drawings for which Östberg completed in 1909 (47).

Came the First World War and four years of Nordic isolation. With the release of peace, there was much travelling southwards by artists and architects. The reaction against heavy nationalism set in. Uncovered brick was out and cheerful coloured stucco was in, embellished with white appliqué motifs and perverted pagan columns. This was the New Renaissance, the period of Hellenic elegance, of Swedish Grace (it became Pseudish Grace to the grave pedants of the next decade). It was eclecticism again but with a new excitement and freed from antiquarian copyism. The names of the period are the Concert Hall, Stockholm (1926, Ivar Tengbom), with its purely decorative portico of Corinthianized columns, and the excellent little Liljevachs Art Gallery, Stockholm (1919, Carl Bergsten). Perhaps the most typical example, however, was the Gothenburg Exhibition of 1923, relics of which can still be seen at the top of The Avenue and in the Liseberg pleasure gardens.

Then Corbusier arrived. Away went "meaningless" ornament. In Sweden, as elsewhere, the architect ruthlessly rubbed out his formalized details, opened out his plans, removed a wall or two, nailed the flag of Function to the mast of Form and concentrated on the stern reality of reinforcing rods and tuberculosis statistics. Between 1930 and 1940 *Funkis* swept over Sweden. Here was a creed whose devotees had true faith, a faith formulated in polemics as well as deeds—for instance, in the publication *Acceptera* of 1931 written by six of the most enthusiastic supporters of the new movement, including Asplund and Markelius. The enthusiasts produced some extremely fine buildings—fine, one now suspects, less on account of the rigid principles behind functionalism than of the creative stimulus provided by the new creed.

High priest was the great Gunnar Asplund, who began his new phase with the courageous and extremely successful Stockholm Exhibition of 1930. This had a profound effect throughout Scandinavia. Here Asplund forgot his Swedish Grace and the discovery of Tutankhamen's tomb (that had obviously influenced his Stockholm City Library) and designed afresh in the so-called international style—with Swedish grace. There followed many more buildings in the same vein, including his little Bredenberg's store in Stockholm. Markelius and Åhren produced their severe but satisfying students' club, also in Stockholm. Other important buildings were those of the Co-operative Society's architectural department under Eskil Sundahl, Markelius's Concert Hall at Helsingborg, and the Swedish pavilion at the Paris Exhibition of 1937 by Sven Ivar Lind. In Swedish town planning and housing, too, Le Corbusier's theories have had a noticeable effect—as, for example, in those Point Houses which have become a familiar feature of the Stockholm skyline.

But time passes. Theory becomes well tried by the ineluctable facts of practice. Today the *Funkis* phase in Sweden is dying, or perhaps, more correctly, is becoming absorbed in a new phase. Another reaction, now against a too rigid formalism, has set in. The first excitement of structural experiment has gone and there is a return to workaday common sense. There is a feeling that buildings are made by human beings for human beings rather than for the cold logic of theory. The word *spontaneitet*, so often on the lips of the young Swedish architect today, perhaps gives the key to the new approach. The Swedish temperament is a compromise between Teuton and Anglo-Saxon. German mechanical perfectionism and love of abstractions is balanced by British individualism and earthy practicality, and now the balance, in architecture at least, is moving towards the commonsense end of the see-saw. Why, they ask, make windows larger than necessary just to show that we can create a wall entirely of glass? Why flat roofs when they always start to leak in the spring? Why avoid traditional materials when they do their job well and provide pleasant texture and colour at the same time? Why eschew fantasy and decoration for which, in our hearts, we long?

Planning has become much freer and far less concerned with the pattern on paper than with the final reality on the site. Fenestration, too, is freer and windows occur at the places and of the sizes which needs dictate and as the pattern pleases. Indigenous traditional materials are used both inside and out, especially brick and timber. In domestic work cosiness is coming back. Buildings are married carefully to their sites and to the landscape, and flowers and plants are made an integral part of the whole design.

This does not mean that the new sociological approach to architecture is passing. Far from it. It is stronger than ever. Nor is there any slackening in the rationalization of building or in technical experiment. Rather is an attempt evident to bring a new science into the picture—that of psychology. A few examples of this latest phase of modern Swedish architecture are: Asplund's last big job before he died in 1940—the strangely moving crematorium at Skogskyrkogården near Stockholm, by which he retained his inspiring leadership in Swedish architecture right to the end of his remarkable career. There is also Nils Einar Eriksson's fine concert hall in Gothenburg which to some extent foreshadowed the new movement, for it was completed in 1935. Another example is the Town Hall and Hotel at Karlskoga-Bofors by Sune Lindström, completed in 1940, which we shall see on our cross-country journey (26). In this last example particularly, the architect has sought atmosphere as well as good function and he has not been afraid to use traditional materials, including brick and even shingles, to clothe the reinforced concrete structure; nor has he inhibited his pleasure in creating imaginative form and detail. In the domestic sphere a good example is the charming Friluftstaden at Malmö by Eric Persson, a garden city with terrace houses designed with considerable technical ingenuity but clothed simply in bricks and tiles.

A young but well-known Swedish architect, Sven Backström, explains the new attitude in these words: "We do not want either reactionary artiness or schematic over-simplification in our architecture, and therefore psychological factors must become our main concern in quite a different way than hitherto. We must attain the positive and life-assenting in architecture as in life itself and allow our whole beings and therefore our feelings to find expression."

From the turn of the century and in harmony with the new architecture, the handicrafts began to flourish and a new realization grew that the Machine has its own aesthetic which, if understood and accepted, need not be out of harmony with hand-made wares, but can indeed by contrast enhance the beauty of both the machine-made and the hand-made. The glass factories of Kosta and Orrefors, the porcelain works of Gustavsberg and Rörstrand, developed their old traditions in the modern idiom and surprised the nations with their beautiful and skilfully made wares. Modern Swedish furniture, too, set a world standard, especially in mass-produced pieces which could be bought by those with limited incomes. Together with these productions, public taste was being educated by such excellent and typically Swedish social movements as the Swedish Institute of Arts and Crafts, founded in 1845 and still going strong, and the Stockholm Citizens' Furnishing Advice Centre, where young couples, who have borrowed money from the municipality at a low rate of interest to buy furniture, can obtain free trained advice on the furnishing and decorating of their new homes.

The general pleasure taken in handicrafts and the good design of everyday things permeates all classes and such home crafts as weaving are practised with enthusiasm but without selfconsciousness, for the old peasant traditions survive in the transformed life of the new industrial age.

ROCK CUTTING AT TEGNEBY, BOHUSLÄN

IV

Gothenburg

FROM the short, steep chop of the North Sea the steamer glides into the calmer waters of Sweden's west-coast archipelago and we enjoy the never-failing, age-old thrill of landfall. We steam through the scattering of skerries, some dark and bare, others covered with pine trees and small red timber houses, a new and refreshing landscape. On our way up the Göta River we pass many kinds of craft—a small white passenger steamer on its way to some coastal resort, a tough fisherman popping powerfully on its Bolinder diesel, a graceful pleasure yacht and then a noble ship of the Swedish American Line. Ahead Gothenburg comes into view, Sweden's Little London, her main port and her second city, housing some 350,000 souls. Now she appears as a panorama of cranes, oil-tanks, docks, shipyards, roofs, spires, all set among rocky bluffs. To the south the scene is dominated by the red brick church of Masthugget with its bold square tower rising from a granite hill. Built in 1914 to a design by Sigfrid Ericson this landmark greets the foreign visitor like a carefully chosen diplomat, for it is an excellent example of that purely national style we have discussed, which developed during the first decade of the century to produce a Golden Age in Swedish architecture and craftsmanship. At last the ship's engine is at peace, the gangway clatters, the crowds surge forward and we march down to the cobbles of a new land.

Most travellers will now enter a taxi, after observing the customs' ritual, and will at once make for the swift electric train which will take them to Stockholm in seven hours. This is a mistake. One should dally awhile in Gothenburg for it is a most pleasant town and has much to show the visitor.

Everything here is clean and orderly. The streets are lively and yet do not hold that nervous tension of the great continental capitals. The shop windows are filled with the best of wares and everyone looks well dressed. Bright signs project over the pavements and plenty of bunting is afloat. Cooling water streams down the plate-glass windows of the *charkuteri* shops, and in the restaurants proud waitresses in black and spotless white move with the dignity of countesses. The crowded narrow shopping streets gain intrigue by contrast with the broad park-lined avenues and with such wide spaces as that where the statue of Gothenburg's founder stands—the great King Gustav Adolph. You will notice the well-designed street furniture, such as telephone booths, bright yellow cycle stands and decorative advertisement posts, the many neat *konditori* displaying rich pastries among the climbing plants, the ubiquity of fresh paint, bright dresses, sleek American cars and handsome policemen who, in their white caps and gloves, swords swinging at their sides, give a gay, light-opera touch to the picture. The girls are pretty, and soon we shall learn to distinguish a definite Gothenburg type with petite features, good complexion, straight back and, of course, blue eyes. We are never out of sight of a tree. Students frequently pass in their white caps with small blue and gold rosettes in the band to signify that they have passed their matriculation, and perhaps a veiled widow in mourning as deep as that of any French provincial. Types of ageing men pass by, also, whom one thought had vanished from the earth decades ago—types bred in the heydays of the Edwardian bourgeoisie. In the local paper, Mutt and Jeff still survive as *Storklas* and *Lillklas* and "Charley's Aunt" is on at the local theatre. In the entrance halls of offices and pensionats we gain our first whiff of a common Swedish smell, one which when sensed years ahead will bring back a sudden, nostalgic pang of memory—a pleasant, sweet smell with something in it of burning birch wood, of varnished pine and simmering coffee.

Everyone in Gothenburg seems to have some words at least of English. Perhaps this is partly because the town has close ties, both cultural and economic, with Great Britain—ties which were greatly strengthened by Napoleon's blockade of the Continent during the first decade of the nineteenth century when the port became the chief depôt of British trade in northern Europe. They say, indeed, that when it rains in London people in Gothenburg put up their umbrellas. The town was built for trade, especially for trade to all ports outside the Baltic. With its seven miles of quays, it is today essentially a carriers' centre and less of a mart than it was once. It also acts as the main market for the West Coast fisheries, and here are important ship-building works and other industries. The place has a cosmopolitan air, not only because it is a port, but because it has been peopled since its foundation by different nations; first by Dutchmen, some of whom actually helped in the planning and building of the town with its fortifications, canals and moat. The Dutch language was at that time during the seventeenth century heard as frequently in Gothenburg as Swedish. Other immigrants were encouraged and many German, Jewish, English and Scottish families eventually settled here, some of which founded large fortunes and established distinguished lines. A few of these patrician families still flourish and have given much through the years to Gothenburg, for it became something of an obligation if one acquired wealth to help the town in some way—by the presentation of a piece of parkland, a new hospital, a museum or a work of art. Thus the city has acquired a proud and self-confident attitude of independence and has always been the most powerful stronghold of free trade in Scandinavia. It is a Buddenbrooks kind of place.

Some of the patrician families were of Scottish descent, the most notable being the Dicksons, who gained a fortune by exploiting the Norrland forests and have perpetuated their name in one of the streets of the town. The best known of their many acts of munificence was the financing of the Nordenskiöld Expedition of discovery through the North-East Passage in 1878. Another well-known local Scottish family is that of the Carnegies, famous for their Gothenburg porter, and it was a Colin Campbell from Edinburgh who was one of the founders of the Swedish East India Company. But these Scotsmen were of the second, and commercial, influx of the later seventeenth century to the eighteenth. There had been an earlier and military Scottish influx into Sweden which began in the 1560's when King Erik XIV recruited a Scottish legion to fight against the Danes. This recruitment continued during the early seventeenth century, when Gustav Adolph, then engaged in the Thirty Years' War, called to his aid Campbells, Crawfords, Hamiltons, Gordons and many other clansmen. Some of these mercenaries were granted titles and land, and took their places in the new House of Nobles. Englishmen, too, were recruited at that time, but the Scots were the majority and were considered the élite, being highly rated as fighters, though wild, arrogant and difficult to handle, as Gustavus found. The levies must have been considerable, for during 1630 alone some 8,000, mainly Scotsmen, were serving under the Swedish colours.

In spite of having become a world port, Gothenburg is no Hot Spot of waterside brothels and night haunts, for the people are puritans all and take their leisure in a balanced bourgeois style. Even the Liseberg Amusement Park, which is owned and run by the municipality, is tidy and well-behaved, with not a hair out of place—perhaps a little too prim. Only now and then (with a certain relief, it must be confessed) does one strike a note of spontaneous jollification as one passes a café where Carnegie porter is being quaffed by loud-voiced men in peaked caps and bright cotton shirts —the nearest equivalent to the English pub in Sweden, and a poor substitute. However, it is cheering to hear the strains of an accordion and the rough laughter coming through the swing doors, in spite of the presence of the stern policeman standing for ever on guard at the entrance.

In the summer the pleasures of the skerries are near at hand—bathing, sailing, fishing—and it is easy to reach the holiday island of Marstrand by boat, or the delightful seaside suburb of Särö by train or car. In the winter the cultural life is rich enough, for the town is renowned for the high standard of its music and drama; then, too, intimate home and social life is enjoyed by all classes.

Though the street vista along the canal by Norra Hamngatan must be one of the finest in Europe, the town's architecture as a whole is mediocre, being mainly of nineteenth and early twentieth century confection. The place has few fine old monuments but, taken as a whole, it has character and cohesion. Remnants of the original town of the seventeenth century exist now only in the Grand Canal, in the remains of the old moat which zigzagged round the town and in the two forts by Eric Dahlbergh called Göta Lejon and Kronan. These forts are simple, strong, stone structures standing on high ground and once formed part of the original outer fortifications of the town. Now Kronan houses a military museum. Gothenburg was built in the Dutch way on a system of canals. These canals not only gave access to the wharves for shipping and acted as drains but served also as protective barriers against the spread of fire, which in those days of timber building was an important consideration. Now most of the old canals have been filled in, but when the town walls were pulled down in the nineteenth century the tract along their line was turned into open plantations. Thus Gothenburg has obtained its brilliant band of green which stretches right across the modern town and creates its special cachet—that of a maritime garden city. The old moat runs through much of the parkland, adding to the garden landscape the charm of water where small pleasure boats or a barge café, gay with bright umbrellas and geraniums, lie moored. How different is the sparkling scene to our own squalid and neglected, yet potentially beautiful, Little Venice at Paddington.

Apart from this canal park, Gothenburg has many other gardens —the Slottskog, the Botanical Gardens with their West Coast glen preserved as a primeval forest, the ocean promontory of Keiller's Park and the English garden of the Horticultural Society where the ghosts of rich and festive Edwardian merchants still linger on the terrace of the fretwork restaurant to sip sweet punsch and listen to the band. One can indeed stroll among the trees on a summer day

23 GOTHENBURG:
The Göta River

STOCKHOLM:
ooking towards
kansen from
Nobel Park

25 GOTHENBURG:
The Square of Guld
heden, with the *Kollek
tivhus* in the backgroun

26 KARLSKOGA-BOFORS:
The Courtyard of the Town
Hall cum Hotel (1941)

through the fragrance of lilac and linden from one end of the town to the other.

In short, Gothenburg is by no means a dull place. Its bustle and internationalism form an antidote to the smugness and boredom which beset so many other provincial towns. Moreover it is not too big—that is to say it is one of those towns of just the right size which you can walk out of in a morning. Today you will sometimes hear proud Stockholmers say: "Life in Gothenburg is becoming much pleasanter than in Stockholm. The capital is growing too large. It suffers now from big-city nerves"—a remark which would have been considered gross treason twenty years ago. In spite of such concessions, a good-humoured, boastful rivalry continues from of old between the two towns.

Among Gothenburg's few old buildings of distinction you will notice the classical Cultural History Museum facing the canal in Norra Hamngatan, which was built in 1750 to designs by Hårleman and B. W. Carlberg as offices for the East India Company. This Carlberg was the younger brother of J. E. Carlberg, Gothenburg's first municipal engineer and town planner. B. W.'s son, the last of this creative Gothenburg dynasty, C. W. Carlberg (1746–1814) was responsible for another worthy old building, the Cathedral of 1808–15, which is a rather heavy, unadventurous but nevertheless dignified Palladian design. It stands well placed among the trees of a public garden which gives a sudden spacious release from the tightness of Kungsgatan.

Of the modern buildings, the finest in the city is unquestionably Nils Einar Eriksson's concert hall. This is one of the group of buildings around Götaplatsen, the town's *Forum Artis*, whose focus is a fine fountain of Poseidon by Carl Milles. The forum lies at the top end of Kungsports Avenue, the grand axis of Gothenburg, usually called simply The Avenue. Eriksson's concert hall was the result of a competition held in 1931 and will undoubtedly be regarded by future generations as one of the best buildings of its kind and time anywhere in Europe.

Around the outskirts of the town and especially to the south-east much new housing is being built both in the form of flats and individual dwellings, including a type which seems to be peculiar to the town—a house containing two flats only, which we would call a Duplex. Housing is a social problem in Sweden and is still very cramped. One reason for this, of course, has been the war and another the recent explosive rise of the birth-rate. Finance is also a problem, for buildings must be well built against the severe winters, the levelling and excavating of the granite foundations are costly

71

and good equipment and general conveniences are demanded. Swedes take readily to new ideas from abroad and delight in new mechanical gadgets for their homes. In that they are like the Americans. Yet they have far greater social conscience than the Americans, and in town planning and estate lay-out they are forging ahead. All over the country the Swedes are now applying the principle of the Neighbourhood Unit, the small planned local community which is based on theories propounded by Lewis Mumford in America and Thomas Sharp in England.

Let us now take one of the blue and white trams from the centre of the town and rattle up to the southern heights, there to inspect one of these modern Neighbourhood Units—that of Guldheden (25). It was barely complete in 1950, for the private company which launched the scheme began work only in 1944, and it has since had difficult conditions to work in. The rocky, park-like site is laid out informally and the blocks of flats of brick or coloured stucco, some of them as high Point Houses, others as lower Long Houses, are set wide apart without stiff regimentation. They are simply designed like most of the new flat blocks in Scandinavia, and their utilitarian appearance is mitigated by the subtle, free landscaping and the use of building materials with pleasing colours and textures. All the conveniences are here. Around the so-called Market Place stand shops, a restaurant, cinema, post office and a large *Kollektivhus*. The latter is a type of building developed in Sweden especially for single people or married couples both of whom go to work each day and have little time for domestic work. The Market Place is charming with its nearby pond and informal garden, its restaurant terrace bright with flowers and orange shop-window blinds. Up among the blocks of flats are other buildings for communal use—a laundry, a plant for heating the whole neighbourhood (fed with local rubbish), a garage and a nursery school. The whole area is served by winding approach roads only and no through traffic can pass across the site. Another amenity is an office in one of the buildings on the Market Place where household help can be hired by the day or the hour and where mutual help among the tenants can be organized.

Most of the flats have splendid views and contain between two and four rooms apart from kitchens, bathrooms, built-in cupboards and home laundries. Below each block is a communal drying room and some of the blocks have large halls which can be hired for social gatherings. As in all modern Swedish flats, rubbish shutes have been built into the walls with access openings at each landing. Here at Guldheden life should be easy and enjoyable, for most of the practical problems of domestic life have been solved, and many of the aesthetic problems too. The place has been built for the less wealthy middle-class resident, though the same general standards are being aimed at in Swedish working-class housing as well. Indeed it is often difficult to distinguish between the two kinds, for the classes are far less disparate than in England and frequently live mingled easily and unselfconsciously together in the same district.

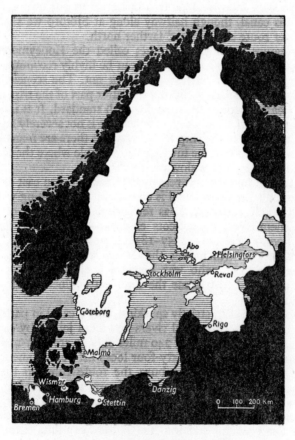

27 THE SWEDISH EMPIRE IN 1700.
Copyright A. B. Kartografiska Institutet

73

V

The Göta Canal

BACK in the town once more you will no doubt stroll down
to the docks to savour the busy life of the waterside. There
you may come to the small dock lying at the lower end of
Östra Hamngatan, where small steamers arrive and depart each
day on the Göta Canal journey between Gothenburg and Stockholm. We shall soon be departing ourselves in our own craft on a
part of this canal, though halfway along at Sjötorp we shall leave
the steamer route and proceed farther north.

The steamer journey, sometimes called the Honeymoon Run,
takes about two and a half days and can be highly recommended to
the traveller, whether on honeymoon or not. The scenery on the
way is beautiful, especially during the latter part of the trip, and the
food on board is up to the usual Swedish standard. It is indeed an
interesting and restful journey on which one is not severely restricted
to the small space of the ship all the way, for there are many halting
places and walks along the towpath are possible where the locks are
thick and the ship makes slow progress.

A digression here on this remarkable link between east and west
is justified, for the Göta Canal is an old and a fascinating waterway
and was largely constructed, as few people know, least of all the
Swedes themselves, by a Scots engineer—none other than the
great Thomas Telford (1757–1834), builder of canals, roads,
harbours, bridges (including the Menai Bridge); also architect
and would-be poet, who was born in a shepherd's cottage in
Eskdale and lived to become the foremost engineer of his day in
the world.

The Göta Canal is, strictly speaking, only a canal in parts, for it
consists of a series of natural rivers and lakes joined by canalized
sections. Of its total length of 240 miles only 59 are man-made, and
in that man-made mileage sixty-four locks lift boats some 278 feet
above the sea. From Gothenburg the route runs up the Göta
River, past Trollhättan Falls, across Vänern, the largest lake in the
country and the third largest in Europe, then through Västergotland
and across Lake Vättern to Vadstena. On through the fertile province of Östergotland and into the Baltic Sea; then through the
friendly, verdant archipelago of Södermanland and so by way of
the short Södertelje Canal into Lake Mälar with its many islands

74

28   At the Midsummer Festival, Trollhättan

29 A modern lock at Troll-hättan

30 An old lock at Sjötorp

THE GÖTA CANAL

and thickly wooded shores to end in the evening glow at the lovely capital, the Queen of the Mälar.

The canal was built originally for both commercial and strategic purposes and, though the western part from Gothenburg to Vänern is still fairly busy with commercial craft which serve the towns round the lake, the whole is now mainly a tourist route. As such it is a valuable national asset and deservedly popular, for the scenery through which it passes has an idyllic, fertile charm and along it a good general impression of modern and ancient Sweden can be gained. The old provinces of the Goths through which it passes have been inhabited and cultivated since early times, and in these districts the period of greatness of the seventeenth century has left many monumental adornments in the form of churches, manor houses and castles, including Vadstena (9). As far as Lake Vänern the route was modernized in 1915; here the locks are worked by electrical machinery and are large enough to take ocean-going ships (29). Strictly speaking this is Trollhättan Canal. The stretch from Sjötorp on the east of Vänern to the Baltic at Mem is the Göta Canal proper, and this part, for which Telford was responsible, is undoubtedly the most beautiful and interesting and still retains its intimate early nineteenth-century atmosphere and scale (30). There the original type of hand-operated lock is still in use, and there, as in most of the old canals in the world, nature has taken an artificial work of man to herself so that the cut winds along as prettily as any river through the woods and meadowland.

What the journey lacks in high drama is repaid by the continual change and contrast as between the closed and open view—between the wide waters of the lakes and the narrow channels where you can pluck catkins from the birch-trees as you stand on the steamer's deck or gaze for a brief moment as you glide along into the soft unblinking eyes of a plump Östergotland cow as she lies chewing the cud on the bank only a few yards away.

Of the lakes along the route, Vättern is the strangest, and is still regarded with a certain awe on account of its moody, unpredictable nature and mysterious habits. Old folk-legends tell of its terror and its magic. The lake is strangely shaped, for it is 80 miles long from north to south but only 19 miles at its widest from east to west. It is like a great fissure and plunges down between cliffs at its deepest point to 455 feet, where the water remains very near freezing point all the year round. Fed by few streams it is in fact an enormous spring—a spring so clear that it is possible to look deep into the cold depths and see the glitter of fish whose ancestors were there when, 10,000 years and more ago, the lake was a bay of the sea. At one moment Vättern is serene and loving. Suddenly the sky darkens and within ten minutes she is a lashing, dangerous shrew. But her strangest habit is her burping—her periodic cannonading which is particularly audible in the quiet days of early spring. This is believed to be caused by gases which rise to the surface when the bedrock settles, but to the sailor out there on his lonely schooner it must seem as though some great primeval monster had suddenly snorted in its sleep.

A waterway which was to link Sweden's west and east coasts had been planned as early as the sixteenth century, but the dream was not to become a reality for another three centuries. Telford explains in his *Life* of 1838 how the Göta Canal was realized: "Near Wenersborg, two connected locks have long existed, each 182 feet in length and 34 feet wide; they were constructed about the year 1600 in the reign of Charles IX by Dutch engineers. . . . In 1793 a plan for passing the Trollhatta Falls was laid before the then King, by a company of subscribers. . . . To encourage the projectors, the lock at Edit, built on the river Gotha in 1640 and that at Akerstrom, built in 1774, were granted to the company. . . . The canal works were completed in 1800. The Count Platen . . . was elected a director of that navigation and very soon perceived the advantages that would be derived by continuing a similar communication between the Wenern and the Baltic . . . the Count (in 1808)* therefore applied to me; and having acceded to his proposal, I, with two assistants, went over to Sweden and commenced operations early in August, and by the aid and judicious arrangements of Count Platen, I executed a regular survey, and laid down correct plans and sections of the country between Lake Wenern and the shore of the Baltic, near Soderkoping. . . . The subscription was opened in May 1810, and at the first meeting Count Platen was appointed chairman and manager-in-chief. . . . From 1813 to 1829, the Count sent me at least once every year a detailed statement of the canal operations; and he uniformly behaved with attention and kindness to the British workmen whom I sent over from time to time, as required."

"When the canal was completed", Telford concludes, "and opened for public use, large gold medals were struck on the occasion, when one of each was presented to me; and as a further mark of the King's approbation, I received a Swedish order of knighthood, and a portrait of his Majesty set in valuable diamonds."

The great advantages of such a canal were obvious. No longer would dues for passing the Sound have to be paid to the Danish

* At that time Telford was at work on the Caledonian Canal.

Government, but dependence on the Sound in times of war could be avoided. Moreover, as Telford pointed out, "an opening would be afforded for exporting produce of timber and iron, also for conveying the limestone (which is chiefly found on the shores of the lakes) to the interior of the country for agricultural purposes."

For over twenty years Telford was connected with the work. It must have been among the most agreeable to him of his many enterprises, for not only were his efforts warmly received by the Swedish people but he made an intimate friend of the amiable, enthusiastic and able von Platen. The Count (1766-1829) had retired early from a high position in the Swedish Navy, was an energetic member of the House of Nobles and towards the end of his life was sent to Norway as Viceroy in order to secure a lasting peace between the two countries. His life's work, however, was the carrying out of the Göta Canal, a task which was at last accomplished in 1832, three years after his death. It was built during times of war, blockade and revolution and in the face of recurring financial difficulties and opposition from members of the Riksdag. It could probably not have been completed without the persistence of the Count, the efficiency of Telford and the close bond between these two honest, sincere and notable men.

In 1813 Telford paid his second visit to Sweden to see how the job was progressing and no doubt to have a word with the fifty or more British engineers and foremen who formed the basis of the staff. He found them controlling several thousand Swedish soldiers who were then engaged in regiments on the digging operations and using tools which Telford had insisted should be imported from England. Though Telford's letters relating to the canal are missing, those of the Count to Telford are now in the Institution of Civil Engineers and give a vivid account of the building of the canal and incidentally suggest how attractive was the personality of von Platen.

He writes a charming note to Telford the day after he has boarded a packet boat at Gothenburg bound for Harwich: "Sir, A few hours after your departure I found how well it would have been to see You once more, Tho' I hope this has had no influence on the bad wind I understand keeps you nearly in the Road . . . Lastly You see mankind are always so foolish either to run away from or run after each other. Now, as in the beginning running away would not do for our business, we soon found since that it would not do neither for our affections; and thats the reason why I now find myself always in the habitude of running or looking after You. Well make of it what you can but I tink of tomorrow morning there is a fresh westerly wind You may as well come ashore once more for to fetch a better wind; seamers always do this and find it answer very well."

In 1822, the year in which King Karl Johan formally opened that section of the Canal which lies between Trollhättan and Lake Viken, von Platen visited Telford in England and spent several months touring the country with him. It was doubtless a happy time for both men and it is a tribute to their characters that the friendship was maintained throughout the many tribulations which faced them in their task. At the end of it all the Count must have been a tired man for he writes in his last letter to Telford: "I have done my duty tho' with little gratitude".

Von Platen lies buried near Motala on the bank of his beloved waterway. Since he was laid there that debt of gratitude has been amply repaid by his countrymen, who to this day regard the Göta Canal with a justifiable pride.

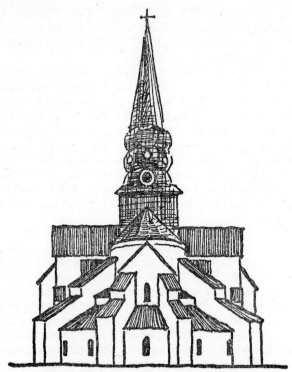

VARNHEM MONASTERY CHURCH: EAST END

VI

Across Sweden by Water

A	T the base of a flight of granite steps we dip our canoe into
	Gothenburg's Grand Canal. Any kind of boat, however
	small, bewitches the Swedes, and a small crowd has gathered
to watch. Then the great god Thor crashes on his anvil up in the
sky to give us a dramatic departure, as through a thundery shower
we glide below four bridges and turn upstream into the wide Göta
River (23).

The wharves and factories are soon behind and the sun bursts
out to light up the vivid green pastures on either bank and the rocky
hills in the distance. A trading schooner beats by on its paraffin
engine, followed by a glossy white yacht on a holiday journey from
the Baltic. On our left lies Hisingen, and soon we reach the con-
fluence with the Nordre River which bounds the north of Hisingen
to make it the second largest island in Bohuslän. There high up on a
knoll stands the old ruined castle of Bohus, its two remaining round
towers, called Father's Hat and Mother's Bonnet, making an
imposing silhouette against the thunder clouds. On that site a castle
stood as far back as 1308, but the scarred veteran we see was built
in 1448 as a border fortress when Norway marched with Sweden
along this river boundary. The castle became the most powerful
stronghold in the North, was beleaguered many times but never
captured. After the last siege in 1678 it fell into decay and formed a
local quarry until in 1838 Karl Johan, seeing its condition when he
was on a river journey, forbade its further mutilation. Below the
castle snuggles the pretty village of Kungälv with its big trees, its
red cottages and old wooden church of 1679 wherein carved angels
trumpet and a fine votive ship hangs forever becalmed.

The hills come closer, grow higher and more wooded and in a
meadow up among the pines we shall find our camping ground, the
first of the many idyllic places where we shall pitch our tent and set
our Primus roaring for the twilight meal.

★　★　★　★　★

Next day we stop for stores at Lödöse, little more than a quiet
village today but once an important, fortified market town and one
of the several local precursors of Gothenburg. Founded early in

the Middle Ages it grew to possess two churches, a monastery and a castle, but in the fourteenth and fifteenth centuries it was thrice laid waste by invading Danes and Norwegians from across the river. It suffered also from the heavy tolls imposed on its ships by the hostile commanders of Bohus Castle. In 1473 the Government moved the inhabitants to Ny Lödöse near the river's mouth and the old town lost its size and privileges. Now, on the mound where backward men once struggled against violent death on the battlements, stands a white timber house, trying to imitate a French château, where backward children play, and on the spot where monks once chanted within sacred walls a cash register tinkles in the neat co-operative store. The ancient churches have gone, too, but on the site of one of them stands a simple stuccoed church of 1845 with a barrel-vaulted ceiling of timber over the nave, around which stand medieval figures of saints carved in wood. An effective feature of the interior, and typical of Swedish country churches, is the flooring of ordinary timber boarding painted in large squares of variegated greys to give a chequerboard effect of stone slabs. Like the frescoes on wood with false shadows painted on the walls of Swedish castles to represent carving, this is a poor country's substitute for rich grandeur. Nothing remains in Lödöse to reveal its great age, and apart from this church the oldest thing revealed to us was the cargo boat from Hamburg which was lying rusting in the boatyard.

After Lödöse the countryside becomes less inhabited. Sometimes the river, with marshy banks, is several hundred yards across; sometimes it narrows between rocks to produce a fast stream where going is hard. The river, however, has been tamed for navigation, and many thousands of years have passed since this river valley was a wide fjord. Trees grow thickly on the banks and oaks are frequent, so that here and there the view is faintly reminiscent of the Home Counties, until the illusion is shattered by the sight of granite rocks, conifers and a typical red timber farmstead.

*　　*　　*　　*　　*

This red of the country farms and cottages is so much part of the Swedish landscape that a digression upon it is called for here. The colour is indeed so typically and exclusively Swedish that Strindberg declared the Swedish national colours should be not blue and yellow but green and red—the green of the pine woods and the red of the houses. Sweden is largely forest land and most of the country buildings are therefore of timber, as they have always been since people settled there. Mostly the timber is softwood and softwood in its sawn state needs protection. No better wood protection exists than this Swedish red paint, but it is remarkable also for two other reasons—its cheapness and the beauty of its colour. There is no lovelier building colour in the world than Falu Red— a rich, warm, ruddy purple which owes something to the matt texture of the absorbing wood surface. It harmonizes in a magical way with the landscape, forming a perfect contrast to the dark green of the surrounding conifers and the grey outcrops of granite and creating vivid focal points to enliven a view which, with its eternal pine and birch, lake and rock, tends to grow monotonous. One never grows weary of the colour itself, perhaps because it varies so subtly in tone from place to place and according to the season and the time of day. Moreover, like wine, it is enhanced by age. Reflecting the evening sunlight on the rocky skerries of the west coast, the colour, though never garish, is fantastic in its brilliance. Among the whites and greys of winter it is more quietly gay. It is a lyrical colour and has been an obvious source of inspiration to a host of Swedish landscape painters, especially to such nationalists as Carl Larsson, Carl Wilhelmsson and Anders Zorn. As the Swedes would say, the colour is so full of *stämning* (atmosphere is our nearest word) that a whole thesis could be written on the subject of "The Aesthetic Influence of Falu Red on Swedish Landscape Painting".

It may be that the paint looks so exactly right in the Swedish landscape because it is a natural, indigenous material and no sort of soulless, synthetic modern import. Certainly the attempts to produce the same effects, either preservative or aesthetic, by synthetic means have so far failed.

What exactly is this Falu Red, this red ochre paint of Sweden? The foreign visitor will have some difficulty in finding out. He will be told with a shrug: "Ja, det är vanlig rödfärg"—just ordinary red paint, as though the question were a foolish one. There is, however, one certain source of information—the *Stora Kopparbergs Bergslags Aktie Bolag*. Founded in the thirteenth century, this claims to be the oldest trading company in the world. It is still flourishing as one of the largest industrial concerns in the country, and owns among other things the ancient copper mine at Falun in Dalecarlia. A by-product of this mine is this *Falu Rödfärg*, and though the *Rödmull*, or Red Earth, from which the paint is made is found in other parts of Sweden, Falun is the main and most famous source of supply.

Right back to the Stone Age red colour has had an appeal, especially among those who live in direct contact with nature. The appeal comes not only from its decorative quality but from its likeness to blood and fire with their mystic associations with the powers of life and heat. In building work in Sweden, however, red paint began to be used to a large extent only in the seventeenth century and then mainly as preservative on those parts of buildings most liable to rot—the outside angles, the roofs and doors. Not until the middle of the eighteenth century did red ochre paint come into its own and the whole of the external walls were then covered with it as a result of a new and large-scale production at Falun. The paint then became cheap enough for use on the houses and barns of the peasants. Hitherto it had been seen only on the more important buildings—manor houses, churches and vicarages. Today it has lost its early snob prestige, and to distinguish them from the common run the more important timber buildings in the country are contrariwise now usually painted in white, grey or buff oil colour— that is, where ardent nationalist architects like Cyrillus Johansson have not had their way.

Though the red colour was no doubt readily adopted for aesthetic reasons, its real purpose was to preserve the thinner sawn timbers of the built-up panel buildings which came to supersede the solid, more durable and untreated axed work round about the end of the seventeenth century. Conservation also became more necessary as the cost of timber rose. As a preservative it is especially valuable today when even Sweden, the land of timber, is worried by the world timber shortage.

Before about 1750 the raw material for red paint came as a by-product of sulphur and vitriol production. Then the large-scale mining of Red Earth began at Falun, where the mines produce not only copper ores but many other minerals, particularly pyrites, sulphides and silicates. Among these products is this *Rödmull* which contains a mixture of certain minerals combined through the centuries by natural physical and chemical processes. After mining, the *Rödmull* is ground to a fine powder, refined, washed and then burned with care to bring out the redness. It arrives in barrels and then has to be prepared. Ferrous sulphate is mixed into boiling water with rye flower, the red powder is added and then the paint is ready to use.

Falu Red is so characteristically Swedish that one feels that if it should ever be replaced some virtue would have left the land, a virtue linked with the strong national pride and independence of the Swedes. Red in Sweden means Falu Red. Its significance is purely national.

* * * * *

An old cottage in its Falu Red dress, squatting below a group of silver birches, peers at us now across the river through the white-rimmed eyes of its windows. Below it a bright green lawn of new corn slopes down to the water. On our side of the river behind the small patch of greensward on which we have bivouacked rises a protective mound of granite and away behind that the dark pine woods serrate the evening sky. Up river the lean chimney of a paper mill projects above the trees, marking the sudden presence of industry and the town of Lilla Edet. Then the daily passenger steamer from Stockholm swirls by on its downstream journey in a glory of fresh white paint, the sky blue and sunshine yellow of a large Swedish flag lolling gracefully at her stern.

We turn inland to pick a cupful of wild strawberries and then to seek water at a cottage. A little girl escorts us to a well, chatting easily and asking many questions, quite unalarmed by two wild-looking foreigners who speak her language with so strange an accent. "Yes," she says solemnly, "there are many languages. They teach us English at the school in Lilla Edet." Then inconsequentially, "Uncle surely has not come all the way from England in the canoe?" Later her father comes down to the river to fish, accompanied by a grown-up daughter who tells us that she works at the hotel in the town. The hours are long, she says, and the pay is poor but she prefers it to working in the paper mill. Many foreigners work at the mill now, she tells us—Poles, Greeks, Austrians, Finns. They are welcome, for labour is short in Sweden. "None of them want to go back home," she says, "they like it here." Then pointing proudly across the river where the red cottage lies, she adds simply, "Is it not beautiful?"

*　　*　　*　　*　　*

Next day at Lilla Edet we rise up through a giant steel lock worked by electricity from the power station nearby, the last scion of a family of locks, the first of which was built here in 1607. Parts of this old work can still be seen. The town itself we shall pass by, for there is little to see there. It is one of those white-painted timber towns which must look something like the towns of the Middle West of America. Unlike them, however, these small Swedish towns, now local market centres depending also on a factory or two, mostly have ancient foundations. Rarely is any evidence left to show that this is so because catastrophic fires have always ravaged them at least once through the centuries on account of their timber construction. Lilla Edet, for example, was last burned down in 1888 and has since been rebuilt. The result of these fires has been that

Sweden unfortunately lacks those delightful old villages and provincial towns of narrow, crooked streets dominated by a church or a cathedral spire and rich in the textures of age, which are found in England and in Continental countries. Throughout Sweden only Stockholm's Old Town, the Town-Between-the-Bridges, retains an ancient character to any great extent, for its plan is still medieval —that is if we except the extensive thirteenth-century German remains of Visby on the island of Gotland.

The old country towns of timber were merely clusters of houses, each built on the plan of the isolated farmsteads with their central courtyards. We shall obtain a hint of their charming style in the old part of Örebro which has happily survived for more than a century. Little remains in Sweden even from the enthusiastic town-planning and building activity of the seventeenth century, when thirty-two towns were laid out afresh in contrast to the five replanned in the previous century and the single one of the century which followed.

Not only fire has deprived Sweden of its old country towns and villages. The *Storskifte* of the 1750's, a kind of Enclosures Acts procedure, did not seriously affect the old communities, but that of 1827 when parcels of land were exchanged and the peasants moved out of their settlements to isolated farmsteads set in the midst of their land, newly united into a whole, broke up the communities drastically. Only a few survived, like Viby near Sigtuna and Remma in Småland. Today the tendency is to congregate in compact villages once again.

The old summer grazing settlements have been less disturbed and one or two examples still survive in the sparsely populated north of a type of settlement which goes back to the Middle Ages. It is called a *kyrkstad* or Church Town. Here peasants from outlying districts foregather on Holy Days and live temporarily, each family in its small hut to which a stable is attached. Lövångers Kyrkstad in Norrland is a delightful example—harmonious, immutable, unselfconscious and in that natural good taste of which the artificial life of modern industrialism has now deprived the people. Tradition still survives here and there also in the industrial villages belonging to the pre-industrial age, such as that of the copper-mining community of Åtvidaberg with its old houses of solid, untreated timbers and tiled roofs which are set without rigidity to form pleasing street pictures.

Today most new buildings in the larger country towns are built of brick, stone or concrete so that the old danger of mass-destruction by fire has disappeared—a danger mitigated also, of course, by organized fire brigades and water supplies. In towns of any size flat blocks are replacing the small, individual houses, a tradition which began in the latter part of the eighteenth century. In Stockholm, for instance, some 85 per cent of the population now lives in flats, not by any means always willingly, for at heart the Swede retains much of the individualism and desire for self-sufficiency of his free peasant ancestors.

★　　★　　★　　★　　★

We pass other villages, noting especially the typical white stucco church tower with copper turret atop at Hjärtum, and then pitch our tent below a wooded, granite cliff at a hamlet called Rosenberg. A plump, contented horse grazes nearby of that special Swedish strain which rightly, but surprisingly, glories in a golden mane like those fairy-tale steeds depicted by Ivar Arosenius. As we finish our *al fresco* meal, soft, mysterious singing permeates the windless dusk. We clamber up the rocks in search of woodland spirits but discover instead a large congregation of human beings, gathered in a clearing around a handsome preacher in lay dress who is conducting the singing. One of those open-air services, held sometimes during the summer out in the unspoiled country by the *predikanter*, is in progress. The people look solemn enough but one senses no great fervour.

On the whole the modern Swede, though steeped in protestant taboos and conventions, has little religious zeal, and his churches are as empty as our own. But there exists an ardent religious minority of non-conformists, perhaps the descendants of that strong Pietist movement which originated in Germany in the late seventeenth century. The movement came as a protest against the creed-ridden and dictatorial Lutheran pastors and gained considerable support in Sweden. In Denmark the support was not so strong, for there its austerity and uncompromising fanaticism had less appeal to the jovial people. Perhaps this movement has had its effect on the growth of the Salvation Army in Sweden, which is remarkably active. Throughout both Denmark and Sweden such pious bodies run hotels, which, being open to all, are a godsend to the impecunious traveller, for they offer excellent food and service at very low rates, and beyond supplying each bedroom with a Bible do not intrude into the spiritual lives of their guests. The staffs at these hotels receive low wages and regard their work as a service to their fellow men.

★　　★　　★　　★　　★

Our next stop is at Trollhättan, the first large town on our journey. There Sweden's greatest hydro-electric power station has been built. We approach through a rocky, wooded defile against a heavy current and then the rocks open up to the right to reveal a flight of three giant locks, the first flight of the five which will lift us, by a way blasted through the living granite, 104 feet up to the town. It is one of Europe's highest lock staircases (29).

The great steel gates seem to boom at us: "We were built for big steamers. Do not expect the mountains to part for your ridiculous mouse." Intimidated we decide to make an energetic portage round the locks and land to investigate. Humbly we approach the engineer in his cabin, impressive with polished keyboard of electric buttons. He is kindly enough and seems to have his beasts well under control. "*Javisst,*" he says, "Of course you can come through, but you must pay 3.75 kronor at the office higher up. We will let the water in gently, so have no fear of capsizing."

We paddle into the first lock and cling to a steel ladder while jets of cold water spout down our necks from the slimy walls. Soon the doors swing slowly and quietly together and, imprisoned in the vast, dank tomb, we rise slowly into the sunshine, lifted more gently than in any small, homely lock on the Grand Union Canal.

To the north of these modern locks of Trollhättan Canal which were built between 1909 and 1916, lies a whole complex of old disused locks and canals. Beyond them the great dams and the modern power station stand, below a rocky precipice where six lashing torrents once poured down. Now the falling water cannot be seen, for it is guided under cover down into a row of mighty turbines. As much water passes through them every second, they say, as would supply the daily needs of 3,200 townsfolk. Sometimes the sluices in the dams are raised and then one can see the old falls in their pristine splendour.

An abortive attempt was made to build locks past the waterfall in 1749, the works being placed in the hands of the first Swedish engineer, Kristoffer Polhem. Several years later the backbreaking work of hewing the lock basins out of the granite was well advanced, when a mass of floating timber roared down and burst the dam. Funds ran out and the work was abandoned. A legend says that the destruction was organized by the local peasants, who were finding it difficult to earn a living from the soil and were adding to their incomes by carting river cargoes round the falls. On seeing that the locks might be completed and realizing the import to themselves, they organized this minor Luddite riot. One of the uncompleted locks is under water but another can still be seen, part being in the form of a tunnel. Near by it, incidentally, is a grotto where royal visitors have carved their names in the rock ever since the eighteenth century.

The next attempt to make a navigation was made towards the end of the eighteenth century and on August 14th, 1800, a ship passed the falls for the first time. Vänern at last had a navigable outlet to the sea. But these were narrow locks, as one can still see, though considerable feats of engineering for those days. When the Göta Canal had been completed new locks were built in 1844. These too can still be seen and appear as though they could easily be put into full working order.

*　　*　　*　　*　　*

Trollhättan itself is a flourishing modern town containing many factories and workshops. Its two most pleasant features are its great market place with modern lamp-posts decorated with great bowls of flowers and its waterside parks laid out on long islands, many of which were formed when the power station was built.

As we arrive an important annual feast is being celebrated in the market place (28). It is Midsummer Eve. Out in the middle of the square a pole has been erected with a cross-piece near the top at the ends of which two wreaths dangle. The whole is wound round with birch leaves and the Seven Midsummer Flowers, while two cut-out figures of a man and a woman in traditional costume stand in full colour on the cross-piece. At the crossing itself is a modern touch in the form of a cluster of loudspeakers. A great crowd has gathered, orderly and sedate, and children are now dancing traditional steps around the pole to the music of an accordion. Now and again an enthusiastic lady sings an old air into the microphone. Many women and children are in peasant costume, a self-conscious anachronism today, but one not to be regretted, for the costumes are attractive with primary colours, spotless white linen and scintillating brooches. Benches have been arranged around the dancers and an officious young policeman is continually shifting them and suggesting to the squatters that it is someone else's turn to rest. He is handsome in his white cap and gloves and his neat blue uniform, and is so clearly well-intentioned that no one takes exception. Other policemen are strutting round the square with swords swinging, now and then saluting an acquaintance who bows and doffs his hat. The personification of the law is always respected—that is, until some inebriate is treated a trifle too roughly, when that dormant individualism of the Swede suddenly awakes and all around give strong verbal and moral support to the bemused drunk.

This Midsummer Festival must be very old, for it shows not a sign of Christianity. Though the new world of electric light has burst some of the bubbles of its former spontaneity, it is still celebrated with enthusiasm. As pagan as the candles on a Christmas tree (or for that matter as a bishop's mitre, which is a fish mouth and a vagina symbol), it reveals how keen is the joy of the sun's return, as also do those other ancient feasts of the north—the bon-fires and songs of Valpurgis Night celebrating the return of spring and the crown of candles of St. Lucia which are lit when the longest night of the year is over.

Birch branches hang everywhere today—in the church lobbies, on the porches of the houses, even on the bonnets of the cars. Today every town and every village will have erected its *maistång*, and through the twilit night couples will swing round it to the lilt of the graceful *hambo* waltz. This midsummer cult seems to be unique to Sweden, for neither in Denmark or Norway is it celebrated; nor, indeed, in Skåne, where traditions are more Danish than Swedish. No doubt it has roots in some ancient fertility rite and maybe the maypole is a tree to be worshipped. No one in the market place at Trollhättan today whom we question seems either to know or to care. The sun is blazing, the rhythm of the music is quickening the blood, the young men's faces are brown and healthy, the girls' eyes are bright and restless. Let us leave these dusty questions to Sir James Frazer and join in the dance.

*   *   *   *   *

In time we return to the canoe. Wherever we land we leave our kit aboard unguarded and now as always we find that nothing has been touched, nothing is missing—a silent comment on the exceptional honesty of the Swedish people.

Above Trollhättan the river is wide on account of the dam, almost like a lake. Soon it narrows again and within a few miles the two long ranges of Halleberg and Hunneberg come into view ahead—a curious formation. The two hills have precipitous sides but their tops are cut off sharply to form plateaux; they are in fact one long range cut into two by a deep valley. Now 270 feet above the sea, they lay in prehistoric times below water. Near the cleft we can see high up on Halleberg the curious scars of some limestone quarries where pillars of volcanic rock have been left standing as supports for the side of the precipice.

At Brinkebergskulle we turn left off the river and enter the old Karls Grav, Charles's Ditch, which was begun in the reign of Carl IX, Gustav Vasa's son, but was not completed until the eighteenth century. The single lock we pass through is, however, large and modern. At the end of the short canal the Vassbotten Lake is entered and the roofs of Vänersborg appear on the right. Under a swing railway bridge, and there before us stretches the great lake of Vänern, 90 miles long and 50 miles wide. It is a small area compared with that of Vänern at the time the Ice Cap receded, for then it covered the whole of south Värmland and a large part of Västergotland and Dalsland as well. At that time it was connected with the North Sea, not by the Göta River alone but by a series of wide sounds. Links with that distant past are the small grey salmon still swimming in Vänern's waters.

Before skirting the lake let us land for an hour at Vänersborg. This town received municipal status from Queen Christina in 1643, but like most other towns of its kind it has been destroyed by fire several times. The last fire occurred in 1834 when, though most of the town was destroyed, the pleasing eighteenth-century church, set in the small formal park among the lime trees, was saved together with the imposing provincial governor's residence of 1754 which faces the market place. The completion of the canal in the nineteenth century brought a new prosperity to the place, though it has not become marred by industry to any large degree. A charming feature of this small, homely town is the fine park situated on a promontory, stretching into the lake to the north, which is laid out with that subtle sensitivity to landscaping which is a Swedish characteristic.

*   *   *   *   *

Across the bay of the lake called Dalbo we skim with sail set through choppy water to the base of Halleberg and there land among the boulders to explore. The thick pine wood is desolate and wild, and the only signs of humanity are the narrow track we follow and an occasional stack of faggots. The smell of pine sap and wild garlic is all around; high up the sunlight dapples the bark of the trees, but below the mossy boulders are dark beneath the undergrowth of cranberry bushes. There is a theatrical grandeur about the tall conifers and a solemnity which keeps our voices lowered. "We must go back", we keep repeating, but the track lures us on. Besides we may have the luck to spot an elk in this lost world where more elks are found than in any other part of the globe. We see none, but their spoor is frequent. This is a very strange place, quite unlike the cultivated countryside around. It is in fact one of the few remaining old royal forests in southern Sweden and is rich in legend. Many signs of prehistoric man can be found here, and Viking burial mounds, too. On the tableland we find a narrow lake lying in a volcanic fissure and farther on we come at last to the far side and scan a high and splendid view across an arm of the lake. The wind has died and as the long evening settles down we select our camping ground for the night lying two miles away across the quiet water.

*   *   *   *   *

Once settled there we search for drinking water and find a well by a cottage. An old lady helps us to fill the canvas bucket and points to some lethal-looking fungoid growths floating in the well.

"It always blooms like that when there's thunder about," says the old lady, "But don't worry. I've been drinking this water all my life."

Then suddenly she asks, "But why come all this way for water?"

"Where should we obtain drinking water then?"

"Water? Why, there's your water."

She points towards the great lake. After that we have no hesitation in baling our drinking water straight from the clear, clean lake and all our water problems are solved.

*   *   *   *   *

The next stage of the journey takes us round the deserted rocky shore of the Vänersnäs Peninsula. The sun burns through a brilliant day; mirage islands float far off shimmering just above the water against a purple haze; above us the white wings of seagulls flash against the blue. We brave a five-mile paddle out across the dead calm water of the Brandsfjord and land to rest in wild country where birds and bees swoop down towards us, angry at our intrusion. On along the coast now thickly fringed with reeds and marsh. Openings in the reeds are rare and at last we plunge straight through the reeds to arrive sweltering at a pool where water lilies bloom. Ahead lies an oak wood like an English park, and there we land to camp and to inspect the fine manor house of Storeberg with its model farm. On again through the maze of reeds to Söne, one of those scattered villages which have been so broken up that all form has vanished. The cottages and farms lie far apart, but a timber mill, a church six centuries old and a modern co-operative dairy give some reason for calling the place a community.

North of Söne an extraordinary strip of land projects straight out into the lake. Though it is only a few hundred yards wide—only a hundred at the tip—it is over three miles long and wooded for most of the way. Beyond Hindensräv, as this queer peninsula is called, we find a passage among islands south of Kållandsö, entering

92

31 LÄCKÖ CASTLE : A detail of the Chapel with its carved and painted wooden
    figures (second half of the sixteenth century)

32 LÄCKÖ CASTLE on Lake Vänern (medieval but largely rebuilt in the latter half of the seventeenth century)

33 Central Swedish Landscape

between two rocks where medieval fortifications once stood; past
the rotting hull of a Väner schooner, along a narrow river and across
a small lake fringed by pines above which a rich, thick cumulus
cloud looms like a Bikini explosion, foreboding thunder. Some old
stone ruins stand near the shore. In the seventeenth century this
was a new palace built for the much-travelled Count Bengt Oxenstierna. It grew into one of the grandest in the country and was
especially renowned for its unique and luxurious Roman, or Turkish
Bath. This must have been something of a Divine Grot, for Linné
wrote of it after a visit in 1747: "The bath house in Lindholmen's
garden was a masterpiece . . . the bath itself, the Calidarium, was a
very high chamber, octagonal in shape, every other one of its eight
walls being encrusted with lustrous stone—quartz, spars, shells;
it was like a grotto. . . . The roof was vaulted and was stuck all over
with crystals and long diaphanous stones like icicles and stalactites."

✶   ✶   ✶   ✶   ✶

Along the Ullersund we reach a road bridge as the storm breaks
and make for a *gästgiveri*, where we eat well and enjoy the luxury of a
bed. From here next day we take bus to the famous Läckö Castle
standing on the edge of the lake on the north of Kållandsö—one of
the finest Baroque castles in the country (32). Its simple geometrical
forms and bold whitened stone walls seem to grow with immense
strength and vitality from the rocky foundations. Because it lacks
the technical finish and sophistication of the Continental Baroque
it gains in vigour.

The castle originated in 1298 and belonged up to the Reformation to the bishops of Skara. Little remains of this medieval work.
The building as we see it was mostly built in the second half of the
seventeenth century by Christina's favourite, Count Magnus
Gabriel de la Gardie, Lord High Chancellor, who inherited the
place from his father, Count Jacob de la Gardie. In 1830 all the
interior furnishings, even to the painted panelling, was auctioned
by the Crown at knock-down prices—a stupid piece of vandalism
by which much of the wall painting was harmed. Some of the
magnificent gobelin tapestries, it is said, fetched as little as a shilling
each and were thereafter used as carpets and horse blankets by
local farmers. Now, however, the State looks after the place and
keeps it open to the public. Much of the original furniture and
panelling has been reinstated, so that here one can obtain a fairly
accurate impression of what a great seventeenth-century Swedish
nobleman's palace really looked like.

The 248 rooms of the palace are grouped round two spacious

connected courtyards and a narrow kitchen yard to the north. Around these yards on the ground floor are the various staff and service rooms—kitchens, larders, armoury, craftsmen's workshops —while to the north-east, at the end of a long, dark passage, lies the dank medieval prison, which was still being used for its original purpose in Gardie's time. Off the kitchen yard is a curious well sunk during the Middle Ages through the rock to a depth of 90 feet. It is connected halfway down to the waters of the lake by a tunnel, which not only gave an inlet to the water but provided a last means of escape for the castle's inhabitants in case of a siege. It is called the *Fläskgrav* (the Pork Well) because it was engineered by the burning of no less than 300 fat hams. In this way the rock was heated; then being suddenly cooled it cracked and could then be removed fairly easily in large pieces with the help of iron tools. The pump of the well is a strange device; constructed originally in 1678 it is operated by a man's swinging on a great oak beam.

On the upper floors lie the state rooms, the finest of which is the Riddarsal, the Hall of Knights or Banqueting Hall. Here the painted ceiling panels of groups of arms and flying cherubim by Johan Werner are the outstanding features, and one will notice here also between the deep window reveals several vast battle-scenes of the Thirty Years' War executed by various painters of those days. At the north end of the hall is a finely carved screen, a servery and above these a gallery where the musicians could play unseen.

The finest interior of the castle is that of the chapel, which is adorned by a set of carved and painted wooden figures of the Apostles set in niches in the window reveals (31). These were begun by Johan Werner, who was a sculptor as well as a painter, and were completed by Georg Baselaque; foreign names, we note. The altarpiece, pulpit and organ here are grand, ornate pieces of "baroquery".

*   *   *   *   *

Back at our hostel we join for a meal with a young medical student on holiday and a loquacious and very old inhabitant of the local town.

"What was Lidköping like when you were young?" the medico asks the old man.

"There were very few restrictions then," he replied, "and living was cheap. Now we have to carry our money about on a cart and put our goods in our wallets. Life was rough but it was lively in those times, and you could enjoy yourself cheaply in one of the many rowdy alehouses in the town. Now only one of them is left, and they are talking of closing that down."

It seems that restrictions, inflation and austerity are not the prerogatives of modern England.

"We used to get all our water from the big pump in the middle of the market place," the laconical old man went on.

"Was there much illness then?" the medico asked, no doubt with typhoid in mind.

"Yes, we had quite a bit. We had one lazarette in Lidköping, but people avoided it if they could. We had a very common complaint called the Fever."

"Some kind of malaria, I suppose?"

"No, just the Fever. We used to cure it with raw potato spirit mixed with salt."

"Was there much cancer?"

"No. We had only two diseases in those days. One was the Fever and the other was Dying. We had many homely cures and, of course, there were a lot of old women about who used to fool people with their magical drinks. Things are much better now in that way."

State medicine is certainly well organized in Sweden now, and in Stockholm we shall be able to see its latest physical manifestation in the giant new municipal hospital on Södermalm, a pile which is almost alarming in its vastness and aseptic austerity. But organized treatment of the sick in Sweden is in fact far older than the old man of Ullersund, for it stems back in a rough and ready way to the days of Gustav Adolph, who virtually founded the modern type of army in which he was the first general to provide field ambulances, hospitals and a staff of surgeons.

*　*　*　*　*

On again, but southwards now down the Kinnevik Bay, to visit the old man's home-town of Lidköping, a small industrial centre containing among other works a match factory, a sugar refinery and the pottery works of Rörstrand, founded in the eighteenth century and as famous as those of Gustavsberg near Stockholm. The town is entered from the lake along the River Lida which divides the place in two—the Old Town to the east and the New Town to the west. It is an attractive small place with its riverside park, its trim rows of moored pleasure craft and its great cobbled square, the largest in the country. As usual few ancient build ngs have survived the usual series of fires. The Old Town goes back to 1446, the first town on the lake; the New Town is only as old as the seventeenth century. This is de la Gardie country and it was Count Magnus who laid out the New Town on a part of the land he owned, giving away building plots and building materials free to anyone who would settle here and so help to stimulate rapid growth.

The only old building in the place is a fascinating timber one standing in the middle of the square. Originally it was a hunting lodge of the Count's which stood among the woods of Kållandsö, but in 1676 it was transported to the town by boat in parts and erected here as a courthouse. This building now has a low projection round three sides containing shops and yet it remains as intriguing a structure as it was in its original simple form—a squat tower on granite base with ogee roof and two stepped-back lanterns above. Its appearance is somehow oriental. In its time it has been a fire station, a police station, a telephone exchange and is now a museum of local handicrafts. During the eighteenth century it served still another purpose—a look-out tower where the watchman would call out the hours of the night while keeping his eyes open for fires, calling out when the hour struck:

> *"Klockan ar tio slagen.*
> *Gud bevare staden*
> *För eld och brand*
> *Och fiende hand."*

which means:

> "Ten of the clock doth sound.
> God preserve this town
> From flame and brand
> And enemy hand."

*　　*　　*　　*　　*

From Lidköping we now make a short expedition by rail to the east to see one of Sweden's important historical monuments— the monastery church and ruins of Varnhem. Nothing is left of the monastery except the foundation walls which have been excavated, but from these the general arrangement of cloisters, refectory, abbot's house, kitchen, monks' common room and so on can be visualized. The church to which the monastery was attached is complete. It is a beautiful building and remarkable not as a medieval church as such but as a medieval church added to and radically altered in the Baroque period. The effect is striking, being neither quite medieval nor quite seventeenth century, yet having an impressive homogeneity. Nothing like it can be seen anywhere else in the world (13, 37) (p. 80).

The present building came about in this way. In 1143 the

34   The painted interior of the medieval timber Church (built about 1323)

35   A detail of the paintings on the Nave ceiling
(painted in 1494)

SÖDRA RÅDA CHURCH

36 NYSUND CHURCH: The painted saucer Dome of timber over the Crossing (1747)

37 VARNHEM MON
TERY CHURCH: Baroc
furnishing in a Got
interior

Cistercians from Clairvaux in France founded two monasteries in Sweden—at Alvastra in Östergotland and at Nydala in Småland. From Alvastra a colony came to Varnhem in 1150 and built a new monastery. This was destroyed in a conflagration in 1234 and was rebuilt in limestone and sandstone between 1234 and 1260 by French craftsmen and overseers. It came to be the most flourishing church settlement in Sweden during the early Middle Ages, thanks largely to the support of wealthy patrons, especially of Birger Jarl, who died in 1266 and was buried in the church. His tomb is still to be seen there at a focal point of the interior. In time this busy, powerful foundation acquired much land in the surrounding district, which it dominated until the Reformation. Then in 1532 its lands were confiscated and distributed among members of the nobility. In 1566 the Danes gutted the place and up to the middle of the seventeenth century Varnhem stood as a ruin. Round about 1650 Count Magnus Gabriel de la Gardie, then Lord High Chancellor and husband of Carl X's sister, visited the ruin and decided to rebuild the church at his own expense as a future burial chamber for himself and his family. The work of reconstruction proceeded between 1668 and 1674. Being an aesthete and ardent to preserve Sweden's ancient monuments, de la Gardie saw to it that the job of restoration was done thoroughly, but unlike our own Victorian church restorers he improved, rather than destroyed, the building's character in a boldly creative way. Stones from the monastery ruins were used for two new narrow western towers and for the thick buttresses round the apsidal east end and along the south and north walls. A splendid timber spire over the crossing and two smaller ones over the western towers were added. Inside, new pews, altar, pulpit, organ and other furnishings were installed and, as we can now see, created perfect foils of intricate workmanship to their background of plain Cistercian stonework.

Externally the east end with its complex roof slopes and radiating buttresses makes a magnificent and exciting composition (p. 80). Here and in the Romanesque east end of Lund Cathedral, we can experience the thrill of the two finest east ends of all the churches of Scandinavia—perhaps even of Europe. The analytical mind of the purist may ask why these fat buttresses of de la Gardie's time were structurally necessary, since the original building of the Cistercian monks managed to stand up for so long without them. But why ask these questions? The fact remains that they look, they *feel*, dynamic and superbly right.

*   *   *   *   *

Farther on in our journey round the lake we land below Kinne-kulle, a great hill which dominates the landscape for many miles—the result of the strange prehistoric upheaval which also formed Halleberg and Hunneberg. Ten thousand years ago it stood up as an island. Now it is part of a district which has become a tourist attraction, and still a paradise for botanists, bird-watchers, miso-gynists and nature-lovers, as it was when Linné came here on a tour in 1746 and remarked that "this region is more delightful than any other in Sweden."

The stiff climb to the summit is well worth the effort, for here a timber look-out tower was built in the 1890's from the top of which a wonderful panorama over the wide forests, fields and waters of Västergotland can be obtained at a height of 900 feet above the level of Lake Vänern stretching below. The name was formerly Kindakulle (*kulle* being a hill and *Kinda* or *kinna* meaning to kindle a fire), because since time immemorial Kinnekulle has been a beacon hill from which warnings of enemy approach in times of strife could be sent out to the inhabitants for miles around.

Many strange rock formations and natural grottos are found among the woods here and a few interesting old buildings also—notably the typical manor house at Råbäck with its detached wings and, to the south-east, the ancient church of Husaby, which was the centre of the first see in Sweden from where Christianity was spread over Västergotland. Here in 1008 Olaf Sköttkonung was baptized to become the first Christian king of Sweden. The tower is the oldest part and was built as early as the beginning of the eleventh century, the rest following a century later in pure round-arched Romanesque. The church was rather over-restored in 1866.

*   *   *   *   *

Some 18 miles of paddling brings us next to Mariestad. For many miles as we approach, the tower of its church has acted as our landmark above the water. We paddle through one of those brilliant summer evenings of the north when all things are so bright in colour and so clearly defined that all sense of distance is lost. Buildings which are miles away seem like toys which we could touch if we stretched out our paddles. Mariestad is a pleasant country town founded about 1582, but there is little to see there. The town's centre was laid waste by a fire in 1895 and was replanned with a wide avenue to form a town axis. The church dates from 1693 but was largely reconstructed in 1903.

We proceed northwards on a Sunday morning. Pleasure boats are dotted about the lake and along the shore stand many small holiday huts where families from neighbouring towns have settled to enjoy a simple week-end and to worship the sun. These holiday huts, called *sportstugor*, are an important feature in modern Swedish life and are virtually a new democratic form of the old nobleman's country seat. Mostly they are freshly painted, well kept timber houses, some in Falu Red, very compactly planned, with bunks for sleeping and a Primus stove for cooking. Set among the rocks and trees they decorate rather than mar the landscape near the towns. Near each hut a white flag post always stands, and every summer Sunday the national flag flutters at the head to add to the gaiety of this charming open-air cult.

At Sjötorp the Göta Canal proper begins (30). From here the locks are in their early nineteenth-century form, and from here the scenery as far as the Baltic becomes more wooded and intimate. Sjötorp itself is a soothing, rustic village with its birch trees, scattered timber cottages and fertile gardens, its small shipping pool and diminutive white timber lighthouse. The quiet, bosky perspective of canal invites us on, but our route is settled. We shall travel farther north by more difficult but possibly more interesting waters.

Up near a village called Årås we are compelled to organize a portage for several miles past a rapid and we are lucky enough to acquire the help of a friendly peasant in the typical peak cap who loads our gear and canoe on to his hay wain and jog-trots us through the pine woods to Gulspång where, above the hydro-electric works, we float again and paddle out into the small lake of Skagern to land finally at a perfect camping site—a grassy patch sheltered by pine trees broken only to the south to give us a *coup d'oeil* across the lake.

*   *   *   *   *

A mile away lies the scattered village of Södra Råda, which is of little general interest except for its jewel of a little medieval timber church. Being deep in the south Värmland countryside, it receives few visitors. Yet it is unique and has rightly been preserved by the State as a National Monument, for not only is it one of the few medieval timber churches left, but it has a remarkable interior (34, 35).

Outside with its dark brown shingles covering solid timberwork, its sloping shingled roof and small projecting porch it is nothing to look at, even though it is about six hundred years old. But let us not turn away but go to fetch the old lady with the key who lives in a nearby cottage. She is small, very clean, very abrupt and does not smile. But she has a sense of theatre and turning the key, she flings the doors open with a sudden flourish. The sight before us is one of splendour. Walls and ceiling are covered with brilliantly coloured medieval paintings in a perfect state of preservation—a great illuminated Bible.

The ceiling is of clover-leaf section with a central barrel vault flanked by two elliptical quarter-vaults, all of timber boarding, the only extant example of its kind. The paintings in the choir are of the same date as the church itself, about 1323, and are the finest of their period anywhere in Scandinavia in colour, line and composition, their inspiration being the illuminated manuscript of Jean de Papeleus's Bible produced in Paris in 1317. The paintings in the nave are not quite so good, yet they have considerable naïve power. They were painted in 1494 by one Nils Amund, a Swedish monk, who is known to have decorated at least twenty church interiors. These paintings were not intended merely to act as decoration but had a didactic purpose—that is, to tell Biblical stories and religious allegories, such as the Day of Judgment scene painted in the tympanum at Södra Råda.

The altar is dated 1707 and is a vigorous, if crude, piece of carved wood, peasant Baroque in character and painted in brilliant colours. The painted pulpit is dated 1689. Another timber adjunct is the carved wooden crucifix of about 1400, which is decorated all over with a lurid pattern of red wounds.

*   *   *   *   *

Up to the Let River now, passing on the way an idyllic holiday centre for the employees of the Degerfors Steel Works which we shall come to farther up river. A portage round the Åtorp Power Station and we are at Nysund, little more than a village and containing a good timber church which, though not completed until 1639, has some of the medieval timber church traditions. Many additions have come to the church such as the galleried transepts, the steeple, the sacristy and the embellishments to the beautiful seventeenth-century carved altar and pulpit, all of which are eighteenth century. Since that time, except for a few repairs, the church has remained untouched. The finest feature of the interior is the flat dome of boarding over the crossing painted in 1747 with flying angels and skyscape in the Rococo manner by one Petter Mård (36). The outside of the church is not unlike some of our own timber churches in Essex.

The scene by the river here is not un-English either; it is happy and peaceful and might almost be somewhere on the upper Thames. Beyond the village the river grows very beautiful, with its banks fertile and wooded. A garden slopes down to the river and there in the tranquil evening air a large, bespectacled man in a white shirt sits in melancholy meditation. He calls out and beckons us over to him. We paddle across and he introduces himself as the local rector in remarkably good English. We begin to talk; we "tire the sun with talking and send him down the sky".

The rector is an almost pathetically sincere man and finally he asks us desperately:

"Why do so few people come to church today?"

Then he adds: "At least I have one consolation. My lovely old church can still offer people peace and beauty. That is why some of my parishioners come there, I believe, although they have little faith. A man I know who lives in these parts is a confirmed atheist, yet he has bought a radio set so that he can listen to the weekly religious service that is broadcast. When I asked him why he does so, he replied that only then can he hear men discussing human values. He is an intelligent man; at least he realizes that Christianity is trying to preserve the value of the individual in society."

At last the Rector rises and invites us to spend the night on the camp beds in his summer house by the river and then, with that true Swedish hospitality which we had already often enjoyed on our journey he takes us up to his house to meet his wife and to share a meal with him. The rectory we find is a delightful old white timber building with classical detailing and spacious rooms built in the eighteenth century and moved to this delectable spot in 1865 from its original site several miles away. The house represents a typical phase in the timber house tradition of Sweden which continues today in the form of the standard, factory-made type. It is significant that this eighteenth-century house is demountable too, and is in many ways not unlike its modern progeny in appearance.

The conversation in the rectory flows on, but the eyes of our host and hostess have a question in them. Suddenly the rector asks simply:

"Are you married?"

We are not taken aback, for the question has been flung at us before. We assure our host that our marriage is of a ten-year-old vintage. He then explains that young couples today in Sweden frequently spend their summer holidays together as lovers un-united by Church or State. It distressed him to find that this was becoming a generally accepted convention. The subject was not pursued though it is an interesting one. Clearly promiscuity is fairly common in Sweden in spite of the puritan traditions, but it is not certain that this is the result of modern emancipation and birth control alone. Very few Swedes are further from the soil than three generations, and on the farm fertility is not regarded as devilish but as a pleasure-giving economic need, supplying useful offspring. In the old days on the farm a young fellow would usually find his girl's bedroom window wide open when the night was auspicious, or he might take her for a tumble in the hay after a village dance. If the girl did not conceive no harm was done. If things went differently marriage would be celebrated officially—partly for the sake of propriety no doubt but partly also because the prospective father was then certain of an offspring who might turn out to be a fine, hard-working boy. Where a nation has a healthy agricultural background what hope has Calvin's pale ghost against the inexhaustible energy of Frey?

* * * * *

Down the lovely Let River on a perfect summer morning we reach Degerfors, a town with a large steel works where a portage is necessary. On the outskirts of the town among the pines is a very strange formation of smooth rocks, clefts, terraces, enormous boulders and round pot-holes in the granite. This formation, covering many acres of ground, is the dry bed of a primeval water-fall—the mighty Sveafall. It is the most remarkable natural pheno-menon in the whole of Sweden. Here the rocks have been so formed by far-off centuries of ice and rushing water that in the mysterious stillness of the terrain, enhanced rather than broken by the distant wail of a factory hooter or the rattle of a train, it is easy to reverse time and retreat in an instant some 10,000 years back in history to hear in the stillness the roar of a huge white jumble of cascading waters. The Ice Cap is receding. Denmark is joined to Sweden, the Baltic is a great inland lake and just here the melting glacier begins to trickle and then as the years pass to pour the Baltic water in a vast cataract down into Vänern and so into the North Sea to join the oceans of the world. Given time even ice and water can mould hard rock, and here we can now see how powerful they can be in the curious pot-holes called *jättegrytor*, or giant cauldrons, which have been ground out of the solid rock through the centuries. So vast were the falls here that those at Trollhättan would have seemed insignificant in comparison, for at their head they were nearly half a mile across—that is somewhat wider than Niagara. If you make a through tour of the whole area, following the course of the five arms of the falls, you will need at least four hours, because their course twists and turns over a terrain where going is hard and where care must be taken to avoid a fall into a crevice or into one of those fantastic giant cauldrons. The whole place holds one fascinated and four hours will indeed not be enough to satisfy one's wonder at this weird place where time itself seems to have petrified.

* * * * *

The river above Degerfors carries us past the neat houses of the factory workers set among the trees, past a riverside bathing place and, after a few miles of tranquil scenery, into Lake Möckeln, which is just an ordinary Swedish lake six miles long surrounded with low hills covered with pine trees, fields and farmsteads. At the northern end we reach Karlskoga, which is now linked with the neighbouring Bofors as one town. Here we find a lakeside pensionat and settle for a day or two. Our host is a charming fellow, who, like many of his countrymen, has spent part of his life in the United States. Over there the Swedes often pine for home. If they succeed they are too busy to return; if they do not they cannot afford the fare back. Thus only those who have done moderately well are found back home again, having enjoyed a period of adventure and acquired an American accent and a broader outlook than the stay-at-homes.

Karlskoga was founded three centuries ago in a hunting forest of Charles IX; hence its name, which means Charles's Wood. Now, with Bofors, it is essentially a modern town, a mushroom expansion of the past twenty years, sprawling out so loosely that though its inhabitants number only some 30,000 it covers a larger area even than Stockholm. Here for once the people live mainly in small houses. No doubt the reason for this dispersal is security, in that the famous armament works and the Nobel explosives factory here would be the first targets of an aggressor. The town exists by virtue of these works, and it was at Bofors that those wonderful ack-ack guns were made whose barking was like music to harassed Londoners during the Blitz.

Through the good offices and subtle diplomacy of a friend we manage to penetrate into the Bofors works, though unfortunately all the machines are still and most of the craftsmen are away on holiday. Nevertheless the tour is interesting enough, and we enjoy the privilege of walking around the enormous artificial caves blasted out of the rock, where gallery after gallery of modern equipment and machine tools were installed during the war out of bombing danger. Occasionally where the rough walls of rock are visible the effect is as dramatic as a Piranesi etching of a Roman prison.

A humorous, hearty foreman with Homburg hat ajaunt escorts

107

us round the works—another Swede who has lived in America and speaks with an easy Texas drawl. On our progress he points out things of interest—tools kept in controlled temperatures giving accuracy to microscopic degree, a great hydraulic stamping machine made in Britain in 1916, and then the half-completed barrel of the latest Bofors weapon, the most deadly ever produced, which will fire 160 shells a minute with the certainty of a hit at six miles distance.

"A terrible gun," mutters our guide, shaking his head with an air of pride mixed with awe.

The market square in Karlskoga is distinguished by its modern town hall and hotel built in 1941 to designs by Sune Lindström. This is one of those typically Swedish institutions where private enterprise co-operates with officialdom. The town hall is designed as a unit with the hotel which is owned by the town. Private enterprise, however, plays a part in the catering. The design is simple and dignified with careful, imaginative detailing and surrounds a generous courtyard open towards the square on one side at ground floor level. Brilliant boxes of flowers decorate the forecourt of the first-class restaurant and a bronze statue forms a fountain to one side (26). The design shows a new trend in using old materials in a modern way—red handmade brick for the outer walls, wide eaves of thick slate slabs and shingles for the walls of the courtyard—shingles which harmonize this sophisticated modern building with the seventeenth-century timber church nearby whose walls and steeple are protected in the same way. As in many such institutions there are three distinct restaurants—first, second and third class. The food is of the same high quality in each, comes from the same central kitchen but varies, of course, in price. In the second-class restaurant we enjoy one of the best meals of our lives, beginning with the traditional appetizer of snaps and that special kind of Swedish *hors d'oeuvres* which is a meal in itself. Everyone knows about this *smörgåsbord*. Some say that it began in the old days when the workers returning from the fields called loudly for food, but the hot meal not being quite ready, the housewife kept her menfolk pacified by placing numerous titbits on the table—cheese, salted herring and odd remains from yesterday.

In this rather formless town, with its eternity of villas and its dark satanic mills, the town square with its fine new hotel-cum-town-hall and its neighbouring park is a cultural oasis promising a better world. But Karlskoga has other compensations. As though allaying its guilt for merchandizing in death, the town has produced two of the most beautiful monuments to death in the world

38 ÖREBRO CASTLE: Originally a medieval fortress

39 KARLSBORG: Fortifications designed by C. F. Meijer (1845)

40 STOCKHOLM : The Heralds making a Royal Proclamation in front of the Riksdag

—the Skogskyrkogård, the Graveyard-in-the-wood, which was founded in 1908, and the new crematorium cemetery lying east of the town which was opened in 1945. The former is the lovelier. It is set in a half-wild wood of pine trees and at its centre lies a deep dell. Paths wind in great curves between the sighing trees, while here and there, among the widely spaced gravestones some lit up theatrically by shafts of sunlight, stone slabs cross cultivated patches of greensward. The graveyard adjoins a natural forest and wild animals occasionally roam in here from the surrounding countryside. Even elks have been seen. The place has an almost unbearable poignancy.

The new crematorium cemetery is of a different character, being a grand, undulating open space, far more deliberately cultivated, but in its way also dramatic and blending subtly with the whole landscape and sky around. The crematorium building itself with its conical roof has some originality of character but is not inspired. Near it stands a timber bell tower, a simple modern example of a very old type of Swedish structure, and its existence here provides an excuse for a digression on Swedish timber bell towers in general.

*   *   *   *   *

Designed and built by local peasant craftsmen these bell towers show great architectural virtuosity and technical skill. No existing example goes as far back as the Middle Ages, the oldest being at Söderköping, which was built in 1582, but without doubt many of the older bell towers are of medieval design and tradition. The reason why these towers were built detached from their parent churches is not clear. The tradition came probably from the Mediterranean countries, where the Campanile at Pisa is an example. Perhaps the risk of fire in the timber churches had something to do with it, in that if the church was destroyed the tower and its bells might be saved. Often the towers were built later than the churches, as at the twelfth-century church at Skäfthammar which has an eighteenth-century bell tower. In cases like this it was easier, of course, to construct separate structures than to build on to the churches, whose foundations might not be strong enough to take the added weight.

But perhaps the main reason for the separate bell tower was an aesthetic one. Villages were, and indeed still are, proud of their bell towers on which much creative effort and money were spent. Moreover the bells were often rung for other reasons than the customary one of summoning the faithful to prayer. The bells had an almost mystic significance in the North, and many folk-tales record how the bells were rung to drive away demons. The witches of old were well aware of the potency in magic of the bronze of the bells and of the grease of the axles from which they hung.

Many of the ancient medieval towers unhappily disappeared in the eighteenth century—one reason being the vandalism of the Russians who invaded the country in 1721 and laid waste by fire a great number of northern towns and villages. Many of the destroyed towers were soon replaced with new structures, which, while retaining the vernacular character of folk art, also reflected the Baroque influence of the time in sharply pointed steeples and ogee roofs. Often they incorporated onion domes influenced perhaps from Russia. The eighteenth century was the golden age of bell tower building. Most of that period are of superb craftsmanship and greatly varied design. In Norrland schools of bell tower builders were founded which recruited students from the peasant class. Some of these students later achieved such fame that their names are still remembered. A splendid Baroque example of 1732 stands in the Skansen Open-Air Museum in Stockholm, whither it was removed from Hällestad in Östergotland. Designed by Nils Uhrberg it is the highest in Sweden at 125 feet, and has the not unusual feature of protective shingle-cladding on the external posts (49). A beautiful example stands also at Leksand in Dalecarlia designed by Nicodemus Tessin for Charles XII.

* * * * *

Örebro can be reached from Karlskoga by water over Lake Toften and along the narrow Svartå River, but the journey, though pleasant, is uneventful and since time is pressing we now pack our folding canoe into its bags and depart for Örebro by car. We find it a large, busy industrial town. The main street is filled with first-class shops much like any main street in any part of Europe, but it has that depressing air which is always to be felt where the width of the street is the same as the height of the buildings on each side. Otherwise Örebro has a number of charms. It has several interesting old buildings. It has a park and a river running through it. It has an enchanting old quarter of cobbled streets and courtyards surrounded by Falu Red timber houses. It has a medieval castle surrounded by the water of the Svartå with four round bastions and thick grey walls of stone (38). The castle originated in the fourteenth century, but has undergone many alterations since, the last, and too drastic, alteration being of the end of the last century. Much of the original building still remains and the whole forms an imposing focal centre to the town, situated as it is on the water and backed by the trees of one of those municipal parks in the lay-out of which Sweden excels. Part of the castle is now a museum composed of a mixed collection of objects from different periods, among which the medieval sculpture is most worth seeing.

Strolling through the park along the river bank one comes soon to an interesting old timber building which is now also preserved as a museum. This is Kungstugan, the King's House, for in 1580 and 1581 Carl IX resided here when he visited Örebro. It is a rare example in solid heavy timbers with a cantilevered balcony and turf roof of a wealthy burgher's house of the sixteenth century. Inside it are some striking allegorical frescoes of the seventeenth century painted direct on to the timber walls.

* * * * *

Down at the quay in the park we board one of the small, white passenger steamers which leave daily on a fifteen-hour journey to Stockholm. After churning our way for several hours across the shallow, muddy water of Lake Hjälmaren, dusk descends at last, the moon rises and we enter the Hjälmaren Canal, an enchanting, narrow water fringed by old oak trees, birches and pines—an old canal originating in the seventeenth century. In a minute cabin we eat an excellent dinner served by a tall, sunburned waitress whose deft movements are like a dance. She is so amiable, smiles with such genuine goodwill and is so unaware of her outstanding beauty that we do not begrudge the high cost of the meal. The whole crew in fact is interesting and seems to be enjoying the journey as much as the restless, high-spirited passengers. Most of these are on holiday, among them three Belgian youths in bright green tights on a cycle tour, a group of schoolgirls with their slacks rolled up to the knees, a rogue of a Finnish sailor who grows ever more talkative as the Pilsner bottles are emptied and a young woman travelling alone who bears her ripe breasts with confident maturity and is soon surrounded by a court of admirers. The captain-cum-purser, king of this small community, has a weather-worn face of an intelligence and dignity that seem to deserve greater responsibility than this modest realm. Perhaps it is to him that the reeds bow twice so obsequiously in the steamer's wash.

In time most of the passengers are asleep. We enter the Arboga River in darkness, steam quietly east through flat farming country and in an hour tie up at Kungsör to unload. Here Charles XII once hunted in the neighbouring woods, here Christina took her summer ease and here we now enter the great Lake Mälar, the third largest lake in Sweden. Mälar has its own special character of pine-filled intimacy, for it rarely appears as a great lake, being filled with innumerable islands, large and small. One might say that it is amphibian, for not only is it half land and half water but it is half lake and half an inlet of the sea. Indeed, to the east near Stockholm, salt water penetrates into the lake and gives rise there to an underwater life which is unnatural to fresh water. The Mälar country is ideal for holiday-making in a small boat, for it possesses endless bays, inlets and sounds for exploration, the country is sparsely inhabited and yet has many old towns that may be visited along its shores.

Among these old towns is Strängnäs, one of the oldest settlements in Sweden, which we pass in the early dawn and can easily distinguish by the square brick tower of its cathedral. This cathedral was begun in the late twelfth century in Romanesque style, and parts of its original structure still remain. The last considerable rebuilding took place in the fifteenth century though the intricate copper lantern and turrets at the top of the tower were built later to designs by Hårleman. Within those walls lies the dust of Carl IX, while in one of the ancient buildings nestling below them Gustav Vasa was declared king in 1523. Apart from that building, the bishop's residence near it and the cathedral itself nothing remains to show the age of this small, quiet city, for since the thirteenth century down to 1871 Strängnäs has been devastated by fire no less than seven times.

Outriders of the capital appear among the conifers—*sportstugor*, summer villas, then an oil refinery, a factory or two, a shipyard and the first of the modern flat blocks. And there at last, framed by the wide steel span of Västerbron, lies the romantic city. On the left, miles of modern apartments, brightly coloured, end at the City Hall, above whose stately tower the gold of the Three Crowns catches the morning sun (47). On the right the cliffs of Södermalm bound along towards Slussen and the old Town-Between-the-Bridges. Our ship steams boldly on towards the Island of Knights to dock below the Wrangel Palace. The Finnish sailor performs his last parlour trick, the captain salutes his passengers and we march ashore and into Stockholm.

41 St. George and the Dragon in the S t o r C h u r c h, wood carving by the Lübeck sculptor, Bernt Notke (1489)

One of the narrow medieval streets

43 STOCKHOLM: The South of Tessin's Royal Palace. The Stor Church is
in the background

VII

Stockholm

THEY say of Stockholm: "It is a beautiful city", and "It is the Venice of the North". The first is true, at least by comparison with other European cities. The second is a poor and over-worked analogy. However, it is easy to see why the phrase has become a cliché. First, there is the ubiquitous water, for Stockholm is built largely on a group of islands; the waters between are mostly natural and few have been canalized. Secondly, the Italian Renaissance has had a great influence not only on the older buildings but on those of the nineteenth century also; even the City Hall, completed in 1923, has sought inspiration from Italy, especially Venice. There the similarity ends.

Stockholm's beauty is the product partly of nature itself, in that the environment of rocks and in particular of water, that basic element in pleasing landscape, is superb. It is also due to an organic but consciously controlled growth and embellishment which has been applied since the town was founded in 1255 by that vigorous ruler of the realm, Birger Jarl.

Here where Lake Mälar pours out its water through the Stream, the shortest river in Europe, into the inlet of the Baltic called Saltsjön, or Salt Sea, lie the three islands which form the centre and the oldest part of the city—Riddarholmen (the Island of Knights), Helgeandsholmen (the Isle of the Holy Spirit), where those architectural abortions of the nineteenth century, the Houses of Parliament and the Bank of Sweden, now stand, and the largest island, Staden Mellan Broarna (the Town-Between-the-Bridges, or the Old Town as it is usually called). Birger Jarl chose the spot wisely, for although the small settlement he found here was being continuously plundered by pirates, it needed only some sound fortifications to make it impregnable. It was also a good centre for trade in being approachable by water for some seventy-five miles by Mälaren to the west and in being in contact to the east by water with the whole of the Baltic. Since Birger Jarl's day the elevation of these islands has risen, and it is estimated that the level of the water was then about ten feet higher than it is now; no doubt the land itself has risen as it tends to do by about a foot a century in most towns.

Of Birger Jarl's original city little remains except a considerable part of the street-plan in the Old Town. Stortorget, the Great

Market, is still in its first position and a part of the original town wall, 18 feet thick, can still be seen in the foundations of Tessin's Royal Palace. Nothing remains of the ancient keep called Tre Kronor, the Three Crowns, which grew into one of the most impressive palaces of Europe until most of it was destroyed by fire in 1697 (10). Something is left from the Middle Ages, however, in Storkyrkan, the Great Church, and in the Riddarholm Church which began as a Franciscan chapel.

Yet the Old Town, on account of its narrow streets, which open out here and there into a small triangular place or a large square and give fascinating vistas down cobbled passageways to the dockside waters, remains essentially medieval in its atmosphere (42).

By the fifteenth century burghers' houses had begun to appear outside the old encircling walls. Many of them were built of stone and a few survive to this day, though not in their original form. At this time the stepped gable from Germany and Holland came to the North, and we can still see three examples in old Stockholm from this time. Some fortifications from the latter part of the fifteenth century still stand, notably the two towers on the west of Riddarholmen, and at this period Storkyrkan had assumed the form in which we see it today.

The town was still small and did not begin to assume its full position as the national capital until Gustav Vasa made his state-entry into the town on the Midsummer Eve of 1523, after his victory over the Danes. At that time the inhabitants numbered only some 3,000. Then in the seventeenth century Sweden suddenly found herself a great country and set to work to expand her capital as one of the most splendid in Europe and a fitting symbol of her new power. Many fine houses stand in the Old Town from that period, especially from the latter half of the century, displaying doorways richly carved in stone in the Baroque manner. Most of the old medieval houses were then either pulled down or modernized and lavishly decorated, and the whole quarter west of Stora Nygatan, which was gutted by fire in 1625, was rebuilt on a modern, grid-iron plan. Foreign craftsmen were mostly employed in this new building, which, apart from the noblemen's new town mansions, included Sweden's two most important historical monuments—the beginning of the new Royal Palace and the Riddarhus, or House of the Nobles, on Riddarholmen (44)—as well as the rebuilt German Church and a splendid new chapel added to Riddarholm Church.

The town now expanded on to the islands and rocks to the north and south of the three central islands. On the south, Södermalm, arose Louis de Geers' Palace designed by a Dutchman and the old Town Hall designed by the elder Tessin, both in Götgatan; also Katarina Church by Jean de la Vallée, which was to be later restored by G. J. Adelcrantz after a fire in the eighteenth century and is the first church in Stockholm to have acquired a dome. To the north, Norrmalm and Östermalm, the new lay-out was in the grand manner of the time with straight, grid-iron streets on which sprang up the grand town houses of the new nobility.

The chief building of the time north of the Old Town lies some distance away to the north-west. This is the Palace of Karlberg rebuilt by Jean de la Vallée in 1670 for Count Magnus Gabriel de la Gardie (16, 46). With its central courtyard, its tiered roof and rows of bold, circular windows decorated with swags, it is a building of strong and unusual character and the best Baroque building in Stockholm next to the Royal Palace and the House of the Nobles. In the eighteenth century Karlberg became a military barracks and long side wings were added to designs by C. C. Gjörwell, who also designed the small Neo-Classic Temple of Neptune in the delightful wooded park lying to the north of the palace.

Towards the end of the seventeenth century, Sweden's first Golden Age of building, which had lasted for nearly a century, came to an abrupt end. The empire, so rapidly gained, was as rapidly lost. The Age of Greatness was over and a dull period of retrenchment and austerity followed. Industry took over many of the empty palaces; Rörstrand Castle, for example, became the famous porcelain works in 1726. By the middle of the eighteenth century, however, the situation had improved and another age of cultural brilliance began under the patronage of Gustav III—the age in architecture of Hårleman, Adelcrantz, Carlberg, Cronstedt, Palmstedt and Rehn. Storkyrkan in the Old Town was largely rebuilt by Carlberg to harmonize with the Royal Palace (43). Its tower, according to Ragnar Östberg, is the finest in Stockholm, but this is a modest belief for the prize must go to Östberg's own lovely tower at the City Hall (47). Hårleman, among other works, built the Observatory to the north in Vasastaden, rebuilt his own house in Drottninggatan, added to Karlberg and completed the Carolinean burial chapel at Riddarholm Church, which had been begun by the elder Tessin and continued by his son (45). Eric Palmstedt, the friend of Sergel and Bellman, altered Cronstedt's designs for the Börshus, the Exchange in the Great Market of the Old Town, perhaps the finest Rococo period building in Stockholm. Carl Cronstedt designed the Artillerigård, now the Army Museum, in Riddargatan with its splendid iron palings. Louis Jean Desprez, best known as a scenic designer, a Frenchman who replaced Piper as royal gardener, prepared a gigantic royal palace project for the Haga Park to the north of the town, which was never completed and reached only ground floor level. The beautiful park at Haga was completed, however, by F. M. Piper and there one can see the influence of Piper's travels to England in search of the picturesque and of his close contact there with Sir William Chambers. Small works of Desprez still exist at Haga in the shape of the playful, "medieval", copper tents and the Chinese Pavilion.

Of the well-known buildings of the early nineteenth century the most imposing are Rosendals Palace in Djurgården, built in Neo-Classic style for King Karl Johan, and the Royal Academy building in Storgatan—both now museums and both designed by Frederick Blom. Of the same period is C. C. Gjörwell's Garnisons Hospital on Kungsholmen.

Before we bring Stockholm's story up-to-date let us look a little more closely at the churches of the Old Town. Like most ecclesiastical buildings in Europe they were not built as a whole in one period, but have been altered and added to through the centuries to make history books in stone and brick. Storkyrkan, or the Church of St. Nicolaus, is the oldest church in Stockholm, although, as we have seen, it was almost entirely rebuilt round about 1740 by Carlberg (41). Nevertheless, here can be discovered no less than thirteen periods of reconstruction during five centuries. It was founded by Birger Jarl in the 1260's, but only in the interior does any part of the old Gothic fabric survive. From the pulpit of this church in 1525 Olaus Petri, the great leader of the Swedish Lutherans, who superintended the translation of the Bible into Swedish—Master Olof as the people called him—sang Mass for the first time in the Swedish language and so inaugurated the Reformation in his country. He lies buried here below the pulpit. The church contains two splendid antiques. The first is the large wooden statue of St. George and the Dragon executed by the Lübeck sculptor Bernt Notke which was presented to the church in 1489 (41). (A modern copy in bronze stands at Österlånggatan in the Old Town farther south.) Ordered by Sten Sture the Elder in memory of the battle of Brunkeberg of 1471, when the Danes under Christian I suffered a sanguinary defeat, this is one of the finest pieces of medieval sculpture in existence. The second antique is the curious painting known as Väderstolstavlan (literally, Picture of the Mock Suns), painted in 1535 by order of Olaus Petri in memory of an extraordinary celestial phenomenon which was observed over Stockholm on the 30th April of that year—five mock suns encircled by coronas.

44   STOCKHOLM: The House of the Nobles, or Riddarhuset, in Dutch Renaissance style. Begun by Joost Vingboons in 1656 and completed by Jean de la Vallée about 1672

45 STOCKHOLM: Riddarholm Church; the Caroline Burial Chapel (1671–1743) designed by the Tessins and completed by Hårleman

46   KARLBERG PALACE, Stockholm: the South side (1670) designed by
Jean de la Vallée (see fig. 16)

47   STOCKHOLM: Östberg's City Hall (1909–1923)

But the picture is less interesting as an astronomical record than as a clear representation of how the city appeared over four centuries ago.

Riddarholm Church may be called Sweden's Westminster Abbey, for it contains the remains of many of Sweden's kings and great men. It was built towards the end of the thirteenth century as a Franciscan Abbey church. A great part of the original structure remains, though the south transept is of the late sixteenth century and the burial chapels are seventeenth-century additions. Of these chapels the most notable is that of Gustav Adolph built in Dutch Renaissance style in 1634. Like many churches both in Sweden and Denmark Riddarholm Church gains in aesthetic power by the application of rich Baroque decoration to the simple Gothic fabric. Johan III in the sixteenth century built a tall tower here which was burned down in 1835 and replaced by the peculiar, ugly but technically interesting cast-iron spire designed by the sculptor E. G. Göthe. Attached to the church is the famous Carolinean Chapel built between 1671 and 1743 to contain the remains of Carl X, Carl XI and Carl XII which has already been mentioned as being the work of the Tessins and of Hårleman (45). Inside the church are some notable frescoes in the vaulting painted when the church was first built; also a magnificent silver chandelier in the choir made in Augsburg during the first half of the seventeenth century.

The third of the Old Town churches is the German Church dedicated to St. Gertrude and built for the German community between 1613 and 1618. Much of the original building still stands, but the tower was rebuilt in 1886 after a fire. The interior belongs largely to the 1640's and is a good, unspoiled example of the work of the period. The royal gallery in the north-east corner was built in 1673 by the elder Tessin with sculpture by one Nicolaes Millich. The richly carved Baroque porch on the south elevation carved in 1643 by Jost Henne is a fine feature of the church.

In the 1850's Stockholm was still relatively small, with some 100,000 inhabitants. Then Europe's bourgeois industrialization began to affect Sweden and great changes came to Stockholm, reflected in much of the existing building of confused eclectic stylism, especially to be seen on Norrmalm. The railways arrived and many other technical developments as well—water and gas on tap, tramways and, before long, telephones, electricity and bathrooms. In the 1860's the authorities were alive to the future and wisely laid out a street plan for coming building development. Stockholmers of today must be grateful to the town officials of that

period for the generous, tree-filled avenues which provide much
of the town's modern character—Narvavägen, Valhallavägen, Birger
Jarlsgatan, Kungsgatan, Sveavägen, Norr Mälarstrand, Ringvägen
on Södermalm and Strandvägen along the waterside which, with
its contemporary buildings, can be regarded as a monument to
Sweden's Victorian age. Hausmann's Paris plan was clearly the
inspiration for this new lay-out of boulevards.

By 1900 the city's population had trebled to some 300,000
inhabitants and suburbs were growing at Lidingö, Djursholm,
Sundbyberg and Saltsjöbaden, pleasant middle-class garden cities
of widely separated villas set amidst gardens of rocks and fir trees.
1900 to the 1920's contained the decades of that distinctly national
style of building, with its stress on natural materials with rich
textures and on handicrafts which reached its final apotheosis in
the City Hall. Then, together with Functionalism, came another
great expansion of the capital and the new blocks of flats so characteristic of Stockholm grew up like mushrooms around the town,
especially in the working-class distict of Södermalm—utilitarian,
ungarnished structures strongly influenced, as was all Functionalism,
by the cubist school of painting (50). On the practical side they
were an improvement on the old courtyard blocks, for they were
built in strips open on both sides. Their austerity and their cramped
interiors are mitigated by useful fittings, by bright stuccos on their
exteriors, by striped sun blinds, by small balconies giving each
family its open-air room and providing form and shadow on the
otherwise bleak elevations, and by sensitive lay-out and landscaping in which trees, water and rocks are dominant elements. One
of the most imaginative flat buildings of the time was Sven Markelius's Kollektivhus in John Ericssonsgatan, which obtained an
international reputation.

The Second World War brought another great expansion, partly
on account of the sudden rise in the birth-rate, partly on account
of the centralization of industry and administration. More and more
flat blocks have been built, but still the housing situation has not
been solved. Stockholm is faced also with a serious traffic problem
which the town-planners, headed by Markelius, are now trying to
solve. One means of easing the troubles has been the building of an
underground railway, running from north to south, which has been
inspired by London's Underground. The problem in Stockholm,
as in all old cities, is to graft the new ways of living of dense popula-
tions on to an ancient foundation economically and without destroy-
ing too many valued old buildings and too much of the town's
cultural inheritance. Stockholm is not an easy town to modernize

for two main reasons—the need continually to cross the ubiquitous waters, and the bottle-neck between north and south created by the Old Town and Slussen, the Lock, which is a narrow piece of land linking the Old Town to Södermalm. At Slussen the difficulties have been largely overcome by a remarkable and intricate piece of engineering in the form of clover-leaf crossings, fly-overs and underground passage ways—an area dominated in the south-east corner by the fascinating Katarina Lift and its hanging restaurant. The new underground railway should greatly reduce that flow of traffic through this bottle-neck which along Skeppsbron, the quay-side of the Old Town, becomes lethal at peak hours. The broad principle of planning is, as in London, to decentralize the city by creating satellite communities around the capital.

The population of Stockholm is approaching a million, and if it grows much more it will be in danger of losing its charm. Arriving from the quiet provinces one is at once struck by the effects a big modern city can have on the national character—the simplicity, kindliness and calm of the provincial Swede is sullied by *angst*, by Americanization, by an unhealthy restlessness, by the cold, calculating, impersonal eye and the loss of the old human courtesies.

Three things may save Stockholm from the final frenzy of the megalopolitan city. The first is the cleanliness of the air which gives to everything a fresh air of gaiety. The second is the wonderful, penetrating system of parks and gardens which, combined with the water and contrasting with the closely built-up areas, bring nature to the centre of the town, provide interesting pictures wherever one looks and give a fine sense of spaciousness. The third is that close contact by water with the surrounding countryside which has produced the summer holiday cult of the Swedish town dweller. Nearly every Stockholmer owns some kind of boat by which he can escape each afternoon or at week-ends into the archipelago or among the islands of Mälar. If he does not own his own craft he can board one of those small steamers lying in flocks along the quays and so travel many miles to some small private retreat where for a brief spell he can fish, swim or just lie idling in the sun. This impulse for the simple life amidst natural surroundings affects the Stockholm scene—on the negative side by giving the town-planners another headache when trying to solve the seasonal traffic problem created by the summer migrations; on the positive side by providing those lively quay-side scenes when the people in relaxed mood mill around the steamers or around those small boat basins where rows of craft from diminutive dinghies to sumptuous yachts lie waiting for a jaunt (24). This sun and nature worship is enjoyed by all classes. The working class has its own type of country seat in the form of allotments on the outskirts of the town. These are not merely patches of ground with squalid shacks of rusting corrugated sheets so sadly familiar in England, but are well laid out with small, trim dwellings, each with its white flag pole and neatly tended garden.

The municipality itself has in the past acquired much of the land in and around Stockholm and has thus through its foresight been able to reserve considerable areas as parks and open spaces. These it has linked up with the old parks and gardens to form a Park System which is unique in the world. Of the old parks there is eighteenth-century Haga to the north, Kungsträdgården at the very centre which was a royal garden as far back as the fifteenth century and Humlegården near the centre which Gustav II laid out in 1619 as a hop garden (*humle* meaning hops).

The chief fascination of the Stockholm Park System is its intimate informality and its acceptance of the advantages and restriction of the natural conditions of thin top soil, granite outcrops and that fairly severe climate which prohibits the cultivation of the English lawn. The style is based on traditions in which the English Picturesque, Chambers's Sharawaggi, and contacts with the Orient made in the eighteenth century by the East India Company are all evident. But the style is at the same time new, functional and organic in being a reflection of a conscious democracy.

Mr. H. F. Clark, the expert on gardening, writes in *The Architectural Review:* "The social democracy of the Scandinavian countries and particularly of Sweden is aptly expressed by the free style, sensitively controlled naturalism of the Swedish park. The visitor is conscious of these values almost at once—the public squares decorated with standing flower pots and flower boxes bright with geraniums and petunias are indicative not only of a national pride in order and seemliness but also imply a highly developed sense of social responsibility. For it is only possible in a milieu where there seems to be no obvious class division into 'we' the people and 'they' our rulers, that the unselfconscious intimacy of a public square decorated like a private garden can be both created and maintained. For the landscape architect on his tour of Stockholm is at once struck by the seeming carelessness and inconsequence of meadows in an urban park, the oddness of the fact that no path has a clear and well-defined edge or verge, that garden shrubs are planted singly or in groups in grass and that clear unpolluted streams and pools are verged by untrampled reeds a stone's throw from the tramlined streets."

48 Eighteenth-century peasant painting of the Halland school

49 The baroque timber Bell Tower from Hällestad in Östergotland (1732)
STOCKHOLM: SKANSEN OPEN-AIR MUSEUM

50 Flats over
looking th
Klara Water

51 Characteris-
tic street decora-
tion at Nybro-
plan

STOCKHOLM

Typical of Stockholm's gardening is that mile-long strip park which lies between the tall flat blocks and the lake along Norr Mälarstrand on Kungsholmen. "This might have been treated as an urban, tree-lined, terraced promenade", writes Mr. Clark, "but has instead been landscaped. The success or failure of the result is a matter of opinion. But, again, it should be remembered that the Mälarstrand was constructed for recreation, for the casual evening stroll, for mothers and their children and for picnic making. Here the lake water and its margin interpenetrate and intermingle. Small inlets percolate the banks, timber piers and summer houses on piles jut into the lake. The margin is loosely defined with casually placed water-worn boulders or groups of reeds and water-loving plants and the only floral decorations are naturalized groups of indigenous Swedish wild flowers."

Swedes have green fingers, and a universal appreciation exists of the value of plant forms in the landscaping of a town or a window box. "In England", Mr. Clark goes on, "the boarding-house aspidistra and the pot plants in cottage windows are all that remain of a fashion that is almost moribund. In the Scandinavian countries, however, this fashion rages with undiminished vigour."

With this informality of garden lay-out and the love of free, organic forms goes a high level of design in street furniture which helps to make the Swedish townscape the least squalid in the world. Add to the general sense of order and love of fresh colours a tradition of good design and high quality in craftsmanship and the results are subtle textures and patterns of paving materials, and excellence of neat, bright rubbish containers, charming ice-cream kiosks, public notices, bus stops, park seats, lamp standards and, not least, those famous precast concrete flower-pots, or portable gardens of Holger Blom, the Stockholm Parks Architect, which decorate Stockholm's public places and have now set a European fashion (51).

Stockholm has no very large central parks like London or New York. The open spaces, the city's lungs, are small, interpenetrating and ubiquitous. Nevertheless, not far to the east of the town, a mere twenty-minutes' walk from the centre, lies the great park of Djurgården set on an island. It might be termed the Richmond Park of Stockholm for it was originally a royal deer park later turned into a public resort. Its appearance is not unlike that of Richmond Park for it is planted in the free English manner largely with oaks, though unlike its counterpart it contains a fair number of buildings, both old and new. Of these the most notable is the Rosendals Palace and the eighteenth-century timber inn of Gröna Lund where Bellman once caroused and sang to his lute. Here also by the water is an open-air café beside a yacht basin where the walker can refresh himself and watch the small white steamers puffing proudly towards the skerries.

To the west of Djurgården on a hill overlooking the town lies Skansen (meaning a small redoubt) (24). This is the parent of all the other Scandinavian open-air museums wherein the culture and traditions of the past are preserved in a park setting in a fresh and lively way. Skansen is also a zoo of indigenous fauna. It began in 1872 when Arthur Hazelius, a teacher of languages who was interested in history, began to collect objects illustrating Sweden's social life. These formed the foundation of the Nordiska Museum of which Skansen is an open-air branch. Skansen was opened in 1891 when the first of the old peasant cottages was re-erected there at a time of growing national consciousness and romantic provincialism. Now in those pleasant, wooded grounds stands a splendid collection of buildings dating from the sixteenth to the nineteenth centuries which characterize the way of life of different sections of Swedish society through the centuries. The buildings come from different parts of the country from Lapland down to Skåne—*inter alia* farmsteads, bell-towers, a windmill, an eighteenth-century church and manor house, all with their interiors furnished in their respective contemporary styles (18, 19, 49). The place is, of course, artificial but, though one senses the presence around the old buildings of puzzled, displaced ghosts, Skansen is by no means filled with the deadness too common in national museums, for the old ceremonies are frequently celebrated here, country dances are enjoyed and in the old town quarter men practise crafts like glass blowing and printing in the ancient, traditional ways. Here, too, one can dance in the open in the modern manner, one can dine and wine well and listen to the band until the sun is sent ceremoniously to rest as the flags slide slowly down their masts.

Many examples of an attractive phase of Swedish folk art can be seen both in the farmhouses of Skansen and on the walls of the Nordiska Museum close by (48). This is the school of peasant wall painting, which flourished roughly between 1750 and 1850, called Bondemålningar (Peasant paintings). Their equivalent can be found nowhere else in Europe, nor even in the other countries of the North. Indeed this vernacular school was restricted in Sweden itself to two districts—Halland with south Småland and Dalarna with Bergslagen and south Norrland. The century's work of the school shows the full round from vigorous primitive beginnings, through the flowering peak to decadence and death. Each of the two districts has its own distinct style.

Ever since Viking times decorations with human figures had been produced on tapestry and embroidery. This tradition, together with that of wall painting, grew in the Gothic churches, continued in the Baroque palaces and brought forth in the gay times of the Rococo period this naïve, joyful and wholly delightful painting in the homes of the people. Probably the links between the church paintings and those of the peasants' houses were the paintings in the manors and the rectories. One might, in fact, regard these peasant wall decorations as the poor man's Gobelins.

In Dalecarlia the dwellings were larger and roomier than in most other districts, and most well-to-do farms had both their work-a-day living-rooms and their special parlours for festive occasions. In these parlours then the wall paintings, laid direct on to the walls or fixed as permanent frescoes painted on canvas or thick paper, were permanently in position and large in size. In Halland where life was poorer no special parlours existed and rooms were smaller. Hence the Halland paintings were always on canvas or paper which could be stored away safely from everyday wear and tear and brought out and hung only on special occasions such as Christmas time.

The artists were themselves peasants who regarded their paintings as a side-line, although some of them became so renowned that they always had some commission in hand. Many names are still on record, among them that of Per Hörberg, a poor soldier's son and the most gifted of them all. Often families became renowned, the skill being handed on from father to son. Colouring was always brilliant, largely primary, and subjects were mostly biblical, the general composition of figures being based, at least in Dalarna, on early bible woodcuts. Dress and architecture were contemporary, and so one may see the Three Wise Men arriving to honour the Child on horseback and dressed in breeches and three-cornered hats—or the Queen of Sheba in crinoline being driven in a stately coach and four. But scenes from the life of the times are frequent— a service or a wedding in the local church, Bernadotte's coronation in Norrköping, some allegorical idea such as the Staircase of Life or scenes from private life bearing a moral. Like all the best phases of creation in any culture, this art form had its firm conventions within which the individual artist had enough scope for his own personal fantasy.

Cheerful decoration rather than naturalism was the aim. When Jesus preaches in the Temple, the top and bottom of the painting have bands of repeated floral or zigzag patterns, while the sky above the Temple is filled with a gigantic Rococo posy of flowers and foliage suspended magically in mid-air. There is no attempt at perspective and colouring is free, so that a horse may be green and spotted and John the Baptist's hair may be pale blue. Horses, naturally enough among peasants, are popular as elements in the compositions, especially in Halland. Paint was either oil colour or a kind of distemper made of chalk and glue mixed by the artist himself until these were replaced during the last decadent decade by cheap aniline dyes.

The Dala paintings are the more familiar and have tended to overshadow those of the Halland school. The southern paintings, however, are both more amusing and of greater artistry and technical skill. They are more formalized and tend to repeat motifs in a more disciplined and decorative way. Since the Halland paintings are generally shaped as horizontal strips which could be pinned across the rafters, their matter tends to restrict itself to such suitable subjects in rows as the Wise and Foolish Virgins, the Twelve Apostles or a series of consecutive scenes from the life of the Prodigal Son.

This vigorous, primitive art which developed within its limitations to a climax of sophistication was killed by industrialism. After the middle of the nineteenth century the old self-sufficient peasant culture rapidly declined and cheap printed wallpapers took the place of this spontaneous folk art of the Bondemålningar—just one symptom in the North of the world revolution. Sixty years ago one could still find examples of these paintings lying rolled up and forgotten in some country attic or perhaps decorating the walls of a farm-yard closet. Then you could buy a piece for a shilling or two. Today these paintings are highly valued and you will be lucky to acquire a good specimen for fifty pounds.

It may be that the visitor to Stockholm will be less impressed by her old buildings, either at Skansen or elsewhere, than by her modern buildings and her social planning and organization as expressed in the whole environment. Much of the new architecture is utilitarian but through refinement of detailing, competent craftsmanship, careful siting and good choice of colours and materials most of it has a decorative quality. The new schools are especially good, for in Sweden children form a privileged class. Paul Hedqvist's Southern Communal School and his Technical School are fine examples. But it is in the work of Gunnar Asplund, one of the great architects of our age, that we can best see the development of this century's architecture in Stockholm.

Asplund died in 1940 at the early age of 55, and though his productive life ran for only 25 years he accomplished an astonishing amount of work. The Stockholm City Library, the Scandia Cinema, the 1930 Stockholm Exhibition which revolutionized architecture in the North, and his last and greatest work, the Woodland Crematorium, are his best known creations. He also designed a great number of smaller buildings in which his charming and individual genius are perhaps best expressed—for example, the Woodland Chapel in the Stockholm South Cemetery of 1918 and the delightful house he built himself at Sorunda in 1937.

Asplund went through several phases of rapid change during his working life. He began in the new nationalistic style which broke with international eclecticism at the turn of the century; there followed the romantic period of Swedish Grace after the First World War, a brief spell of almost academic classicism, the return to internationalism through *Funkis*, and the final phase as expressed in his crowning work, the Woodland Crematorium, which shows a departure from functional puritanism to a freer manner where landscaping is of major importance.

Through all these phases Asplund was in the lead and always with a fighting sincerity. In spite of its supple adaptation to changing ideas, its youthful and often fanatical belief in new fashions, his work was never just *à la mode*; it was always creative in a fresh, adventurous and intensely personal way. This was so even when his individualism was under the restraint of Functionalism, for in his 1930 exhibition and in his small Bredenberg Store in Norrmalm, which is in the uncompromising style of Le Corbusier, some individual quality of gaiety, fantasy and grace comes bubbling through.

Today most of the young architects reach a high standard of design, but none has yet achieved such international renown as either Asplund or that star of an earlier generation, Ragnar Östberg, for the tendency is towards co-operation, utilitarianism and an austere effacement of the individual spirit in the name of that uncommon, if not mythical, creature, the Common Man. However worthy this new architectural approach may be, something has been lost to all men of that fantasy and drama which imbue the work of Asplund and Östberg. Never again are we likely to see quite the same kind of brilliance as is displayed, for instance, in the City Hall of Östberg, for it is the belated swan-song of an age of handicrafts that has vanished (47). The social realist of today will no doubt spurn the bourgeois escapism of this *tour de force*, and the architectural puritans of architecture, whose high priest is Le Corbusier (in his way the greatest romantic of them all), may still regard it, though with decreasing conviction, not as a piece of architecture at all but as a piece of theatrical scenery. Nevertheless one returns to it again and again and always with fresh delight and enthusiasm. Whatever one's viewpoint one must in the end come to accept the Stockholm City Hall as a masterpiece of its kind. It is a fairy-tale told so vividly and with such conviction and imagination that we believe it is true in spite of our cynical selves. In the end is it not just this fairy-tale quality which is the hall-mark of a work of art, a quality of personal creation which forms something larger and more wonderful than life?

Clearly the City Hall is a work of infinite care and patience. The craftsmanship throughout cannot have been surpassed at any other time in history. Here the sense of texture, colour and materials is hyper-sensitive, especially in the red brick tower with its subtle entasis and elegant copper belfry. Here the best of Sweden's artists, designers and craftsmen were called in to pool their skill under the controlling hand of the master architect. Every detail from a tower balcony to a small font carved in the paving of the waterside terrace, from the grand and gilded mosaics of Einar Forseth in the Banqueting Hall to the wrought-iron curls on the spire of the Moon Tower, from the chandeliers of the Council Chamber to the frescoes in the ceiling coffers of the South Portico—all things have been conceived and executed with a loving care and an uncommercialized pride.

There is no more fitting place from which to say farewell to this land than the tower of the City Hall. From the top the town can be seen in panorama all around, and not far off, just across the water of Lake Mälar, we can look down at the Old Town, the kernel from which Stockholm grew. But it is in the depths of the Old Town itself that we shall prefer to make our last visit. We shall sit in a café overlooking a small cobbled place where the sunlight is warming the stones of the old town pump just as our spirits will be warmed there by the intimate atmosphere, that moving *stämning* of the ancient community, which only the passage of the centuries can form. At noon the bells of the German Church will begin to sing: "Glory be to God on High".

DENMARK

VIII

Land and Livelihood

LOOKING at a map of Denmark unrelated to the rest of the world the country looks large. But this is an illusion, caused maybe by its splintered look and by the number of small islands which make the mainland and the two largest islands appear extensive by comparison. The area of the whole country is in fact only 16,575 square miles. That is about half the area of Ireland or of Scotland. Yet the coast lines add up to 4,622 miles (p. 141).

Apart from the peninsula of Jutland, which is attached to the Continent of Europe where it borders Schleswig-Holstein on the south, Denmark is made up of some 100 inhabited and 400 uninhabited islands. The largest of these islands is Zealand on whose eastern shore the capital city of Copenhagen lies.

The country divides naturally into two parts. West of the Great Belt, which is 20 miles wide and is crossed by ferry, lie Jutland and Funen. These are joined by a great bridge which strides across the Little Belt. To the east lie Zealand, Lolland, Falster and white-cliffed Möen, also joined by bridges. Compared with Norway and Sweden the country is certainly flat. Himmelbjerg, the Sky Mountain, in Jutland is called by the Norwegians a hole in the ground. Nevertheless it is 530 feet above sea-level. Jutland also has a waterfall. It is 4 feet high. Denmark has some rocks, but these are only found on the island of Bornholm. In spite of this lack of drama the aspect of the country is not dull, for there are wide fjords along the coasts and inland lies much woodland (beech being the national tree) and much rolling, fertile, homely land which, studded with small white farmsteads and spanned by the wide sky above, has that cheerful, friendly charm without ostentation which characterizes the people who inhabit it (54, 55). The landscape smiles at one in a friendly way.

A Dane has described his country thus: "An English writer once declared that Denmark resembled a red cow in an enormous green field. Add that it is a gay cow and a pleasant field and the remark is true enough. But there are also broad streams and blue lakes about the country, idyllic fjords, beaches where water laps the white sand, unexpected cliffs that you can fall over if you lean out too far; there are stretches of moorland so flat that you stop believing the world is round, dunes with masses of sand almost indistinguishable from a sample of African desert, damp rich marshes, woods with pale green beeches and picnic baskets, and Rebild's heather-covered hills and dales. Dotted about amongst it all are thousands of gardens, surrounding thousands of small white farms, and ancient parks surrounding ancient castles that are haunted by grey and white ladies who look down from the mullioned windows upon real white swans on the green waters of the moat. There are hundreds of gay, queer, amusing towns where gay, queer, amusing people go around speaking twenty different kinds of Danish."*

Long ago Denmark did not look like that. It did not look like anything, for it lay under the sea except where the lava of Bornholm raised its head above the water. Through the centuries millions of tiny armoured creatures sank to the bottom of the ocean where, compressed, they formed in time the bed of chalk, limestone and flint which is Denmark's foundation. Upheavals lifted this bed to the surface. The cold years came and the ice covered all the North carrying with it the moraine of the sand, gravel and clay which now form the surface of Denmark. The glacial rivers ground out shallow valleys to produce the characteristic rolling hillocks, the fjords and that range of hills running down Jutland which divides the undulations of the east from the flat sandy heathland of the west. The weather grew milder, the ice melted and floods burst across the country to produce the Three Channels—the Sound, the Great Belt and the Little Belt—(now symbolized as a trade-mark on the famous Copenhagen porcelain in three wavy lines of blue). The Baltic became linked with the salt oceans of the world and the forest grew on Denmark's soil—first fir trees and later oaks and beeches which were to be of value to the men who came wandering up from the south.

In time much of the forest was cut down and slowly the land came through human effort to acquire its present aspect. Today the most beautiful part of the country lies in Jutland, in the district round Silkeborg which is still forested. This is Denmark's Lake District. Jutland also contains the dullest part of the country in the endless flat farm land on the west which is not improved by wire fencing and overhead electric cables. The coast on the west, however, has a fascination and provides the right holiday conditions for those who want no more than to lie in the sunshine and to bathe in the sea (59). The east of the mainland where the towns nestle in the fjords is more amiable than the west, and here the typical

* Mogens Lind in *We Danes—And You* (National Travel Association of Denmark).

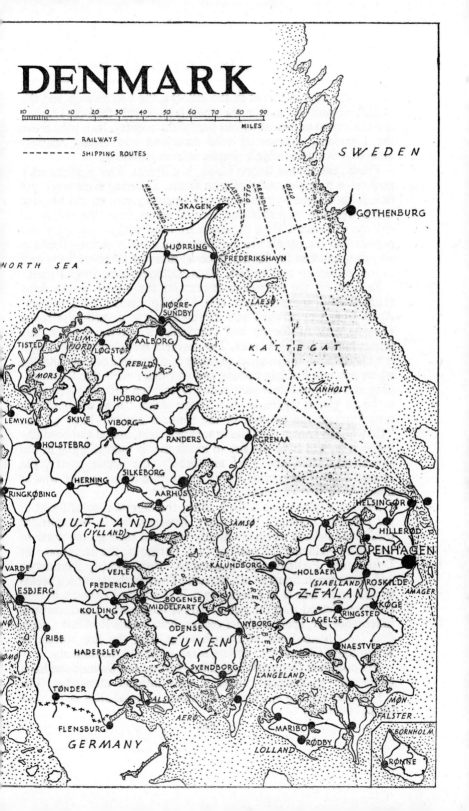

Danish charm is apparent in the hillocks, the beechwoods and the overall verdure. Jutland on the whole is less fertile than the islands; it is the leanest and most serious part of the country. Its north, above the Limfjord, consists of wild moorland and dunes, sparsely inhabited but possessing a simple, solemn grandeur.

Funen, the second largest island, is different. This is Denmark's garden—a happy country of trim farms, flowering fruit trees and rich fields hedged by hawthorn and bramble, with an old but still living tradition of cultivation handed down from the monks of Odense monastery. Here the roads are lined with willow trees and poplars and the people are the liveliest of a lively nation. Funen is also distinguished for having fathered many of Denmark's greatest artists, musicians and writers. Hans Andersen came from Funen.

Zealand on the east, since it contains the capital, is the most sophisticated, industrialized and built-up district of Denmark. Apart from Copenhagen and its suburbs it is nevertheless rustic enough, with its forests and cornfields, its pretty villages, fine manor houses and park lands. The northern area above Copenhagen is a playground, the summer paradise of the people of Copenhagen, where you will find gay bathing and yachting resorts like Klampenborg and the great deer-park called Dyrehaven with its 3,500 acres of beech glades where, as two Danes write, "it is wonderful to walk through the twilight of the summer night". They go on: "He who has known the Danish summer night, unreal and bewitching as it is, will have the key to much that is unintelligible in the Danish character, the quiet melancholy, the gentle poetry, the strange dreams simmering under the surface of the people who at first sight appear so realistic and prosaic."*

Here in Zealand also is Grib Skov, the biggest natural forest in the country. Zealand's chief glory, however, lies in her splendid castles and palaces which are mostly scattered through the north of the island—Hamlet's Kronborg (77), Sorgenfri, the Hermitage of Dyrehaven, Fredensborg, Jaegerspris, Frederiksdal, Marienlyst and, most magnificent of all, fantastic Frederiksborg, which seems to float on its lake as in a dream (75). The north of Zealand, in fact, has been blessed with the richest part of the country's architectural inheritance for, apart from its castles, here stands Roskilde Cathedral (56), mausoleum of Danish kings, and the five towers of Kalundborg Church (61) among many other old monuments.

But how does Denmark live? Like Norway and Sweden she has a democratic government under a constitutional monarchy. The

* Kirsten Halberg and Carry Hedemann in *Introduction to Denmark* (A. C. Normann).

53   The fortified Round Church of Østerlars, an early medieval type of building
      showing influences from eastern Europe

54 Pibemølle

55 The hills of Holbaek

DANISH LANDSCAPE

people number four million, of which as many as a quarter live in Copenhagen and its suburbs. The four largest provincial towns are in order of size—Aarhus, Odense, Aalborg and Esbjerg. Seventy-five per cent of the productive area of the country is used for agriculture on which about a third of the population earns its living on some 1,000 large farms, 100,000 medium-sized farms and 100,000 smallholdings. The farming is well organized, highly progressive and based on mutual aid. Those are the factors, rather than fertility of soil, which have made Danish farming what it is. It is significant that the buildings which dominate the Danish landscape are the church, the manor and the co-operative dairy. Though the co-operative movement was born in England, it has been left to the Danes to develop it in farming in a practical way, and now the Danish Co-operative Movement in agriculture has become a world model. Its ideals brought into being the Folk High School Movement for adult education which has had such a profound effect on the country. The schools are attended mainly by the farming community and have been largely responsible, by widening the outlook of the peasantry, for the intelligent way in which farms are run today in Denmark. This humanist and liberal movement began in the middle of the last century and now there exists throughout the country a number of Folk Schools where anyone can study in his spare time for sheer pleasure if he wishes, for examinations are not a part of the curricula.

About 30,000 Danes fish for their living and their industry has strong government support. Otherwise Danes live by a considerable number of industries which all together employ about a third of the population. Denmark has no black coal, steel or oil—and no drab industrial areas either. As in Sweden, industry is well dispersed with a tendency to congregate at the ports and around the capital. As in Sweden also the factories are mostly small. Industries include cement works (especially round the Limfjord), shipyards, engineering shops of all kinds especially for making farm implements, some brown coal mining, timber works obtaining their raw material from the country's 850,000 acres of forest land, porcelain factories especially for electrical insulators, clothing and footwear factories, brickworks, the famous Copenhagen Porcelain and Jensen Silverware works and, of course, breweries. As the Danes say: "The Danish national drink is beer. The Danish national weakness is another beer." They also say: "We export silver, porcelain and oysters. We completely control the markets of the world in flints."

A few words now on Denmark's history and cultural inheritance. A Dane has summed it all up very nicely thus: "The Danes display a possibly surprising conviction that they are a thoroughly civilized nation. . . . They feel so closely bound up with Hans Christian Andersen's fairy tales, Thorvaldsen's statues, the East Asiatic Company, the Round Tower in Copenhagen, Roskilde Cathedral (56), Østerlars church in the island of Bornholm (53), Burmeister and Wain's ships, Professor Niels Bohr, and the Viking planes that they almost believe themselves to be the creators, inventors, builders, organizers, or in some way responsible for the whole lot. They seem to be on most intimate terms with Bishop Absalon, who put Copenhagen on the map in 1167; and they really genuinely regard themselves as related to Christian IV, who turned Copenhagen into a beautiful city, and to Christian X, who reigned during the period when it transformed itself from a provincial town into one of the world's great cities—in a small way." The writer concludes that Denmark is stacked with Art, old and new. "There are, for example, the Pearls of Architecture distributed evenly over the countryside. Among these pearls are our castles and manors. Nobody can afford to live in them today, but they are attractive all the same." Finally he sums up his countrymen thus: "The Danes are democratic. Nobody looks down on a man who is a millionaire. . . . Certain class distinctions must be admitted, but nobody has yet discovered where to put the distinction."*

How has this state of affairs come about?

* Mogens Lind in *We Danes—And You* (National Travel Association of Denmark).

IX

History and Heritage

THROUGHOUT her history Denmark has been affected by her central position as a transit country between Europe and the Baltic countries. From early times invading tribes and cultural currents have crossed the country coming from Europe and the south. Her position was bound to bring conflicts if she was to survive as an entity—especially with Germans on the border country known as Schleswig-Holstein and with Swedes in Skåne and Norway. These conflicts have dominated her history.

Prehistory. When the ice receded the first men wandered up into Denmark hunting reindeer, and later as the climate improved and deciduous trees grew they lived as huntsmen of woodland animals. During the last era of the Stone Age, the hunters began to settle down as farmers who cleared the forests to grow corn, cultivated domestic animals and built houses for the living and tombs for the dead—barrows which were crude versions of those at Mycenae. This was before 2000 B.C.

From the Hungarian plains then came the Beaker Folk, bringing the Bronze Age and a new aristocratic civilization to the North, which produced fine works of handicraft expressed by example in beautiful, curved bugle-horns of bronze, 6 feet long. Came the Iron Age, the plough, the runic alphabet and the muddled, expansive times of the Folk Wanderings. For many years there is restless change and upheaval of which we know little, but in the fighting of the migratory period when tribes were organizing for strength, the Danes emerge as a kind of nation ruled by leading land-owning families. The population lives in villages depending partly on strip farming and communal grazing land as in England—a system which affected agriculture in Denmark right up to the beginning of the nineteenth century.

* * * * *

The Viking Age (A.D. 800–1050). The raids began in a small way, partly to secure trade routes and partly as a check to the thrust of the Frankish-German empire, but from 850 to 892 the large-scale raids on England began and Wessex was finally captured and settled by the Danes. About 900 Alfred the Great succeeded in beating the invaders. The raids were then aimed at

Normandy, and round the year 1000 the last powerful drives secured for the Vikings a short-lived empire around the North Sea. South-east England was re-captured by Sweyn Forkbeard, and his son Canute became King of England, South Norway and Denmark. His empire, however, collapsed soon after his death in 1035. Meanwhile Christianity had been gaining ground and already the first Harold had been baptized in 826, largely for political reasons and to placate the Germans. After him Canute appointed English bishops at Odense, Roskilde and Lund. Odin was transfigured into Christ, the Viking chiefs were embodied in the Saints and Valhalla was renamed Paradise. The Church was not firmly established in Denmark, however, until the time of Canute the Holy after 1080.

* * * * *

The greatest existing monument of the Danish Vikings is the famous fortress at Trelleborg on the west of Zealand. We shall be visiting this fortress and shall there see that these Vikings were far from being undisciplined, rapacious gangsters, but, on the contrary, excellent organizers and engineers.

* * * * *

The Middle Ages (1050–1536). A Danish primate was at last established free from the power of Hamburg, whose archbishop had been the head of the Scandinavian Church. Centres of learning were established, notably by Archbishop Absalon, the man who founded Copenhagen as a defensive position against pirates. During these early years there was much struggling with invaders from the south, but by 1220 the Danish king Valdemar I had fought his way to control of an empire extending from the Elbe to Estonia. Like the empire of Canute it had feet of clay. Valdemar was kidnapped by a German prince, and from 1241 until 1340 Denmark was in a state of continual warfare and discord. Only the Church remained stable. Then arose the able young Valdemar Atterdag to reunite the kingdom and to challenge the power of the Hanseatic League in the Baltic. After his death an old dream was fulfilled. Sweden, Norway, Denmark, Finland and Iceland were united under one Regent Queen, Valdemar's daughter, the remarkable Margaret. She had been married to Haakon, King of Norway, in 1363 at the tender age of ten, and by that marriage Norway was united with Denmark and remained so, though somewhat loosely, until 1814.

Margaret was one of the colourful personalities of Danish history.

"A woman without womanliness", she has been called, but for all that she was a remarkable character—the Queen Elizabeth of Denmark one might call her. "When men saw the wisdom and strength that were in this Royal Lady," the old Chronicle of Lübeck records, "wonder and fear filled their hearts." At the Union of Kalmar in 1397 this Royal Lady persuaded the representatives of Denmark, Sweden and Norway to accept her great-nephew, Eric, as successor. Though the Swedes then strictly reserved the right to elect a king and later, as we have seen, separated from the Union, the Union lasted, nominally at least, until 1521, more than a century after Margaret's death.

In 1479 the University of Copenhagen was founded, two years after the foundation of the University of Uppsala in Sweden, where the Separatist Movement gained many young followers. In 1500 the Danish King Hans led a disastrous expedition to Ditmarsh in Holstein with the aim of subduing the troublesome peasants there, and the Swedish Separatists took their opportunity. An uneasy peace between the two countries was affirmed but another clash soon came between two outstanding representatives—the next Danish king, Christian II, and Sten Sture the Younger of Sweden. Christian, a brutal despot who nevertheless brought many reforms and a Renaissance spirit to his country, after a first defeat in 1519 outside Stockholm, made a last effort, in the name now of the Holy Roman Church, by sending a fleet round the east coast of Sweden and an army over land northward. Sture's peasant army was defeated on the frozen Lake Åsunden and Sture himself was killed. Christian entered Stockholm, was proclaimed hereditary king of Sweden and treacherously instigated the Stockholm Blood Bath. The Danish success was not to last, for the young Gustav Vasa was soon to settle the question of Sweden's succession. Meanwhile Duke Frederick, Christian's uncle, had invaded Denmark from Holstein and laid siege to Copenhagen. Christian unsuccessfully sought the aid of his brother-in-law, Charles V, and ended in prison. In 1523 the Duke became Frederik I, King of Denmark and Norway.

Luther was at this time busy pamphleteering and had already nailed his protest on the church door at Wittenberg. The Reformation was gaining ground, for the demand from Rome for Indulgence Payments, a large part of which went to pay for the building of St. Peter's, was unpopular. Even Christian II had flirted with Luther's ideas and had helped to pave the way for the Reformation in Denmark. The great landowning lords who had been struggling with kings throughout the Middle Ages now held the real power—

a power they managed to retain until 1660 when a period of Absolute Monarchy set in. During the earlier Middle Ages the peasantry had flourished in spite of the general strife and the large landowners. An expression of this early prosperity can be seen even to this day in the many delightful twelfth-century village churches, with their stepped gables, which are scattered so thickly over the Danish countryside. In the late Middle Ages, however, the free yeoman sank into poverty and dependence on landlord, Church and king. He was not to arise to full emancipation again for three centuries.

★   ★   ★   ★   ★

In architecture the Middle Ages are formalized in such brick cathedrals as those of Roskilde, Odense, Aalborg and Ribe, in strong castles like that at Nyborg, and in the innumerable village churches. Of these churches, the most impressive are the distinctive round churches of the island of Bornholm, powerful structures used also as fortresses in times of strife, having a form influenced from the south-east rather than the south (53). Except in the early Romanesque cathedrals like that at Viborg, and in the castles, which were in stone, brick was the chief building material. Influences were French, German and Dutch.

★   ★   ★   ★   ★

Reformation and Absolute Monarchy (1536–1814). Strife continued. There was trouble with the Lübeckese who wished to destroy their naval rival in the Baltic and a two-year struggle called the Count's War began between the Lutheran king, Christian III of Denmark, and Count Christopher, who was in command of Christian II's army. Gustav Vasa saw his opportunity of defeating the Lübeck and Hansa forces, joined the Danish fleet and destroyed Lübeck's naval power. Christian III then laid siege to Copenhagen, and by 1539 was in control of both Denmark and Holstein. Moreover he was now head of the Church and had made the Crown hereditary. There followed the struggle of Christian III's son, Frederik II, with Sweden in the Seven Years' War of 1563 to 1570. By this Sweden became mistress of the Baltic while Denmark retained Skåne and Gotland, and her command of the Sound.

The latter part of Frederik II's reign was marked by the encouragement given to the sciences and to education. It produced the most renowned figure of the time, the great astronomer and scientist, Tyge Brahe, who received lavish patronage from the king.

From 1588 to 1648 Frederik's son, Christian IV, reigned. His was a long reign and, if he had not taken part in the Thirty Years' War and suffered defeat by Sweden, his era would have been a glorious one for Denmark. The king was a man of enormous zest and vigour, a great patron of the arts, an ardent builder of cities and fantastic castles, explorer, soldier, sailor, scientist, debauchee, sire of forty-eight (acknowledged) offspring and founder of the Danish mercantile marine—a typical Renaissance figure. During the first part of his reign things went well. He virtually rebuilt Copenhagen and extended his building activities to Norway where the capital city was rebuilt and named after him. He himself, indeed, took a hand in the planning of Christiania. During his reign were founded the Danish East India Company, the West India Company and the Danish colonies in West Africa—colonies which were finally sold to Britain in the middle of the last century.

Christian made the mistake of going to war, first with the Catholic League in Germany, when Gustav Adolph of Sweden had to come to his aid in order to keep back the Catholic Empire from the Baltic shores, and later with Sweden itself. The king, now an old man, with remarkable energy and courage, led his fleet in person against the Dutch who were assisting the Swedes and then against the Swedish fleet which he put to flight. But at last the combined Dutch and Swedish naval forces defeated him, and, without an effective navy or army, he was forced to sign a humiliating treaty in 1645 by which the islands of Gotland and Ösel and the province of Jämtland were ceded to Sweden while Halland was given as security for the exemption of Sound dues. Christian IV's reign ended in catastrophe, but though it had been politically and militarily ruinous to Denmark it had been a great age for the arts and sciences. Though a poor statesman, the king established himself as a national hero, a man of outstanding physical courage, of many good intentions and of a voracious appetite for life.

Christian's son Frederik III inherited a poor kingdom. He was a weak character dominated by the nobles, who had now concentrated land and wealth into their hands to the impoverishment and enslavement of the peasants. In 1657 Frederik declared war on Sweden under Carl X, who was in difficulties in Poland, the idea being to preserve with the help of Denmark's ally, Holland, the freedom of trade in the Baltic which was threatened. The result was Carl's brilliant march across the frozen Belts. The Danish peasants, understandably enough, refused to fight for their masters, and by the severe treaty of 1658 Denmark was compelled to cede to Sweden the Scanian provinces and the island of Bornholm, while Norway was forced to hand over Bohuslän and central Norway round Trondheim, thus splitting Norway in two. Carl, stimulated by his success, decided to make Denmark a Swedish province, and in 1658 invaded Zealand and marched on Copenhagen. Frederik, strongly supported by the burghers, who demanded in return for their support a Free City and the same privileges as the nobles, made an unexpected resistance. Once more the Danes displayed their traditional resilience. Carl laid siege to the city, but the Danes sent a relief fleet, the siege failed and Carl's army was routed on Funen. At the peace conference Denmark regained Bornholm and the Norwegian provinces but, because Europe wanted balance of power in the Baltic, Skåne remained in Swedish hands. Now the nobles began to lose some of their power, thanks partly to a steady fall in prices and partly to the alliance against them of "Town, Crown and Gown". In 1660 the monarchy was declared absolute and hereditary by the parliament in Copenhagen and under the Crown all estates were to be equal. From then until 1848 the Danish kings ruled without a parliament or assembly.

When Christian V (1670–99) succeeded his father, a new aristocracy was formed, its members being selected according to the king's whim. Once more a war broke out with Sweden, but in spite of a brilliant victory by Admiral Niels Juel, Denmark was compelled, mainly on account of French pressure, to conclude a ten years' alliance with her enemy. In the decades which followed trade was vigorously developed but the state of agriculture went from bad to worse. The new landed proprietors wanted quick profits and so exhausted the land. This condition did not improve under Frederik IV (1699–1730). During his reign, the time of the Great Northern War when Carl XII of Sweden was defeated at Poltava, Denmark once more attacked Sweden in the hope of regaining Skåne. In 1720, two years after Carl's death in Norway a peace was concluded by which Sweden had to pay an indemnity and a Sound toll, and Slesvig came under the Danish Crown. The encirclement of Denmark was broken and the country could at last enjoy a peace which was to continue until the end of the century. During Frederik IV's reign Greenland was colonized and popular education was inaugurated in Denmark.

Frederik's sex life had been erratic and did not receive the approval of his şon, Christian VI (1730–46). This king, educated by pietistic German teachers, brought to his country a stern, puritanical life highly disagreeable to the lively Danes. In spite of his bigotry he patronized learning, founded the Academy of Science and a School of Arts, and rebuilt Copenhagen University which had been destroyed by the great fire of 1728.

56   ROSKILDE : The brick Cathedral of the twelfth century

From a painting by Jörgen Roed
(1808–88)

57   RIBE : A medieval street

58   The Beach and Sand Dunes

59   Figurehead of Lord Palmerston   60   An Islander in local peasant costume

ON THE ISLAND OF FANØ

The following reign of Frederik V (1746–66) saw a violent reaction in the form of a twenty years' debauch whose practical outcome was the foundation by the king of the first hospital in Europe for venereal diseases. During these two reigns German immigrants controlled Danish politics while the Danish nobility enjoyed itself. The peasants were under tighter bonds than ever.

At Frederik's death absolute monarchy was in decline throughout Europe and a period of social reform was beginning. Cultural tendencies were middle class and romantic individualism was growing out of bourgeois German pietism. During Christian VII's reign (1766–1808), one of the strangest characters in Danish history strutted on to the political stage, a provincial German physician who became confidant and master of the licentious and half-mad king. His name was Johann Friedrich Struensee. This man was an atheist with a machiavellian mind strongly influenced by the ideas of Rousseau and Voltaire, a sinister but gifted individual who for a brief eighteen months became Denmark's all-powerful dictator. He took as his mistress the young and attractive Queen Caroline Matilda, sister of George III of England, apparently without any objection from the king, gave to his none-too-gentle friend, Brandt, the task of keeping the king under control, and set to work in the king's name to institute ruthless reforms, many of them laudable. Curiously enough, the first thing he did was to abolish all press censorship. Then he instituted proper auditing of state accounts, set up a Court of Appeal, decreed that brothels should be open to all and free from police supervision, abolished the penalties for begetting children out of wedlock, abolished torture, established pauper commissions and a royal orphanage, turned Rosenborg Park into a public recreation ground, centralized government control so that Copenhagen lost her autonomy, restricted villeinage and in sixteen months passed in all one thousand and sixty-nine new enactments. The pace was too hot to last, and the public sense of tradition was outraged. Besides, Struensee was a German who could speak no Danish and lacked the support of an adequate personnel. A plot was organized against him which had the support of the king's stepmother, Juliane Marie, and of her son, Prince Frederik. One night in 1772 Struensee, now a Count, was seized at a fancy dress ball by the conspirators and later executed in public with his friend Brandt.

The triumvirate which followed composed of the Dowager Queen, her son and one Guldberg did its best without discrimination to undo all Struensee's reforms. Anti-German feeling was strong and by the Ordinance of 1776 all foreigners were excluded from posts in the Forces and in the State Department. Ardent nationalism set in and produced a Golden Age of Danish art, especially in literature—the age of Hans Andersen, Blicher, Ohlenschläger and, above all, of Gruntvig (1783–1872), the great poet, preacher, politician and educationist, Denmark's Wesley, to whom must be attributed the birth of the famous Danish Folk School movement which indirectly did so much to improve Danish agriculture. Indeed one must attribute a great deal of the balanced social democracy of all modern Scandinavia to that movement.

In 1784 the young Crown Prince Frederik assumed a Regency, the mad king being still alive. He devoted himself conscientiously to his job with the help of his able minister, Bernstorff. On the death of his father in 1808 he became King Frederik VI and held the throne until 1839. Valuable humanitarian reforms were carried out during his reign, notably the development of higher education, the abolishment of slavery in the West Indies and that emancipation of the peasantry which was the foundation of Denmark's present agricultural prosperity. By this emancipation the old communal village system was abolished, land was distributed and the peasants moved into farmsteads each set amidst its own fields—something of an Enclosure Act. But the reign was a hard one. In the Napoleonic wars Denmark backed the wrong horse. The economic war of the times burst into military war on Denmark when on two occasions, in 1801 and 1807, the English fleet attacked Copenhagen. Frederik then made the mistake of joining Napoleon in the Seven Years' War against England. By 1813 Denmark's world trade was ruined, the country was bankrupt and Copenhagen was in a badly battered state from fire and from Nelson's bombardments. In 1814 the king signed the Peace of Kiel by which Norway, after a union with Denmark for 450 years, was ceded to Sweden. With the close of the Napoleonic wars a new and hopeful epoch began in all the Scandinavian countries.

*   *   *   *   *

In architecture the three centuries from the Reformation to the epoch of National Liberalism cover the styles of Renaissance, Baroque and Rococo. As in the Middle Ages, brick continues as the national building material, which finds its most vigorous expression in the Renaissance castles and other buildings of Christian IV with their red brick walls, stone dressings, curly Dutch gables and intricate towers of gold-leaf and green copper—Rosenborg, Frederiksborg and Copenhagen's Stock Exchange (75) (69). The influence in this period came from the Netherlands and indeed much of the Danish Renaissance building was carried out by immigrant Dutch architects and craftsmen.

In the Baroque period were built the royal and noble palaces like Christiansborg, Charlottenborg and Frederiksberg in Copenhagen, magnificent royal church monuments like those in Roskilde Cathedral, town planning like that which incorporated the King's New Market (Nytorv) in Copenhagen, and churches like that of Our Saviour, also in the capital. Influences were partly Dutch but now much more French and Italian and the Danish architect was beginning to emerge in his own right.

The Rococo of the eighteenth century produced the outstanding Amalienborg Palace (72, 74) and the Prince's Palace, both in Copenhagen. The absolutism of the age is expressed in the capital city's firmly controlled planning and design carried out by Nicolai Eigtved around Amaliegade.

* * * * *

National Liberalism (1814-64). Denmark suffered greatly through participating in the Napoleonic wars and from 1814 to 1830 faced the poorest period in her history, especially in her agriculture through the loss of English and Norwegian markets. In spite of this, an important reform took place in 1814—the introduction of universal education for all children between the ages of six and fourteen. The result was revolutionary in its political effects because it made the peasantry and working class articulate. From about 1830 the attacks against the absolutism of the monarchy began. The national liberals hoped for great things when in 1839 Christian VIII followed Frederik VI on the throne. The new king was conservative, but under popular pressure he at last consented to constitutional reform. Before this could be ratified he died, and in 1848 the vacillating Frederik VII (1848-63) succeeded him. Soon the barricades were up in Paris, thrones were tottering and the effects of the February Revolution began to spread over Europe. The leaders of Schleswig-Holstein were agitating for a free constitution and for the incorporation of Holstein as well as Slesvig in the German Federal State. The councillors of Copenhagen marched to the Royal Palace to demand a change of government at the head of a crowd of 10,000, which was further excited over the separatist movement in the south, from where a deputation was on its way to the Palace. The king gave way, declared himself a constitutional monarch and the bloodless bourgeois revolution was over.

The movement to keep Denmark extended to the Eider started

immediate revolt in Schleswig-Holstein, the separatists being supported by Prussia. England and Russia, not wanting revolutions at that time, intervened, the *status quo* was maintained and nothing was settled. The new government was then faced with another trouble. The peasants would not accept the leadership of the bourgeois National Liberals and forcefully demanded equality. The outcome was that a new radical constitution was established on June 5th, 1849, a day which has ever since been celebrated as Constitution Day, for the new Act was the foundation of modern Danish democracy.

Now the economic situation began to improve, especially for the farmers. This was partly due to the great increase in exports to England after the repeal of the Corn Laws and partly to the establishment of full freedom of trade in that by 1857 the last effects of medieval trade monopoly were dissolved. Then the smouldering Schleswig-Holstein question flared up again. In 1864 at Bismarck's order German troops crossed the Eider. Denmark took up the challenge with a romantic but ill-considered fervour and despite the courage and toughness of her small, and heavily outnumbered, army she was badly defeated and was at last compelled to give up her ancient frontier province with its 200,000 Danish inhabitants. This disaster eliminated the National Liberals, and a Conservative government, mainly representing the large landowners, took over. The liveliest epoch in Danish history was at an end.

In spite of the troubles, this period was culturally rich—the age of middle-class romanticism and national aspiration. Poets, painters, sculptors, musicians and scientists could flourish under the patronage of the wealthy merchants. Perhaps the early introduction of universal education and the general respect for education in Denmark were mainly responsible for a refinement in the nineteenth-century bourgeois culture of that country not noticeable in other European countries which were at that time producing works of vulgar vigour and ostentation. This was the age in Denmark of the writers Grundtvig and Andersen, of the great theologian Monrad, of the sculptor Thorvaldsen, who used serene, classical form with such romantic sensibility. Moreover it was an age of moderate social distinctions in Denmark which possessed no exploited proletariat, as did Great Britain, to smear the middle-class conscience with guilt. Social conscience was already well developed and a common aim in Grundtvig's words was "to make Denmark happy in a decent manner".

Grundtvig might be called a poetic realist, for he reacted against

61   KALUNDBORG : The brick Church, with its five towers (late twelfth century)

63   The Open-Air Museum

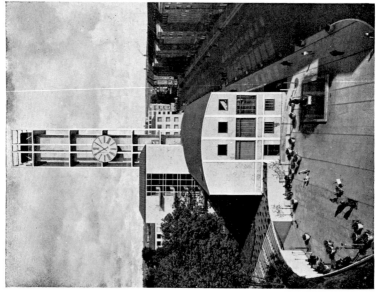

62   The Town Hall (1938-42)

A A R H U S

the escapist tendencies of the romantics. "We were not born to grandeur and magnificence," he said. "To stick to the earth will serve us best." In more violent opposition to romanticism and to the established Church was Soeren Kierkegaard, who is significant to us today, not only as an early Existentialist, but as the supreme individualist who believed that objective science could never reveal reality. He held that reality could be revealed only through personal experience. Only subjectivity is truth. Though the philosophy of the future may not accept Kirkegaard's religious fervour, it may well be that his philosophy of subjectivity may in time have a profound effect on human life, for it is to the study of the measuring instrument, the human mind, rather than to the study of external "reality" that the physicist is now turning in his search for truth.

★   ★   ★   ★   ★

In architecture this epoch is first expressed in the Neo-Classic reaction of the Empire style against the Rococo. Brick, as always, is the chief material but now, in order to imitate stone, it is covered in plaster like our own Regency buildings. The discoveries at Pompeii affect interior decoration. C. F. Hansen is the outstanding name of this period, for he was largely responsible for the rebuilding of Copenhagen after the great fire and Nelson's bombardment. His buildings, though rather heavy, are restrained and simple—of necessity since funds at that time were very short. Typical of his work is the Church of Our Lady, now Copenhagen's cathedral, and Copenhagen's Law Courts, originally built as a city hall with a portico supported by unfluted Ionic columns. Another typical building having the simple classical lines of the time is the famous Thorvaldsen Museum in Copenhagen designed by G. M. Bindesbøll in 1839.

★   ★   ★   ★   ★

Modern Times (1864–1950). Denmark had now lost a third of her territory. She had received a profound shock. She began to realize that she was no great power in the world and that the best thing to do under the circumstances was to cultivate her own small garden. This she has been doing with relative success ever since. In politics the period from 1864 until the turn of the century was dominated by a bitter struggle between the large landowners and the smaller farmers and peasants. In the end the latter won the day largely as a result of the effects of the Folk Schools on the farming community. As steamships and railways opened world markets in grain, especi- ally for North America, Denmark was forced to revolutionize her farming. New methods were introduced, and butter, bacon, eggs and special crops superseded corn-growing. In 1882 the first co-operative dairy was opened and the seed of mutual aid was planted. It has flowered into the effective co-operative movement of today. At Esbjerg a port for exports was established, industries developed and produced an industrial working class, Copenhagen expanded like yeasty dough beyond its ancient ramparts. On June 5th, 1915, during the reign of the esteemed Christian X (1912–47), on the same day of the year as the 1849 constitution was born, a revised constitution came into force based on universal suffrage—the most democratic of its time in Europe.

After the First World War the Schleswig-Holstein question was reopened. A plebiscite was held with the result that a new border was established, North Schleswig becoming Danish. The German Occupation of the Second World War, when the Danes developed a strong resistance movement, the dissolution of the Danish-Icelandic Union in 1945, the succession of Frederik IX in 1947 and the participation in 1949 in the North Atlantic Pact brings Denmark's history up-to-date.

This century saw the growth of democratic government, of the co-operative movement, of social services, of industry and of farming methods. In architecture the restrained classicism of Hansen was followed by the eclectic stylism of the Victorian Age. J. C. Jacobsen and his son Carl made a fortune from their Carlsberg brewery and patronized the arts lavishly, founding the Carlsberg Fund by which all the future profits of their company were to be spent in supporting the arts and sciences. One outcome was the refurbishing of Frederiksborg Castle, another the building of the Copenhagen Glyptothece where, amidst palm courts and down endless galleries, Carl Jacobsen's magnificent collection of antique and Egyptian sculpture is housed.

*　*　*　*　*

At the end of the century, as in Sweden, a revival of national romanticism is evident in Copenhagen's red brick Town Hall of Martin Nyrop's—a mixture of medieval Danish and Italian styles. Though a competent and lively design it cannot be compared with Stockholm's City Hall. As in Sweden also, the influence of William Morris brought about a development of the crafts, the result being that in furniture, fabrics, pottery and silverware Danish design became as excellent as Sweden's, which is to say the best in the world. In domestic architecture and in garden design the influence of the English architects, Voysey and Lutyens, is apparent. In town planning the theories of Camillo Sitte, the Austrian, had their effect in the desire for medieval, curved streets, blocked vistas and informal open spaces. In the early 'twenties the young architects turned against romanticism to produce a brief Classical Revival. Then, as a result of Asplund's 1930 Stockholm Exhibition, many young Danish architects ardently embraced Functionalism. Now the new international style has become humanized and absorbed into the national brick tradition as, for example, in the fine university buildings at Aarhus by C. F. Møller.

In Copenhagen the 1939 Building Act revolutionized flat building and made freer, more open planning possible. One result was the introduction of the tower-like Point Houses, inspired by Le Corbusier but imported from Stockholm. As throughout Scandinavia, architecture in Denmark was at last being properly linked with town planning and to the general well-being.

*   *   *   *   *

In conclusion let us briefly survey the development of Danish building through the centuries from a particular aspect—that of the continuity of the brick tradition and its effects on the simple Danishness of design which runs consistently through seven hundred years. Though naturally affected by the changing European fashions, this design adapts the fashions to the limitations imposed by fired brick, a medium forced on the builders by the scarcity of other materials in the country. It reduced the splendour of the styles maybe, but always produced a characteristic simplicity and restraint. This restraint does not produce mere dullness; it always has charm by virtue of its unique feeling for texture, pattern, colour and sound craftsmanship.

Originally forest covered a large part of the land and provided, together with straw for thatch and clay, the main source of building material. The tradition still survives in the half-timbered farmhouses so typical of Funen. Then the monks came from France and Germany. They taught the Dane, who had few quarries, to make artificial stones in the form of tiles and "monk stones" by baking the morainic clay of which the country possessed almost inexhaustible supplies.

Thus the brick tradition began. Its continuity and its adapting of foreign styles to suit its particular characteristics is partly the result of external conditions, but the national character has also influenced it. The Dane is both sailor and farmer. As a sailor he sees the world and brings home new, strange and exotic notions. As a farmer he is conservative, practical and shrewd; he does not swallow these notions whole but assimilates them cautiously, adjusting them to his own tried methods and to his sense of human comfort without luxury, that sense of ease and solid well-being he calls *hygge*.

Moreover brick enforces simplicity. It does not allow structural fireworks. Especially does it impose simplicity of plan and therefore of the disciplined roof forms which bring homogeneity to a whole building however large and complex. The modern flat roof, whose one excuse in the North is that it allows great freedom of planning, is not necessary when brick has already compelled the use of un- complicated, rectangular plan-shapes. Thus the pitched roof, which gives far better protection in the wet, northern climate than the flat roof of the Mediterranean countries, is accepted as a legiti- mate modern form in Denmark. From the old Jute farmhouse (always turning its back, like the cows in the fields, to the prevailing winds from the west) to the great new university of Aarhus, all the brick buildings of the years show the long tiled roof line and simple combination of rectangles.

The Romanesque style could be adapted without force to this brick discipline. The Gothic on the other hand could not and there- fore such Gothic cathedrals as those of Odense and Roskilde display none of the thrill of daring engineering in stone found in the Gothic fanes of other countries. But compensation is provided outside by the texture, solidity and patterning of the unbroken areas of beautifully weathered brickwork, and inside by an air of lightness, simplicity and spaciousness. There, inside, the plain vaulting and the whitewashed walls provide a perfect foil for the brilliant frescoes and the intricate jewellery of the Baroque monuments.

The Renaissance style in Denmark had already been adapted to brick, for it came from Holland. The Baroque offered either effusion or restraint and in its latter mood could be fairly happily adapted to brick. The Rococo and Neo-Classic used brick as much as any other age but now would not accept it at its face value and covered it with stucco which could be moulded to the desired superficial forms. Today Denmark is using another indigenous material— cement. Combined with imported steel for reinforcement, it helps to make those concrete structures which have revolutionized architecture in other lands. Sometimes brick and concrete mate quite happily in Denmark, but in general brick remains the most common material. The brick tradition lives on, eternally young.

X

The Provinces

THE sea, the windy sky, long low flat land rising just above the water surround the clustered brick walls and red roofs of Esbjerg. A great medieval keep towers above them. The effect as we approach from the sea is one of Dutch eld. But as we enter the town from the docks the illusion is shattered. The buildings are not old and the medieval keep is but a water tower.

Eighty years ago Esbjerg housed but thirty souls. Today the population is over 43,000 and Esbjerg is still growing as one of Denmark's most valuable ports. The town has few beauties apart from those incidental pictures and sculptural forms which all ports present. But let us stay here a day or two, nevertheless, in order to visit both the neighbouring island of Fanø and the unspoiled medieval town of Ribe which lies but a few miles to the south.

We reach Fanø from Esbjerg by ferry and land at the small Skipper Town of Sundby—a bright, pleasant old place of single-storey brick and tile houses, some with curling Dutch gables, all with trim gardens. A bus then takes us past some large, cosmopolitan holiday hotels and then strangely along miles of flat golden beach (59) to the end of the island where the village of Sønderho lies—another old haven of seafarers and fishermen. It is a pretty place of low houses snuggling higgledy-piggledy close together for comfort against the storms. In spite of their age all are fresh, and many are decorated with curling wrought-iron dates and initials and brick window arches painted in stripes of white, green and black. Even that speechless figurehead of Lord Palmerston which some islander rescued from the sea some eighty years ago to dignify his garden gate, has been treated respectfully with a new coat of paint (59). Here among the lanes and across the small grass patches old women pass the time of day dressed unselfconsciously in the traditional local costume (60). This lacks the usual brilliant colouring of peasant dress for it is mostly black. It is, however, intricately embroidered and practical too, for the tight-fitting headdress is so designed that the lower part can be lifted to protect almost the whole face from the sand that flies up from the dunes.

* * * * *

Ribe is well worth visiting (57). It has a history of at least a thousand years and is claimed to be Denmark's oldest town. It was

165

certainly at one time one of the most important towns in the country and the chief port of the west before the sea receded across the marshes. Its former importance as a trading centre has gone, and now from their roof nests the storks gaze down on winding, cobbled streets that have changed little for 600 years. For 400 years the population has remained the same and four times each day the cathedral bells call the people to prayer as they once called the monks who settled here so long ago.

In the centre of the town the cathedral rears above the old roofs —an impressive conglomerate of German Romanesque stonework and Danish brick dominated by a mighty square tower. As far back as the ninth century Ansgar, who carried Christianity to the North, built a wooden church here. Then about 1160 the cathedral was rebuilt in stone carried here by ship from the Rhine. Much of this structure still remains, notably the apse at the east end which is somewhat like its contemporary at Lund. In 1250 the brick tower was constructed as a stronghold and a look-out. In 1402, after a fire, the wider red brick aisles were added in Gothic style. Notable things here are the carved tympanum above the main door depicting the Removal from the Cross, the oldest and most important piece of early medieval sculpture to be found in the country, and, inside, the fine seventeenth-century monument to Admiral Skeel and his wife. The lofty interior with its Gothic vaults and Romanesque piers and triforia is, they say, inspiring but it cannot be compared in dramatic power with the interiors either of Odense or Aarhus.

From the top of the cathedral tower we look out over green marshland through which the River Ribe flows towards the sea some miles away. There we can see Fanø and Manø hugging the coast. Below and all around in informal patterns lie the pantiled roofs, narrow streets and small cottage gardens of the town, and among them we can pick out the thirteenth-century monastery of St. Catherine, the best preserved Dominican foundation in the North.

Up here, too, we can trace the lines of the old town walls. Above one of the gates, set in these walls, an iron hand once hung to remind the visitor that if he misbehaved he was likely to have his hand chopped off with that axe which is still preserved in the town hall. So harsh was Ribe justice in the past that one might be beheaded either for adultery or the adulteration of honey, and they will tell you still of a mother who cried out when she saw her son hanging from the gallows in the town of Varde, "Oh, my son, praise be to God that you were not tried before the Ribe Court."

On the west of the town we can see the rise of a grassy mound

surrounded by a reedy ditch—all that remains of the royal castle of
Riberhus where Valdemar the Victorious held court in the thirteenth
century. In 1644 it was occupied by the Swedes and stood for
another fifty years. It has attained immortality, nevertheless, in
many a popular ballad.

Our last sight in Ribe is a vivid one. A street of worn brick and
stucco with its carved corbels and window sills filled with flowers,
a street where no line is straight, carries the eye away in perspective
to the green marsh and a sky of thunder blue. The evening sun
suddenly bursts out and sets the wet cobbles glinting. Around the
corner, wheeling his cycle, comes the postman in his coat of brilliant
red. The picture is complete.

★   ★   ★   ★   ★

We now cross Jutland, pass over the bridge of the Little Belt to
Funen at whose centre Odense, the island's capital, lies. This is
Odin's town, inhabited long before the coming of Christianity and
now known chiefly as the birthplace of Hans Andersen (1805–75).
For several centuries it was a place of pilgrimage because here lay a
great monastery and the Cathedral of St. Knud (to us, Canute).

Odense is today a happy, lively centre with a number of factories,
a sophisticated shopping street, a river, a canal, many tinkling trams,
two charming public parks, countless cyclists and several old
buildings of interest. Of these the most important is, of course, the
brick cathedral. St. Knud's was at one time called St. Albans and it
was in the original Romanesque stone church which stood here that
King Canute the Holy was murdered by incensed peasants in 1086
when they were being pressed too hard by the zealous king both for
tithes and for military service. The old church was destroyed by
fire in 1247 and towards the end of the century the church was
rebuilt in Gothic style. Five of the ten sections of the vaulting of the
present interior, those towards the west, belong to that period. The
rest is of rather later date and the west tower was added after the
Reformation. The church has a crypt, which is unusual in a Gothic
church and must be the remains of the original structure. At the
end of the sixteenth century the floor of the church was lowered and
the crypt covered, but the original arrangement was restored in
1874 and in the crypt now one can see two interesting shrines. One
of these contains the skeleton of St. Knud and the other the remains
either of the English St. Alban or of Knud's brother Benedict; no
one knows which.

The church is the largest and the most beautiful Gothic building
in Denmark. The interior, with its white-washed walls and simple

167

grandeur, is magnificent and is adorned with a gilded altar-piece carved by Claus Berg in about 1520. The pulpit and organ are Rococo. At the east end of the south aisle is the grand Ahlefeldt Chapel built in 1701 for the Lord Lieutenant of Funen, Hans von Ahlefeldt of Glorup and his two wives and son. The church walls are decorated with several Baroque monuments which give evidence of the wealth of the merchants of Odense during the seventeenth century. Off the north aisle is another chapel built in 1633 for the Valkendorf family, which is graced with a splendid iron gate wrought by Caspar Fincke, a prominent smith of the period.

In Montestraede is a museum worth visiting. Not only are the buildings which house the collection interesting as examples of brick and timber design of the sixteenth and seventeenth centuries but the collection itself contains some rare and beautiful things from medieval wood sculpture to eighteenth-century cast-iron stoves, from inn-signs to peasant pottery.

A short step from the museum stands the small house where Hans Andersen lived from the age of two until he was fourteen, and where his father carried on his trade as a cobbler. Attached to the house a museum has been built containing a hall decorated with some unexceptional modern frescoes and a statue of the great man reading to a group of children. Above is a library displaying an astonishing number of editions of the Andersen fairy tales in a great many languages, including Japanese. The building also houses a collection of Anderseniana—his silk hat, his famous umbrella, his portmanteaux and the length of rope he always carried on his travels in case of fire. Many portraits and photographs of the man are hung around the walls and reveal a striking face, long, thin and sad, with a long poet's nose, a huge sensitive mouth and soft, kindly but defensive eyes—a very definite presence.

From the centre of the town a short tram journey will take us to an open-air museum called Fynske Landsby—a village of about a dozen representative old Funen houses and farms of half-timbering, white stucco and thatched roofs surrounding wide courtyards where hollyhocks grow. In the village is also a windmill, strangely made of thatch and timber, and an inn where refreshment up to the usual high Danish standard is served. The houses are fully furnished in the old styles, mostly of the eighteenth century, and they display that quiet charm which runs through the Danish centuries.

*   *   *   *   *

On our eastward journey our next stop will be at Slagelse, near which lies the famous Viking fortress of Trelleborg with its great

64   AALBORG: The rococo Entrance to the Town Hall (1767)

65 COPENHAGEN: Nyhavn, with its eighteenth-century houses

circular rampart and moat. Intelligent research has revealed how this fortress must originally have appeared in its first form in the eleventh century at the time of Canute the Great, when it served as a well-defended barracks housing a garrison of over a thousand warriors. Inside the rampart in regular arrangement stood sixteen timber buildings, each 100 feet long and shaped rather like upturned boats with bows and sterns chopped off having porticos of timber pillars. Just outside the rampart stood another fifteen of these buildings of slightly smaller size arranged in an arc. A reconstruction of one of these structures has been built near the entrance to the camp showing how seventy-five men, probably a ship's company, could sleep comfortably within on the wide benches round the walls, lying with their feet pointing inwards. The camp is laid out with almost pedantic accuracy and so indicates that Trelleborg was one of many such camps where order and discipline of the strictest kind regulated the lives of the men who lived there.

Trelleborg required more than 8,000 fully-grown trees, mostly oak, for its construction. It was a huge work, and its building may well have been organized by the king himself—probably either Sweyn Forkbeard who conquered England, or Canute the Great who dominated the North Sea. The unit of measurement in its layout is Roman, which suggests that the traditions of the camps of the Roman Empire had been carried up to Denmark, perhaps *via* England, where the Danes could have seen the ruins of Roman camps like that at Warham in Norfolk, which, with its circular form, is strikingly like Trelleborg.

*   *   *   *   *

Our next stop is Roskilde which lies but a few miles west of the capital. It is one of Denmark's oldest towns, a charming country place beautifully situated on a fjord. Here rise the two slender copper spires of the twelfth-century cathedral, the most important national monument in Denmark (56). The site of the cathedral has been holy ground for 1,000 years, for here in 960 the first Christian king of Denmark, Harald Bluetooth, built the first Danish church in wood. Under Sweyn Forkbeard, the Viking who attacked England in 991, an Englishman was appointed first bishop of Roskilde —one called Godebald. Round about 1080 the old wooden church was replaced by a grander limestone basilica, but within a hundred years this too was replaced in its turn by the present Gothic brick structure at the time when Absalon was Bishop of Roskilde. Eventually Roskilde grew into the richest and most important ecclesiastical centre in northern Europe and in the town, besides the cathedral, in time stood twelve parish churches, eight large monasteries and a number of charitable foundations.

The cathedral has from early times been the burial place of Danish kings. Harald Bluetooth is himself buried here in one of the pillars behind the high altar. In all thirty-six kings and queens and 100 people of royal blood have been laid to rest in the cathedral. Thus all round the building burial chapels have been added to the main structure from time to time through the years and now present a kind of history of architectural design in Denmark. Particularly fine are the four sarcophagi in the inner choir of Christian V, Frederik IV and their respective queens, and the magnificent wrought-iron screen in the chapel of Christian IV on the north side of the cathedral—a highly ornate and complex piece of craftsmanship executed about 1618 by Caspar Fincke. The carved oak altar-piece, made in Antwerp in 1580, and still retaining its original gilding and paintwork, is also worth seeing. Nor should one miss the curious late medieval clock high up in the south-west corner with its two groups of mechanically operated wooden figures of St. George and the Dragon and two bell-ringers. When these bell-ringers strike the hour St. George's horse rears up and tramples on the Dragon who utters a piercing cry of death and despair. In the chapel of Christian I (1448–81) is another curiosity, a pillar on which, for some obscure reason, many royal visitors from Peter the Great of Russia to the Duke of Windsor have marked their heights.

Today Roskilde gives little indication of its former importance, for it is just a moderately sized country town, showing but few medieval remains. One can still see the Cathedral School, however, in front of the cathedral—the oldest grammar school in Denmark, founded in 1020. The ancient bishop's palace on the south-east of the cathedral has gone and in its place stands around a courtyard an unpretentious palace built by Christian VI in 1733 as a *pied-à-terre* for his convenience when he passed through Roskilde or stayed here for royal funerals and other ceremonies. It was in this palace that the foundation of Denmark's democratic constitution was laid. Now the place is used for municipal offices. Its simple entrance portico of stucco, backed by a low roof of rich red pantiles and bearing a tympanum decorated with crossed cornucopias filled with flowers, is a serene and refined little composition.

*   *   *   *   *

Half-an-hour in the train will bring us to Copenhagen and the end of our eastward journey. We must leave the exploration of the capital until the next chapter and meanwhile continue our journey over the Danish provinces to the west and north. Our first stop will be at the small port of Kalundborg on the west of Zealand, "a pratie old toun" as Leland might say, with colourful narrow streets, a fishing harbour, a railhead, the Danish radio station and a small clean railway hotel where in the evening a fiddler and a pianist will play us Bach and Boogie-Woogie. It also has a picturesque market square in one of whose houses Sigrid Undset, the famous writer, was born. Kalundborg, like Trondheim in Norway, is a place for townscape painters, though few painters seem yet to have discovered the great possibilities of these towns as sources of inspiration.

Kalundborg's main point of interest is the unique brick church, at one time, like many old Danish churches, also a fortress, which was built towards the end of the twelfth century by Absalon's twin brother, Esbern Snare (61). The plan is a Greek cross and is peculiar in having five towers surmounted by spires above it—one over each of the four wings and the fifth above the crossing, rather higher than the rest. The four outer towers date from about 1170, but the middle one was rebuilt in 1871, some time after the old one had collapsed. This one is dedicated to Our Lady and the others to the saints, Anne, Catherine, Gertrude and Mary Magdalene. The church stands on a hill and the effect of these towers, whether seen at a distance from the water or as one approaches up the curving road lined by old houses on the east, is strangely exciting, perhaps because the form of the five clustered, pointed towers is so extraordinary and so romantic. Inside the church is a good carved wooden reredos of 1650, a pendant votive vessel and a notable granite font.

*   *   *   *   *

Now we take ship for Aarhus, touching at the island of Samsø on the way. Aarhus is a busy port and has grown within a century twenty times in size to become the second largest town in Denmark. Its industrial life is thriving and it boasts examples of Denmark's best modern architecture—Arne Jacobsen and Erik Møller's courageous reinforced-concrete city hall, delightfully detailed though having a somewhat crude tower (62), and C. F. Møller's simple but imaginative yellow brick university buildings which spread themselves in a wide, undulating park north of the town.

But Aarhus respects its past and is proud both of its cathedral and its Old Town, which next to Stockholm's Skansen is the best of the several open-air museums of Scandinavia (63). Founded in 1909 it now forms a fascinating monument to 300 years of Danish urban culture. Here have been set up in a park a representative collection of forty-eight old Danish houses. They are not mere copies but the real things saved from demolition and destruction in different parts of the country and rebuilt here to form a complete village with streets, gardens, a market place, a river and old-world shops. All the houses are furnished in styles ranging from the sixteenth to the nineteenth century, and include such types as a smithy, a bookbinder's, a printer's, a saddler's, a school, a rope-works, a watermill and an Aalborg merchant's house in half-timbering of the year 1650. The furniture from the end of the eighteenth century is especially interesting in showing the strong influence of the classical English taste of that time—a time when the fashionable cabinet-makers of Copenhagen called themselves "English chair- and cabinet-makers".

Aarhus Cathedral is another of Denmark's Gothic brick monuments with copper-covered roof, stepped gables and buttressed red-brick walls embellished with Virginia creeper. As it now stands it belongs mainly to the thirteenth and fourteenth centuries, though the original church was built in the twelfth century in stone Romanesque. It is the longest cathedral in northern Europe and produces a grand effect within with its spaciousness and its whitewashed walls decorated with bold, free and brilliantly coloured medieval frescoes and intricate Baroque monuments of wealthy burghers and their wives. Largely because of its fine frescoes it is, to this writer at least, the most pleasing of all Danish church interiors. Of these frescoes one will note especially the panel on the north aisle of St. George and the Dragon dated 1495 and a lovely angel in a reveal between the nave and the south aisle. Other things of interest are the pulpit of 1588 and the fine organ of 1730.

*   *   *   *   *

On our way to the west and north we shall pass through the hills, lakes and woods around Silkeborg, which create the loveliest part of the country. We shall not stop at the garrison and assize town of Viborg, for it is a dull place which has failed miserably to make use of its two lakes to beautify itself; moreover its Romanesque cathedral of granite, though on ancient foundations, is a large, sad reconstruction of the last century with nothing to recommend it—not even the murals of Professor Skovgaard. The landscape continues to be enchanting as far as Aalborg and on the way we pass through the famous Rebild Hills which rise in the Forest of Rold. Here a large tract was bought by wealthy Danish-Americans in 1910 who presented it to Denmark as a National Park where each year on

66   COPENHAGEN : The Fish Market

67 BOGENSE: The
medieval Church
with its characteristic
stepped gable

68 COPENHAGEN: The
Grundtvig Church, a
modern dramatized essay

July 4th, America's national day, Danes and Danish-Americans gather for a summer festival.

Aalborg on the Limfjord is a lively modern town with a past going back a thousand years. From here Viking raids on England were launched. Now, however, the inhabitants are peaceful. They build ships, make cement and cigarettes and distil excellent Aquavit. They also eat well, dance, sing and sometimes stroll through a park to a hill where they rise still higher in a lift to the top of an alarming steel look-out tower. Up at the top in a round nest they drink Carlsberg to prevent that sinking feeling.

Modern Aalborg is found elsewhere than in its factories and in this interesting piece of structural engineering of its look-out tower —for instance, in the wide new thoroughfare of Vesterbro. But old Aalborg is always near in the narrow, medieval side streets (where perhaps you will glimpse a sweep in his traditional top hat); in the great Renaissance house of Jens Bank built in 1624; in the eighteenth-century town hall with its fine Rococo doorway (64); in the half-timbered Castle begun by Christian III in 1539 which looks like a huge farmhouse; in the Helligaandsklostret which still houses the old and infirm as it has done for the past five centuries, and where you can inspect the original frescoed vaulting; in the old Budolfi Church which stands in the market place and was once a cathedral (p. 194).

Budolfi Church was one of the last cathedrals to be built in Denmark and dates back only to 1440 when it was dedicated to St. Botholphus, the English saint and protector of seafarers. Though built in yellow brick painted white with post-Reformation transepts of 1553 and a noble Baroque spire of 1779, it somehow manages to achieve a unity which is barely Gothic. Inside is much colourful decoration—a rich pulpit of 1692, a carved Baroque altar-piece and a very attractive Italian marble font of 1727, its support decorated with bas-relief panels and angels' heads and its basin carved like a giant shell.

From Aalborg we continue north through the wide spaces which lie above the Limfjord and we soon reach the port of Frederikshavn. From there we shall travel through the night to Oslo and a very different land. But before leaving Denmark we must explore its capital and so with a flick of the page we are back in Copenhagen.

XI

Copenhagen

To many folk in the world Copenhagen is a country somewhere in the north of which the capital is called Tivoli. Others know it as the Paris of the North, presumably not because it looks in the least like Paris but because it is a gay place and contains open-air pavement cafés and many places of entertainment. The most famous of these places are the Tivoli Gardens. Since these lie in the very centre of the capital we may well begin our perambulations there and, in a festive mood, enjoy a spree on the switchback or a meal beside the lake in one of Tivoli's many restaurants. Then, sustained by good food and wine we may feel, according to temperament, either aggressive enough to smash china in the Merry Kitchen or soothed enough to listen to a classical concert. Or perhaps we may goggle with sweating palms at the trapeze artists as they gracefully risk their necks for our pleasure, or watch the ballet dancers pirouette in the open-air theatre, or take a turn ourselves in the Dansett, or just stroll about in relaxed mood as the evening closes and ten thousand coloured lights come on among the trees, the fountains, the flowers, the oriental pavilions and the friendly faces of the restless, chattering Danes.

If we are lucky we may see a Tivoli speciality—the marching of the Tivoli Guard. This is a replica in miniature of the King's Guard, being composed of over a hundred boys resplendent in red and white uniforms and bearskin hats led by their colours and their own highly trained band. They make a grand sight as they swing along and summon up the blood as only peace-time military ritual can. Is it not in its way a kind of ritual dance?

Tivoli is unique. Nothing like it has been seen in Europe since the passing of Vauxhall and Cremorne. Although other Scandinavian towns have copied it, none has managed to capture its special atmosphere. No doubt its vintage helps this special tone, for its turnstiles have been revolving since 1843. It was in that year that the talented architect and writer, George Carstensen, managed, to everyone's astonishment, to obtain the royal assent to using this valuable site in the very heart of the town for a festive garden. The 1840's were unstable years in Denmark, and it is said that he gained the favour of King Christian VIII by putting forward the old bread and circus argument. The monarchy was still absolute, but the king was standing at bay before the forces of Liberalism and perhaps hoped to gain popular favour by his support of the project. Carstensen went to work with enormous enthusiasm and produced from the raw material of the glacis and part of the moat of the old fortifications a pleasure garden in the idyllic and romantic manner of the day which owed much to the English garden landscape tradition. His planning was particularly good, for he made imaginative use of the existing zigzag formation of the old fortifications to provide a winding promenade which, by retaining the element of surprise, entices the stroller on to discover what lies round the next bend, so giving him one fresh vista after another.

Of course, Tivoli has been changed a good deal since its foundation and the moat has been reduced to a small lake, but this charming, picturesque informality is still there and dominates the lay-out. Most of the original buildings have gone, which is a pity, because old illustrations show what light, graceful and playful adaptations they were of styles borrowed from China, Turkey and Grenada. The old tradition continues, however, as one may see, for instance, in that pagoda tea pavilion by the lake which was built in 1900. As a piece of light-hearted fantasy, just right for the setting and purpose of the gardens, it could not be improved. Another good piece of existing *Chinoiserie* is the open-air theatre where traditional pantomime is still enacted each day and where the children still cry in unison, as they have for a century past: "Say something, Pierrot." This, too, is imaginative and in keeping with the spirit of the place with its curtain formed like a huge peacock's tail which folds up like a fan as the play begins.

Tivoli's opening season in 1843 was a phenomenal success. Since then more than a hundred million people have passed through the turnstiles. The place remains as popular as ever among all types and classes, for its appeal is universal. Tivoli provides the impossible —democratic gaiety without vulgarity and physical and spiritual food of fifty-seven varieties all in one larder to suit all tastes without any self-consciousness, snobbery or sense of guilt in enjoyment. As the evening ends with the flash of fireworks and we drift out with the crowds past Plaenen, we lift our hats high in the Danish fashion to the statue there of Georg Carstensen. He made but a small fortune from his venture and others reaped the financial benefits of his zeal. But he himself has gained immortality and a lasting monument. Justly so, for Hans Andersen was right when he called that good-hearted patriot "a real genius".

When Tivoli was first laid out, Copenhagen was still enclosed by its defensive ramparts and each night the town gates were locked. Then the population was only about 120,000. Today with the suburbs it is ten times as many. Greater Copenhagen is therefore largely modern, but within the fortifications many old buildings from different centuries remain to tell the city's history. The general street lay-out in the old part is, indeed, like that of Stockholm, still mainly medieval. Like Stockholm, too, Copenhagen began as an undefended settlement of merchants and fishermen. Then in 1167 Absalon, bishop, soldier and statesman, built a fortress to protect the town of Havn, as it was then called (*havn* meaning harbour). Only later did it become known as Köpmannaehafn or Merchants' Harbour. Absalon not only built the castle but fortified it generally with moats and bulwarks. In return for this work Valdemar the Great turned the town and neighbouring districts over to Absalon, which resulted in over two centuries of conflict between kings and bishops as to who should possess the town. The feud was finally concluded when Erik of Pomerania took the town and turned it into a royal city. From then Copenhagen grew in importance as the country's political, cultural and economic centre until it became the largest town and the largest port in the Baltic.

Of medieval Havn little remains apart from the ruins of Absalon's castle below the Palace of Christiansborg and the general lay-out of crooked narrow streets which lie between the two main places of Raadhuspladsen and Kongens Nytorv. Many of the odd names of these streets are probably medieval too—in translation: Neighbour-less, Lavatory Lane, Take-it-easy Lane, Goose Street, Dear Buying; there was a Cheapside once, as well.

Of all the kings the great builder Christian IV gave most to the town and several of his Renaissance buildings remain. The most imposing is the Stock Exchange built between 1619 and 1630—the oldest building in the world to be built as a bourse (69). It is still used as such, though now trading is limited to stocks and shares; originally it was a place where commodities were exchanged and where booths could be set up and goods stored—almost, in fact, a warehouse. It is typical of its time in being of brick with ornamental stone dressings and copper roof in the Dutch manner, and it is remarkable for its long row of gables which front the canal and its fantastic central spire of four intertwining dragons' tails.

Another fine building of Christian IV is Rosenberg Castle. This also has that vigorous, life-loving character of the period. Built between 1610 and 1624 as the king's country place, it now houses a fine collection of the furniture and personal effects of the Danish kings who have ruled during the past five centuries. Its lovely

69 COPENHAGEN: Christian IV's Stock Exchange (1619–1630) with its spire of entwined dragons' tails

70 Morten Farums Courtyard (1751) off Amaliegade

71 Our Saviour's Church: a detail of the baroque Altar (1707)

72 The Amalienborg Palace (1760) by Eigtved. The Marble Church, begun in the eighteenth century, is in the background

3 The Marble Bridge over the Frederiksholm Canal, leading to the baroque entrance to the courtyard of Christiansborg Palace

74   COPENHAGEN : A sentry at the Royal Palace of Amalienborg

184

gardens are now a public park, the oldest park in the town. In this palace Christian IV died in 1648.

Christian also erected that curious Round Tower which stands near Rosenberg in the midst of the old university quarter. It was built as an observatory and is mounted by a spiral ramp so wide that Czar Peter the Great was able to drive to the top in a horse-drawn carriage. It is not a beautiful building, but it does provide a convenient look-out from which to see over the city. Immediately below it is the Regensen, built in 1623 as a free dwelling for 100 students and still used as a students' hostel.

Other works of Christian still standing are the Nyboder, north of the town, built as quarters for naval officers in the form of rows of standard terrace houses. They are still happily inhabited by members of the Royal Marines. Christian also greatly improved and enlarged the town's fortifications and earthworks and built a naval dock.

From the end of Christian IV's reign the shape of the city hardly changed for three centuries, though it continued to grow slowly within the fortifications. Frederik III, who followed Christian IV, could not afford much building owing to the expensive failures in the Swedish wars, but for military reasons he erected the huge fortification by the water north of the town known as Kastellet, the Citadel, which is now incorporated in a public park.

The next phase of building, the Baroque, occurred at the time of Absolute Monarchy when the old nobility had lost its power and the king was forming a new administrative aristocracy. As in Stockholm, the new noblemen built their own houses in the capital on sites presented by the Crown. In their design, verticality and pomp give place to the playfulness and horizontality of the Renaissance, though the restraint of the Dutch Baroque is evident in them. Two of these grandee palaces can be seen in Kongens Nytorv (the King's New Market Place), which was laid out by Christian V (1670–99). One stands at the corner of Bredgade. It now houses the French Legation, but it was built for the naval hero, Niels Juel; its façade is unfortunately not the original. The other is Charlottenborg, now the Academy of Art, which was built by Gyldenløve, the king's half-brother, with bricks from his old fourteenth-century castle of Kalø in Jutland and survives in its original condition. Round the corner in Bredgade are two more Baroque houses—the Moltke Palace and the so-called Opera House, now used as a court of justice.

In the centre of Kongens Nytorv rides Christian V himself. The original piece by the Frenchman, l'Amoreux, was cast in lead and languished through the hot summers until in 1946 it was replaced by a copy in more resistant material. It is known simply as The Horse. "Meet me at The Horse," one says in Copenhagen. When the students have passed their matriculation and have jubilantly donned their white caps, it is here that, by old tradition, they express their joy by dancing in a ring three times round The Horse, a demonstration which during the Occupation was forbidden by the Nazis as a dangerous expression of national independence.

By far the most fascinating piece of Baroque in the city is the Church of Our Saviour, whose strange spire with its external spiral staircase rises above the picturesque tree-lined canals of Christianshavn (*frontispiece*). Christian V laid the foundation stone in 1682, but the main building was not ready until 1696, when it was regarded as one of the noblest buildings north of the Alps. It was the work of a master-builder named Lambert van Haven and Hans van Steenwinkel the Younger, and is distinctly Dutch in character. The copper-covered spire, surmounted by a gilded figure of Our Saviour bearing a flag of victory and standing on a ball representing the Earth, is of slightly later date than the main structure, for it belongs to the reign of Frederik V, the architect being de Thurah. The folk of Christianshavn still tell you the story with a twinkle in their eyes of how, when the king saw the spire for the first time and derated the architect for having made the staircase screw the wrong way, de Thurah took the criticism so badly that he threw himself from the top of his edifice.

The church is a piece of High Baroque at its best, built of red brick and sandstone with vertical pilasters rising the whole height of the building and high, wide arched windows giving a festive internal light. The altar-piece is one of those violent, restless Baroque affairs in gilded wood, marble and plaster with trumpeting angels, flying cherubim, a great sunburst and a flaming heart (71). It is said to have been made in 1707 from a model designed by the Swedish architect, Tessin the Younger. Being of a type familiar in southern Europe but a unique piece in Scandinavia, it gives the visitor a shock of surprise and pleasure when he first sees it. The carved organ, contemporary with the main building, is another grand and elaborate piece made by the craftsman, Christian Nerger. It is supported on plasterwork brackets in the form of elephants and other elephants are incorporated in the wood carving of the case. They commemorate the foundation of Christian V's Order of the Elephant with which he honoured his new nobility. Also contemporary with the church is the font, which is supported by infants carved in white marble and surrounded by a balustrade of other infants carved in wood. Above it hangs a gilded cover richly decorated with flowers and cherubim.

Frederik IV (1699–1730) brought in the Italian manner in the castle of Frederiksberg (not to be confused with Frederiksborg), a modest piece of Baroque lying in a park south-west of the town. It has been altered considerably since it was first built and is now a military college. During Frederik's reign the town suffered considerably, first from a plague which killed half the population in 1711 and then from a great fire in 1728 which destroyed 2,000 of the old brick-and-timber houses. The city was rebuilt mainly in pure brick and a simple, standard type of house was developed by one, Johannes Cornelius Krieger, of which many examples still exist in the centre of Copenhagen, notably in Nybrogade. They are attractive small bourgeois mansions, three storeys high, and are known as the Fire Houses.

Christian VI (1730–46) was the keenest builder among the Absolute Monarchs. His finest existing edifice, designed by de Thurah, is the small palace called Eremitagen (The Hermitage) in the Deer Park north of the town. It is still a royal domain. His main work, however, was the rebuilding as a royal dwelling of Christiansborg Palace in the centre of the town next to the Royal Exchange. The Palace is named after him, but the present fabric is mainly the work of 1903 designed by Thorvald Jørgensen, the sixth palace to be built on the same spot. Christian decided that the old palace was not grand enough and had it blown up with gunpowder. On the site he built a magnificent structure which stood but for a few decades, for it was burned down in 1794. From that fire only the spacious riding ground with its surrounding arcades and two entrance pavilions on the south by Frederiksholm Canal were saved and can still be seen. The Marble Bridge on the south by which the riding ground is approached is of later date and in the Rococo style (73). Today part of Christiansborg houses the Parliament, the Ministry of Foreign Affairs, the High Court of Appeal and the Royal Reception Rooms where the King regularly receives any among his subjects who considers he has something of importance to discuss with his monarch. The Royal Library, Christian IV's Arsenal (built in 1604 and now a military museum) and the eighteenth-century Court Theatre (now a theatrical museum) help to make up this huge complex.

The Rococo period is marked by the work of Nicolai Eigtved, who served both Christian VI (1730–46) and Frederik V (1746–66) as architect and town planner. He introduced the Rococo to Denmark in his Prince's Palace which now forms part of the National

Museum, but his main work was the Amalienborg Palace of 1760 with its fine octagonal place, where the picturesque Royal Guards parade like toy soldiers in their busbies (72, 74). Amalienborg was first built as four palaces for noblemen, but the whole now serves as the king's town residence. In the centre of the octagon stands an extremely fine equestrian statue by the Frenchman, Saly, which was presented by the Asiatic Company to Frederik V, the weakest of the autocrats who hardly deserved this imperious monument. To the south, linking two of the palaces, is Harsdorff's noble Ionic colonnade built rather later than the Palace, while behind that lies a small yellow mansion where our Queen Alexandra was born.

The quarter round Amalienborg, called Frederiksstaden, was laid out as a suburb by Eigtved acting under royal orders. It includes the streets of Amaliegade and Bredgade which run parallel to each other. Amaliegade stretches north from the Palace towards the Citadel and is a street of many fine old mansions occupied these days by legations and shipping companies, among which is the Italian Legation with a peaceful courtyard to show that half-timbering had by no means disappeared by the eighteenth century in town construction (70). Bredgade still contains a number of elegant patrician palaces of the period, built under the controlling hand of Eigtved—notably the Palace of the Odd Fellows with splendid wrought-iron gates, now a club, and the Frederiks Hospital, designed by Eigtved himself, and now the Museum of Applied Arts.

Eigtved intended to include a large domed church in his scheme to close the vista west of the Palace down Frederiksgade. He prepared an excellent design for this himself but the French architect, Jardin, in the end designed the building, which began to take shape in 1749. Funds ran out, and in 1770 the work stopped. It was not begun again until 1894, when a wealthy banker named Tietgen grew tired of seeing the ruin each day and spent a fortune in completing the job—a curious case of an eighteenth-century monument being built in the nineteenth century (72). The dome is the seventh largest to be built of stone in Europe, and its size seems to ask for a rather more monumental approach than it, in fact, possesses. One should ascend to the lantern, not just for the view at the top, for the spire of Our Saviour's gives a better one, but for a sight of the remarkable and gigantic timber framework between the outer and the inner cupolas through which one climbs in the half-light.

In 1795 another disastrous fire destroyed a quarter of the town's dwellings. This gave the opportunity to rebuild under firmer regulations, such as fixed heights and minimum wall thicknesses.

75 FREDERIKSBORG CASTLE (1560–1620): The Main Approach and the Barbican

76   The Great Hall of the Knights, two hundred feet long

77   From the Sound

KRONBORG CASTLE: Hamlet's Elsinor (about 1570–1650)

About the year 1800 four-storey houses, controlled by these regulations and designed in the restrained classical style of the Empire period, began to grow up in the districts which had been ravaged by fire. Examples of these pleasant, quiet houses of the time of Frederik VI can still be seen in Copenhagen.

Then in 1807 came the English bombardment to lay waste large areas of the city and to end a period of prosperity. Balls from the English guns can be seen to this day embedded in the wall at 13, Nørregade. In spite of the new poverty, rebuilding had to go on. C. F. Hansen was the outstanding architect of this time, a designer who had a great influence on future trends. He carried out a number of public buildings in a simple Neo-Classic manner with stucco-covered brickwork, notably the new Christiansborg which, in its turn, was burned down in 1884, except for his church there of 1810, which still remains. Hansen also built the Church of Our Lady in the university district, the church which has served as Copenhagen's cathedral since 1924. It is a severe Roman building with a coffered barrel vault over the nave and side galleries, the nave being embellished with Thorvaldsen's famous marble figures of Christ and the Apostles.

The most interesting structure of the early nineteenth century is Thorvaldsen's Museum, which stands by the canal at the side of Christiansborg. The architect was G. M. Bindesbøll, a far more imaginative designer than Hansen, who lived well on into the century. Having played an exuberant part in the Battle of the Styles, Bindesbøll created a revolutionary style of his own in house building of a simple, functional quality quite alien to his time. The Museum is one of his earlier works, being completed in 1839 to house all the great sculptor's work either in the original or in cast form. It is a simple building in yellow stucco without columns but with Greek detailing and is unique in its external frieze by Jørgen Sonne depicting events in Thorvaldsen's life. This frieze is a successful technical experiment in external decoration and is known as graffito-work. Strangely enough it does not seem to have been developed to the extent it deserves, for the designs, executed in coloured cements, have worn remarkably well.

In the open courtyard in the centre of the Museum, Thorvaldsen himself (1770–1844) lies buried. Born of poor parents, his father being an immigrant Icelandic woodcarver, the son of a clergyman, he lived to become Denmark's greatest artist. Thorvaldsen, who worked mostly in Rome, was a very serious man and applied himself to his profession with such fervour, concentration and proficiency that he became world-famous and executed a vast number of commissions, all of which can be seen in this Museum, together with his collection of paintings and classical antiques. He had great technical skill and a sensitive feeling for the human body, but those white Graeco-Roman effigies set all together here in endless rows tend to grow boring in their perfection and passionless restraint. There are no unexpected fireworks, no sudden developments—just unflagging competence. Perhaps his bas-reliefs are the most pleasing, and his bust of Byron is good but, by virtue of contrast, one may be most delighted to come across a case containing Thorvaldsen's collection of ancient classical figurines. They include a formalized figure in bronze of a man with penis rampant between thin wiry limbs—a tiny piece but one with amazing vitality and spontaneity.

During the middle of the nineteenth century Denmark began to recover economically. Industry came with technical advances and an industrial working class was forming from the country people who had migrated to the capital in search of work. The city still enclosed by Christian IV's ramparts grew seriously overcrowded, until in 1852, the year before the great cholera epidemic which was no doubt brought about by bad housing, the boundaries were given up and the town could expand to the west. There gloomy tenements soon began to appear. In 1867 the last of the reserved areas lying between the ramparts and the lakes to the west was given over to more new tenements containing small, dark apartments. A new building act of 1889 helped matters by laying down minimum sizes for rooms and, at the same time, wider streets were planned.

In the decades of the middle of the century the lakes to the west and the moat and fortifications were regulated to form a delightful series of parks, including Tivoli, which now run like a green belt through the town. Soon an artery was cleared through the centre of Copenhagen linking Kongens Nytorv, the old centre, with Raadhuspladsen, which, as the town expanded to the west, became the new centre. Though this artery incorporates several streets in its length, it is always known colloquially as Strøget, the Stretch, and forms the very spinal cord of the city. It is both a lively shopping centre and a fashionable ambulatory—the Bond Street of Copenhagen, or perhaps, more appropriately, its Kärntnerstrasse of pre-1914 Vienna. Along the route by Amagertorv lies Højbroplads, an open place at the lower end of which rides Absalon. Here is the traditional fruit and vegetable market where the market gardeners of Amager, the large island east of Copenhagen, dispose of their produce—some of them descendants, maybe, of those 300 Dutch peasants whom

Christian II, a lover of Holland, persuaded to settle in Amager early in the sixteenth century to teach his people better ways of agriculture. Since then Amager has been the market garden of Copenhagen and still on its far side retains a Dutch character of landscape in its trim fields.

Højbroplads, incidentally, debouches on to the wide spaces around Christiansborg and the Frederiksholm Canal. Here we find Gammelstrand and its fishmarket which also purveys a Dutch feeling, largely on account of the fishwives in their large white hoods who sit along the quay-side disposing of the morning's catch, kept all alive-o in tanks until sold (66).

Strøget ends on the south at Raadhuspladsen where the red brick Town Hall of Martin Nyrop was begun in 1905. It epitomizes the national romanticism which, as we have seen, also found expression in Sweden at that time. A more interesting example of the phase and a much later one is the unusual and theatrical Grundtvig's Church on the outskirts of the town to the north-west at Bispebjerg (68). The work of Jensen Klint, it was built as a memorial to the great educationalist Bishop Grundtvig and is a powerful, elephantine and self-conscious version of the traditional Gothic church of the Danish village with whitewashed brickwork and stepped gables (67).

Today we have reached the age of planning and social building, and so, like most modern cities, Copenhagen has its plan for the future. A century ago the population of the capital was 130,000. Now with the suburbs the population is over a million and it is still growing. Clearly this growth must be controlled in order to prevent haphazard, unco-ordinated sprawl. The new plan is imaginative but realistic. It can be visualized best in the form of a gigantic hand with the palm placed on the present built-up area. The five fingers stretch out westward and north-westward into the country, since the town cannot spread to the east where the water lies. The fingers represent future built-up areas each with its own industries, residential areas and community buildings. Between them the country will penetrate deep into the enlarged city and here new woods will be planted. The fingers will be of such length that travelling from the extremities into the centre of the town will not exceed three-quarters of an hour. In time the centre of the town will be replanned and the fingers will be linked here and there by concentric ring roads.

This is sound development and one can hope that Copenhagen will thereby not destroy her past but merge it organically into her future. In this way that Spirit of Place which only time can bring will be preserved in the city (65). Copenhagen's Spirit of Place is a charming and a friendly one with the bustling streets, quays and waters, the peaceful parks and the romantic copper spires, green with the patina of age. Less beautiful than Stockholm, Copenhagen has a liveliness which is both gay and relaxed. In Stockholm one can become aware, without any apparent reason, of the underlying sadness of life. In Copenhagen it is difficult to be sad.

BUDOLFI CHURCH, AALBORG

XII

Two Castles

BEFORE leaving Denmark we must travel for an hour or two north from Copenhagen through the beechwoods to visit the country's two most famous castles—Frederiksborg at Hillerød and Kronborg at Helsingør.

Though of less historic significance than Kronborg, the Keeper of the Sound, Frederiksborg is the more interesting and the more splendid of the two (75). It may, indeed, be placed among the outstanding Renaissance buildings of Europe and is certainly the grandest monument of any period which Denmark possesses. Apart from that, it is worth visiting because it now contains the National Historical Museum, a vast collection of portraits, paintings, furniture, armour from different times, as well as a number of large models of famous Danish buildings.

In 1560 Frederik II built himself a new castle here on the site of a manor house, and here Christian IV was born in 1577. Of Frederik's castle the two round towers by the so-called S-Bridge and the adjacent buildings running towards the town bridge are still standing. Christian IV did not think that his father's castle was grand enough and pulled most of it down. In its place he caused to be built, between the years 1602 and 1620, the present edifice in the red brick with intricate sandstone dressings of the Dutch Renaissance, employing two brothers from the Netherlands, Hans and Lourens Steenwinckel, as his architects.

The castle stands on the edge of a lake on three small islands. Rising out of the water and backed by woodland, its walls of rich red brick, its copper roofs and curling gables, its fine statuary and ornamental stonework, its spires and splendid barbican fantastic with curving roofs, golden balls and arcaded tiers tapering to ethereal, gilded finials, Frederiksborg makes a grand sight. It seems hardly real, something that could not be conceived in solid form but only in a fading dream or in the magic words of a fairy tale.

To approach the inner depths of the building is an architectural adventure at its most exciting, for it is an adventure not in the usual three dimensions of building but in four. Time and movement play their parts in appreciation, as they always do in the finest architectural conceptions where the principles of landscaping have been applied. The whole is not seen at once but from different, and frequently contrasting, aspects as one walks along, to be surprised, perhaps startled, as each new vista suddenly appears.

We cross the moat and pass below an entrance arch richly carved in stone. Ahead, beyond a slight bend, lies a wide, long, gently rising passage of cobblestones between brick walls and pantiled roofs. It ends in another triumphal archway behind which part of the main building can be seen rising in the distance. Nearer, the great barbican soars up from its square base of banded brick. Through the arch the route takes a sudden defensive S-bend across an inner moat to a third archway which pierces the base of the barbican. We are still enclosed by walls but new vistas have opened up on each side down the moat. We round the end of the S and ahead we are given a tantalizing glimpse of the powerful climax —an appetizer. We hurry on and suddenly we find ourselves released into a great courtyard and then ahead the palace bursts upon us in all its splendour.

But the adventure is not quite over and, as in a symphony or a play, the climax may not come right at the end of the composition but near the end. Here in the courtyard we can linger awhile to admire the bronze figures of the great Neptune Fountain. (It is but a copy, for the original, created for Christian IV by the Prague sculptor Adrian de Fries, was removed as war booty by the Swedes in 1659 and then erected by Charles X in the gardens of Drottningholm, where it can still be seen.) Then we can wander out of the courtyard by the side entrance and admire across the water the sandstone Audience Chamber with a richly decorated doorway and an approach from the main building by a passage across the moat. Back in the courtyard we cross a bridge between two roaring lions of stone over a third and narrow moat to enter the inner courtyard and so at last to the arcaded entrance.

The building has twice suffered from fire, the second time in 1859 when most of the interior was gutted. The walls remained intact and the external appearance, though partly reconstructed, is still in its original form. When it was built, however, it may have looked even more magnificent when its sandstone ornamentation was painted in bold colours and even in gold. Inside the walls were first decorated with gobelins, paintings, and furniture of silver and exotic woods. Most of these things were carried off by the Swedes but the chapel, where all Danish kings were crowned between 1660 and 1840, still retains its former glory—perhaps too much so, for it seems over-ornate, restless and a trifle vulgar to our eyes. Among the paintings we shall be struck by the many portraits of King Christian IV with his great nose, his sensual lips, his eyes bright with the lust for life, his hair decorated with a strange little pigtail —an aesthete and a hearty, that rare synthesis which the Renaissance seemed able to produce more easily than has any other age.

After the great fire, Frederiksborg was restored partly by funds raised by a special lottery, partly by individual donations and partly by a generous gift from J. C. Jacobsen, the founder of the Carlsberg brewery. The copy of the Neptune Fountain was made at the same time. Today the museum forms a section of the Carlsberg Fund and receives a share of the annual profits of the brewery.

★　★　★　★　★

Our last visit in Denmark will be to Kronborg Castle, which has played an important part in Danish history in having guarded the narrow Sound and the only approach by sea to the Baltic (76, 77). In 1426 Elsinor became a herring town. Eric of Pomerania, then King of Denmark, Sweden and Norway, built a castle here called Krogen and, in 1430, Sound dues were imposed. From that time until 1857, when they were finally abolished, these dues formed an important part of Denmark's national income. In the narrow waters here for four centuries ships would anchor by the score, sometimes by the hundred, waiting for clearance and taking on stores from the town of Elsinor, which as a result became a lively and a prosperous place of taverns, ship chandleries and warehouses, many of them owned by Englishmen. The town thus depended on the power of the Castle to defend the Sound and prevent ships sneaking by into the Baltic without payment. Though Helsingør today has a shipyard and several industries the general atmosphere of the place is that of an old quiet town, which dreams of its vigorous youth.

Because the Sound dues were so valuable, Frederik II decided to rebuild the Castle and to incorporate Krogen in a stronger and more impressive fortress, and imposed new Cargo Dues to provide the large funds needed. The new castle, however, was to be not merely a utilitarian structure but both a grand palace where a king and his family could suitably reside and a symbol to all who passed by in ships of the glory and might of the Danish kingdom. At first the castle bore the same character as Rosenborg and Frederiksborg in the Dutch Renaissance style. The architect was a Dutchman, Hans van Paeschen, and the craftsmen employed also came from the Netherlands which was then the leading European country both in art and commerce. The Dutchmen were no doubt glad of this large commission, for times were becoming difficult in their home land where the war with Spain was restricting creative occupation.

In 1577 another Dutch master-builder was called in, one Anthonis van Opbergen, for then the king, having visited Germany, had decided to replace the roof tiling with copper and to cover the brick walls with Scanian sandstone to give better protection against cannon-fire. In 1585 the castle stood complete, when it looked something like it does today except that now, unfortunately for the general composition, the main corner tower with its enormous spire no longer exists. This tower was destroyed in a fire in 1629, which more or less gutted the whole building.

Christian IV with his usual energy ordered repairs to start at once, but these were not finished when Christian died in 1648. In 1658 the castle suffered again—this time from Swedish bombardment and conquest. When the Swedes eventually left, they carried off, as at Frederiksborg, much booty, including another splendid fountain. This fountain has never been replaced in the courtyard, though one can judge its appearance from a model which is preserved in the palace. In the eighteenth century Kronborg became a barracks, which it remained until 1922, when a general restoration took place. Now it houses a maritime exhibition and various national treasures.

Kronborg lacks the splendour of Frederiksborg, but internally it scores heavily by virtue of the wonderful Hall of the Knights with its stone floor of pink and grey flags, its ceiling of great exposed joists painted red, its deep, arched window reveals and two enormous and highly decorated fireplaces. The hall is 200 feet long, and is said to be the largest hall in the North (76).

If we follow the guide, we will be shown the very ramparts where Hamlet met his father in such a questionable shape. Then some "beast, that wants discourse of reason", will tell us primly that Hamlet probably never existed, but if he did he lived a long time before the castle was built and then not in Zealand but in Jutland. Why does he spoil a good story and harm the tourist trade? Besides, the tale gives a good excuse for using the Kronborg courtyard as a delightful open-air theatre wherein to enact Shakespeare's masterpiece. If we feel inclined to believe the sceptic in an objective way, let us give our thoughts no tongue. In any case, is not subjectivity the only truth? Does truth not lie "in my mind's eye, Horatio"? Here then at Elsinor let Hamlet forever "rest, rest, perturbed spirit".

NORWAY

XIII

Land and Livelihood

THE short summer night of Scandinavia is over and as we steam north up the Oslo Fjord the sun rises to trumpet our entry into a strange, new scene. On either hand across the water lie the primeval rocks of the North clothed in conifers—small courtiers of the regal mountains which rise somewhere up there ahead of us crowned with eternal snow. The homeliness of Denmark already seems far away and we sense the intimations of a nature which is wild, cruel and impersonal. Up there lie deep fjords and valleys, creeping glaciers, dark forests and, beyond the cold, barren wastes of Ultima Thule, the beautiful white death at the top of the world.

Whether one's father was a religious maniac or not, one can hear the cry of Edvard Munch echoing faintly from the granite—that cry of anguish the great Norwegian painter depicted so vividly and of which he wrote: "My friends went on and I stood alone again, quivering with anxiety. It seemed to me as though all Nature was emitting a terrible, endless scream" (p. 208). Some old peasant who has lived well enough all his life in the fertile Hardanger Valley would no doubt find such talk ridiculous and, switching on his radio for the weather report, would inform us that even he knows that the vengeful gods of the mountains died long ago.

Let us look at Norway in another way then, and say bluntly that the country is like the figure 6. The top of the stroke curls over the north of Sweden and Finland and then runs down very thinly as far as Trondheim sometimes so narrowly that the sea penetrates to within a few miles of Sweden's border. The strip is fringed with numberless black skerries on its seaward side and is itself composed of a bleak terrain, partly forested, having a coast of jagged, naked rocks rising from the sea, where for miles an occasional fishing settlement and the constant flash of gulls are the only signs of life. Up there are the three counties of Nordland, Troms and Finmark —the wild, sparsely inhabited country of the Midnight Sun of summer and the long, long night of winter—ending at the desolate North Cape, a steep headland rearing more than a thousand feet above the ocean, the most northerly point of Europe (p. 206).

Half Norway lies within the Arctic Circle and in spite of the warming Gulf Stream the high latitudes are almost treeless. There the Lapps and their reindeer roam—a bleak country made even more desolate during the Second World War when the Germans retreated southward, driving the people before them and laying waste all human works as they went. But in the perpetual light and clear air of summer-time when all things stand out far off with a strange clarity, this wild country, especially where the granite of the Lofoten Islands leaps high out of the sea, has a fascination which can be found nowhere else in the world and is hardly possible to capture in words.

The southern circle of Norway's figure six contains the greater, most populated and most civilized part of the country. Here are the three other regions—Sørlandet, the South Country from the mouth of the Oslo Fjord to Stavanger; Østlandet, the East Country from Oslo Fjord in the south to Trondheim in the north; and Vestlandet, the West Country which has Bergen as its capital and contains most of the famous fjords with their steep, sombre walls and glacial depths. Here lies Sognefjord, the deepest and the longest, being 4,000 feet in depth at one point and penetrating 110 miles inland until it reaches the foot of Skagastølstindane, a pile of impressive peaks rising more than 7,000 feet to overlook the vast Jotunheim massif. In the West Country, too, but farther south, lies the Hardangerfjord, the most spacious and idyllic of the fjords with its shores covered with friendly orchards and bearing few of those sublime but fearful aspects common to most of the other fjords. In the West Country is also found the incomparable Romsdal Valley (101) and the highest of Norway's mountains, Jotunheimen, the Home of the Giants, which stretches from the great glacier of Jostedalsbre, 400 square miles in extent, eastwards to Gudbrandsdal and the Dovre and Rondane ranges where Peer Gynt played and dreamed. More than a hundred of the Jotunheimen peaks rise over 6,000 feet and two of these, Galdhøpiggen and Glittertind, are over 7,500 feet, the highest peaks in Europe north of the Alps.

Over half of the whole country lies above 1,600 feet, and this fact suggests why Norway has a population of only three and a quarter millions in an area larger than that of the British Isles. Mountains and glaciers, indeed, take up 72 per cent of the country's area so that only 24 per cent is left for productive forests and only 4 per cent for agriculture. Of the population one third lives in towns. The rest live in coastal fishing villages or in scattered farmsteads in the valleys. One third of the population now earns its daily bread in industry, but the majority still exists, as it has done ever since men moved up here when the Ice Cap receded, by farming

78 NORWEGIAN LANDSCAPE: The Naero Valley from Stalheim

79 NORWEGIAN LANDSCAPE : The country on the Norwegian-Swedish border, in the south

and fishing. One third of the people now live by agriculture and one third by commerce, fishing and shipping. Farming, as in Sweden and Denmark, is based on peasant ownership, 45 per cent of farms being smallholdings of only a few acres each and about 50 per cent of medium-sized farms of about 18 acres each. There are few very large farms. Dairy farming is the main agricultural pursuit because this permits the use of every patch of soil, even high up in the mountains where the cattle are driven in the spring at the melting of the snows. There the livestock is tended through the summer by a member of the farmer's family who lives in a small summer-house called a *seter*, a tiny symbol among the huge monuments of nature to human courage and tenacity.

The sea, however, rather than the land, is Norway's greatest economic aid. More fish is brought to land in Norway than in any other European country, mostly cod and herring, a great deal of which is exported. This is not surprising when one learns that, from north to south, Norway's sea border runs for 1,100 miles as the seagull flies and for no less than 12,500 miles if one adds up all the bays, fjords and indentations which lie behind the protective barrier of the 150,000 skerries—a distance of one half the circumference of the Earth at the Equator.

Norway lives on the sea for other reasons than fishing for cod and herring—first for the whaling industry and secondly for shipping, which is of the first importance to the country as one of those invisible exports of which the economists talk, one of those intangibles as mysterious and ghostly as the inflations which spiral so viciously across the western world. Norway's commercial shipping has a tradition going back to the days of the Vikings, but it was eclipsed by that of the Dutch, the English and the Hanseatic League for several centuries. In the middle of the nineteenth century, however, Norway again began to assert herself as a seafaring nation to such good effect that by 1875 she possessed the third largest merchant fleet of sailing ships in the world. The coming of steam vessels caused some difficulties, but before the First World War her fleet was again one of the world's largest. During the Second World War half her mercantile marine was sunk, but now once again Norway's is among the largest. Norway builds few ships herself, and then mostly small craft, but all over the globe tramps and passenger ships can be seen flying the Norwegian flag. So valuable is this industry to Norwegian economy that when shipping slumps the standard of the people falls at once.

The land is too poor to support the whole population, though it manages to produce about 60 per cent of the country's food. Coal

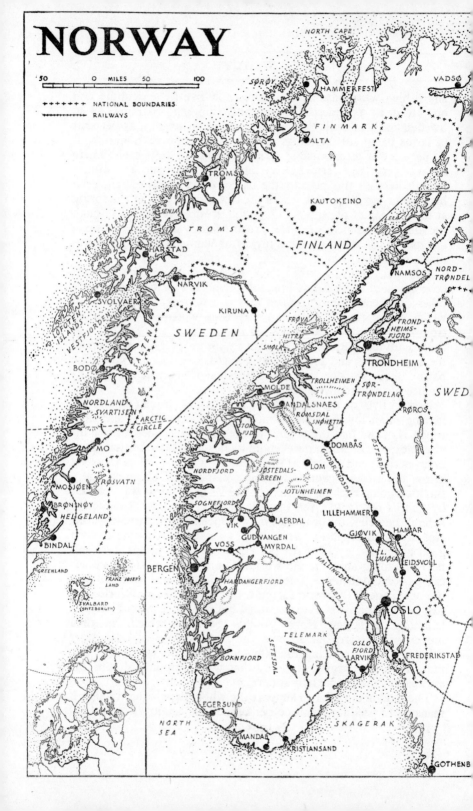

and grain are both imported but some Norwegian coal is obtained from Svalbard (Spitzbergen) up in the Polar Sea. Norway's greatest potential wealth lies in her White Coal, her waterfalls, for at present she uses but 16 per cent of the water-power available. By harnessing the falls electric light and power has been made available to the most remote farmhouse where otherwise life still proceeds much in the way it has done for centuries. By using this water-power large-scale export industries have been established at certain points which engage in electro-chemical and electro-metallurgical production. Norway also has some mines of iron and copper ores, and her wood pulp and paper industries are important. Finally tourism has been of increasing value ever since the British "discovered" her mountains and salmon rivers more than a hundred years ago. In those early days of the great climber, William Slingsby, and his redoubtable sister, Edith, when the English milords were rich, they added to the Lord's Prayer in the valleys, "Give us this day our daily Englishman". But those days have passed and now all nationalities, and their currencies, are welcome in Norway.

The Norwegian standard of living is fairly high and the social services are well developed, thanks largely to the great feats of road and railway building accomplished through very difficult country during the past century. These are modern developments from the ancient, limited system of communications which have existed since 1393 when King Haakon Magnussøn ordered the setting up of a chain of hostelries along the main tracks through the valleys and around the coast where travellers could not only obtain food and lodging, but transport too, mostly in the form of pack horses. This system of posting by pack horse developed into that of the horse cart or *kjerre* in the last century, as one can learn by reading an odd little book published in 1857 and called "Unprotected Females in Norway, or The Pleasantest Way of Travelling There". The anonymous authoress of this work records that only one railway then existed in Norway. She writes: "We set off (from Christiania) at seven A.M. to Eidsvoll on the Miøsen Lake by the only piece of railway in Norway; but alas! just as we were trying to think what the Norske for 'Guard!' was, he ran up, saying, 'Can I be of any use to you, ladies?' showing a real British physiognomy; the line having been the work of English engineers, and the porters dressed in the same greasy corduroy material, with white hieroglyphics on the collar, as their brethren of London Bridge."

The three main railway lines now run from Oslo to Bergen, to Trondheim, to Stavanger. Each journey takes about ten or twelve hours and each is spectacular, especially the famous Oslo–Bergen run which, like the Oslo–Trondheim route, traverses the mountains above the timber line. Rising from sea-level the track passes through cultivated valley and wild forest, by waterfall, torrent, rock and lake, reaching the mountain heights of over 4,000 feet where snow and ice still lie at midsummer. Along the 300 miles of this line some 40 are taken up with 179 tunnels, a fact indicating how remarkable an engineering feat is the Oslo–Bergen railway. So far the railway running northward from Trondheim has reached Lønsdal, just beyond the Arctic Circle, and many years will pass before it reaches the extreme north. Meanwhile the present road, ferries and coastal steamers must suffice. These steamers, which ply along the fjords and behind the skerries are an important part of Norwegian life and are, one might say, the local buses of the coastal people.

THE SCREAM

By Edward Munch

XIV

History and Heritage

THE paucity and difficulty of communications in the past have, of course, greatly influenced the history and economy, as well as the culture and national character, of the Norwegians. Except in the large ports like Oslo, Bergen and Trondheim, foreign influences have infiltrated but slowly, and the ancient peasant culture has survived until very recent times, less in a national way than in local ways, each one confined to its own valley.

Isolation has resulted in great independence and self-reliance among the people, and tended to curb feudal domination. The struggle for existence has been confined to the fight against nature rather than against other men—at least since the Viking raids. Norway's history is thus of limited importance to the rest of the world, especially in that the country was for centuries a Danish province having little independent effect on European events. Norway's history, then, can be briefly told.

Some sort of organized government in Norway can be traced back to the Bronze Age. When men began to extract iron ore from the bogs to make axes, trees could be cut down and this brought a sudden extension of the settled areas inland along the valleys. Even so, during the time of the Folk Wanderings and later in the Viking Age (800–1050), the coast lands were over-populated and caused the raids and colonization from Norway of Scotland, North England, Ireland, the Orkneys, the Shetlands, and later of Iceland, Greenland and the Faroes.

Harald Haarfagre (the Fairhaired) finally dominated Norway towards the end of the ninth century and his descendants were kings for many generations thereafter—for 450 years to be precise, Norway's most brilliant period, called the Saga Age. The year 1000 is important, for by this time the coastal districts, being in close touch by sea with the rest of Europe, had become Christian. Moreover, at about this time Leiv Eriksson, called Leif the Lucky, discovered North America some five hundred years before the first visit of Columbus, when, setting out for Greenland he was driven off his course and came to a land where he found "self-sowed fields and where vines grew". In the interior during this period, pagan beliefs were strongly held for a long time—to such an extent that, when King Olav Haraldsson tried to christianize the whole country, the peasants of Trøndelag banded together and defeated the king at the Battle of Stikelstad in 1030. There followed the short-lived empire of Canute, the canonization of the dead King Olav and the building of the cathedral over his body at Trondheim, where the only Englishman to sit on the papal throne, Hadrian IV, established an archbishopric in 1153. This indeed was a time when the bonds between Norway and England were far closer than they have ever been since. The Cross had been brought to Norway by English missionaries, the two countries had a common ancestry, a common folklore and their languages were closely allied.

By the thirteenth century Norway had attained a leading position in the North Sea, but because she became dependent on grain imports from the Baltic countries, her power soon gave way under the economic pressure of the Hanseatic League. The Black Death in the middle of the fourteenth century, which hit Norway far harder than the neighbouring countries, further reduced her vitality. During these centuries there was constant bickering over the royal succession, until at last the line begun by Harald Fairhair ended with the death of Olav V.

In 1389 Erik of Pomerania, who had married a daughter of England's Henry IV, was crowned King of Norway at Trondheim and then, in 1397, came the Kalmar Union by which the three Scandinavian countries were united under Erik's rule. From that union Sweden extricated herself, while Norway remained under the Danish monarchy right up to 1814.

In 1536 the Lutheran faith was introduced and that tightened the bonds between Denmark and Norway. Between 1563 and 1570 the Nordic Seven Years' War raged between Denmark and Sweden, the outcome being that Härjedalen, Jämtland and Bohuslän were ceded to Sweden. During this century the Hanseatic power was waning and a new middle class was rising in Norway to oust the Germans from their monopolies. This class was particularly concerned to exploit the great forests, for a growing demand for timber was coming from the Netherlands and from England, an exploitation greatly helped by the introduction of sawmills worked by water-power.

From the end of the seventeenth century the peasants, no doubt helped by this new market for timber, entered a period of prosperity and regained that independence which they had lost to some extent during the twelfth and thirteenth centuries. The number of freeholders grew rapidly as the Crown was compelled to sell the enormous estates it had acquired at the time of the Reformation. A result was a flourishing time for the peasant arts which, as in

Sweden, bloomed between about 1750 and 1850. This culture is distinguished by its painted roses, bright hand-made tapestries and costumes, its rich woodcarving, silver jewellery and strange music, alternately sad and gay, played on the ornamented Hardanger fiddle with its two sets of strings.

In 1814, when Napoleon fell and the Treaty of Kiel was signed, the Great Powers set about redrawing the map of Europe. In a high-handed way they decided that Norway was to be presented to Sweden under the rule of Karl Johan *alias* Bernadotte, Napoleon's former general. The Norwegians, fortified by a nationalistic middle class and the European trend towards Liberty and Equality, if not Fraternity, did not accept the idea gladly, for the Swedes had always been far more unpopular in Norway than the Danes. On May 17th in the same year, when Karl Johan was away on the Continent with his soldiers, a representative assembly of Norwegian patriots met at Eidsvold where it laid down that national, democratic constitution, which still forms the basis of Norway's politics, and at the same time founded the Norwegian Parliament, or Storting. But the Great Powers were firm and, after a little military feinting on the border, Norway sullenly gave in. The negotiations which followed, however, produced favourable conditions for Norway, in that the new constitution was retained and Norway's right to self-determination under the new monarchy was recognized.

May 17th is still the great day in Norway. Known as Constitution Day, it is now chiefly a festival of youth, when processions of students and children take place all over the country with flags flying and bands playing—an idea developed by Bjørnstierne Bjørnson in 1871. Bjørnson was one of the five great writers of the latter half of the nineteenth century who, with Ibsen, Lie, Kielland and Garborg, made the Golden Age of Norwegian literature. They produced part of the spiritual and economic development which occurred after Eidsvold in the stimulating atmosphere of a growing national pride. The union with Sweden could not be tolerated indefinitely under the circumstances, however loose the bonds and however tactful the Swedish sovereign. Thus in 1905 the final move came to full national independence. In 1906 Prince Charles of Denmark, husband of our Princess Maud, was crowned King of Norway in the great cathedral of Trondheim under the historic name of Haakon VII.

* * * * *

In architecture Norway is not an important country, which is not surprising in view of her geographical position and character, and of her history. Nevertheless, Norwegian architecture, though presenting few great monuments in lasting materials, has some interest, particularly in its modest but charming vernacular tradition of timber building. What brick has been to Denmark, wood has been to Norway. The tradition goes back at least as far as the times of the Vikings, who produced ships, as we know from excavated finds, and no doubt also buildings, of a remarkably high technical and artistic quality. The tradition has run through the centuries and is found today in such delightful small modern houses as those to be seen around Oslo designed by the architect Ove Bang.

The oldest timber buildings Norway possesses are the few remaining medieval stave churches—those fantastic, almost oriental-looking structures which have no parallel in any other country (81, 82, 89). At one time at least five hundred existed. Today only twenty-two are standing, and most of these are not in their original form. That any should have survived at all is remarkable considering their timber construction, which could have been so easily destroyed by fire, and considering also the destruction by the Protestants who wanted better-lit buildings and had little respect for papist works. It is probable that in these stave churches we see a combination of the Anglo-Norman stone church in wooden form and the heathen timber temple. Indeed, their dark interiors have even now a strangely disquieting sense of pagan mystery. The intricate carving of intertwining animals and grape vines round the doors and on the walls, and of dragons' heads on the roof pinnacles is clearly linked with the ornamentation of the Viking boat builders. Borgund Stave Church in Sogn (81), built about the middle of the twelfth century is, perhaps, the most famous and beautiful of its kind, with its pyramidal form and recessed shingle roofs rising naturally from the plan and the structural frame of upright posts. Other fine examples can be seen at the Oslo Open-Air Museum, at Lom in Gudbrandsdal (82, 89) and near Bergen in the Fantoft Church.

The stave form of construction, with its upright framework and timber infilling, had probably been developed from primitive beginnings within the country and had close links with boat construction. The other traditional form of timber building, that of solid, horizontal timbers laid one on top of each other and joined at the angles of the walls, was on the other hand an import from the Mediterranean—perhaps from as long ago as Homer's day. Examples of both types of construction can be seen still in the Norwegian countryside, notably in the old kind of farmstead where the small buildings with untreated wooden walls and turf roofs compose themselves on the slopes around a courtyard in a delightfully

81   BORGUND STAVE CHURCH (twelfth century): in Sogn

82 Medieval: the Stave Church at Lom in Gudbrands-dal. The transepts and spire were added in the 1630's

83 Klaebu Church, Sør-Trøndelag with octagonal plan (1789)

TIMBER CHURCHES

natural and harmonious way (86). One will note especially among those farm buildings the storehouse, or *stabbur*, set on pillars clear of the ground and often highly ornamented with carving. The easiest way to study this timber tradition, however, is at one of the several open-air museums where such buildings have been carefully preserved.

With the development of the sawmills powered by waterfalls in the late seventeenth century, a technical innovation of the greatest importance to Norway, a change came to Norwegian timber construction. Wooden planks replaced the solid axed logs and pantiles replaced the turf on the roof. Construction was lighter and cheaper and more floors, fittings and partitions could be added to the houses. Panel wall construction was now possible and cabinet-making became a new and rapidly developing handicraft. In the interior of the country the new sawn timber technique was grafted on to the old solid timber tradition slowly and the change is less marked there than in the coastal towns and villages, where the houses received a finished outer garment of overlapping planks or vertical siding and the old rough, tough methods were considered crude and commonplace. The classicism of Europe was adapted with great skill to the new technique in the form of decorated doors, windows and balustrades and so produced at its best such fine patrician houses as Stiftsgaarden in Trondheim, now a royal domain (90, 93).

The new thin boards needed protecting with paint. To begin with, paints of different colours were used, like blue, green, ochre and red, and this variety created a gay effect in the streets—an effect rarely found today, though it can still be seen in the grand riverside warehouses of Trondheim. In the nineteenth century white paint became standard and remains so, as we see in the snug White Towns of the south coast. Something has been lost by this uniformity of paintwork but something has also been gained in freshness and cohesion.

Of the more enduring architecture in stone and brick which has survived, Norway has little to show. Belonging to the medieval period are such edifices as the great Nidaros Cathedral at Trondheim, which is partly a reconstruction (88), the cathedral at Stavanger, St. Mary's Church at Bergen, Vangens Church at Voss, a few small, simple village churches, the Archbishop's Palace at Trondheim and the Bergenhus Fortress at Bergen. Of the Renaissance period there is Christian IV's Akershus Castle at Oslo (85), the Rosenkrantz Tower at Bergenhus Fortress. Of the Baroque there are the manors of Austraat on the Trondheim Fjord and Rosendal in Hardanger, and a few satisfying fortresses like Christian-sten at Trondheim and Kongsten near Fredrikstad, with its concise form, rough texture and restricted, well-placed ornament. Of the eighteenth century there are several good churches, such as that in the mining town of Røros (87) and Sør-Fron Church in Gudbrandsdal, both by Sven Aspaas and both with an unusual octagonal plan, a shape which permitted a large, accommodating gallery around the whole interior. Another octagonal timber church is at Klaebu (83).

The early nineteenth century is distinguished by the buildings of King Karl Johan in Oslo in the austere but noble Empire style—a style which required stone for its proper expression but which, owing to the poverty brought by the separation from Denmark, could in Norway be carried out only in brickwork with a plaster finish. The most important of these buildings are the Royal Palace (84) and the University. Later in the century came a time of commercial prosperity and bourgeois individualism which brought the stylistic chaos to Oslo, mainly of a Germanic nature. Now Oslo and the other large towns began a rapid expansion accompanied by some inadequate town-planning, the erection of depressing courtyard tenements and huge, ugly State works like the Law Courts and the National Theatre in Oslo. In the country the Swiss chalet style and the Dragon style with its spurious imitations of ancient Norwegian detailing, were introduced.

At the turn of the century the younger generation of architects began to escape from the nineteenth-century eclecticism and sought for the threads which would link them again with some kind of honest tradition. In their search they found the English domestic atmosphere and the charm of the eighteenth-century Swedish dwelling, but not until after 1910 could this younger generation make itself felt, when neutrality brought prosperity during the First World War. Many excellent and well-constructed buildings of individual character resulted, such as Arneberg's house of 1916 at Forneby, Baerum and Poulsson's office block of 1917 at No. 1 Karl Johan's Street, Oslo. Then, after a brief attempt at reviving classicism, Functionalism rebounded upon Norway from Stockholm, bringing the modern detached flat block set in parkland, a great improvement on the old courtyard type. It also produced such buildings as the new Oslo University building by Bryn and Ellefsen, with its cubistic blocks of brick, and the distinguished Artists' House in Oslo by Blakstad and Munthe-Kass, who were also responsible for the excellent Klingenberg Cinema built in Oslo just before the Second World War. Now a reaction against the cold impersonality of Functionalism has set in, as it has in Sweden, and the young architects are once more finding inspiration in the native timber tradition.

XV

Oslo

OSLO was founded to the east of the present city on the side of Ekeberg Hill about the year 1050 by Harald Haardraade. This man, called the Hard Fisted on account of his ruthlessness, is known to our own historians for his invasion of England and his death in 1066 at the Battle of Stamford Bridge. The city's site was well chosen, for not only did the fjord give safe anchorage deep inside the country, but around it lay several areas of fertile land on which the city could be supported.

The Royal Palace which Harald built proved to be insecurely placed and so towards the end of the thirteenth century Haakon V erected the Castle of Akershus to be his residence and the main stronghold of Norway. The Castle has survived all attacks and at least three fires during its history and has come to have symbolic value to Norwegians. From the tower of this castle the flag of the new and independent Norway was first flown in 1905. As it now appears above the harbour its stone and brick character is more Renaissance than medieval, for it was rebuilt and extended by Christian IV of Denmark when he reconstructed the city after the great fire of 1624 (85).

The new town he built stood to the west and north of the old town and it was renamed Christiania in his honour, a name which persisted until 1924 when the ancient name was revived. Though Christian commanded that the new city should be built of more durable material than wood, little of it now survives beyond a few stone buildings such as the Garrison Hospital and two or three houses in Raadhus Gate.

Most of the fabric of Oslo as we now see it is of the nineteenth century and later. On the whole its streets are dull, but two things save the town from banality—first, its magnificent surroundings of hills, forests and fjord which are never far away and provide wonderful natural recreation grounds where the citizens can enjoy walking, ski-ing, bathing and sailing within a few minutes of their doorsteps; secondly, the main street, Karl Johans Gate, which holds the town together as a unity and gives just the right amount of monumentality to be in scale with the whole place. The street is seen at its best about halfway along looking west. Across a dip it rises beyond the Students' Grove with its flower beds and lime trees and sweeps up a hill towards the wooded Palace Park, edged with rocks and lilac bushes. Beyond that at the highest point stands the Royal Palace which Karl Johan built in order to make a suitable impression on his new subjects. It is not a great building but with its plain portico and stuccoed walls it has dignity, and forms a suitable climax to the street vista (84).

The king had a good architect in H. F. Linstow who could not, unfortunately, carry out the grand design he at first prepared for the Palace because the economic conditions of the time were desperate. So Linstow's final building as it now appears is smaller and less impressive than was at first intended.

A more prolific architect than Linstow was his contemporary, C. H. Grosch. In Christiania alone he built, among other large works, the Stock Exchange, the Maternity Hospital, the Observatory, the Ministry of Justice and the University buildings which face the Students' Grove on Karl Johans Street. In designing the latter, Grosch was assisted by no less a man than the great German architect, Schinkel.

We shall notice two other buildings in Oslo—the red brick Church of Our Saviour and the new City Hall. The church, Oslo's cathedral, which stands in the flower market by the main square, was first built in 1697 but was greatly altered in 1850. Inside are several good pieces—a carved altar and a pulpit, both of Dutch workmanship dating from 1699, a splendid organ case of 1729 and a font of 1720. The whole ceiling has been decorated with modern frescoes by Hugo Mohr; in spite of their size and competence, they seem to mean very little.

The City Hall, down by the water, had been building for many years and was opened at last in 1950 on the occasion of the town's 900th anniversary. It is composed of a large rectangular block from which rise two towers, the whole being in dark red brick with stone dressings—a heavy, insensitive, rather pretentious structure, crudely detailed and decorated inside with many vast frescoes which try to be Great but achieve only self-consciousness and mediocrity. The fine site facing the harbour deserves a better national monument.

Dispensing the same heaviness is the Vigeland Plan in Frogner Park lying just outside the town to the north-west. It should certainly be seen as one of Europe's greatest visual curiosities. If it were less serious in purpose and so less alarming in effect, it could be called Oslo's Municipal Folly. Here, disposed about an endless, rigid, primitive axis stand about 150 pieces of sculpture in stone and bronze by Gustav Vigeland. (He died in 1943 at the age of

OSLO : 84   *Above :* Karl Johans Street, with the classic revival
Royal Palace closing the vista

85   *Below :* The Castle of Akershus, rebuilt by Christian IV after 1624

86   NORWEGIAN LANDSCAPE: A Farmstead in mid-winter

87 RØROS: A mining town in central Norway. The church has an octagonal plan (1784)

88 TRONDHEIM: The Nave of Nidaros Cathedral

89 LOM: The Interior of the Stave Church (see fig. 82)

74 before his master-work was complete.) The composition of entrance gates, bridge, fountain, flower beds and individual pieces of sculpture are dominated by a huge monolith, 57 feet high, raised on a stepped plinth and surrounded by thirty-six groups of granite figures. The monolith itself is composed of a writhing scrum of human beings, all in a dangerous state of panic. Clearly this represents the male lingam, a symbol which is presumably responsible for the epithet "Courageous" so frequently applied to the scheme. Many yards behind this monolith stands another huge erection in the form of a wheel of whirling, frenzied figures in bronze. Clearly this represents the female yoni. Unhappily the lingam and the yoni are both doomed to eternal frustration for they can never meet. The various nude figures set about the Plan represent heavy-boned beings at various ages from infancy to senility, all engaged in some violent activity. A baby is bawling lustily and stamping in a rage which may turn at any moment into a dangerous fit, an old woman with drooping dugs is giving some advice of a sinister sort to a young girl with fat thighs, a man with a thick neck is kicking a lot of children about, another is hurling his girl to the ground. The whole thing seems to be a kind of hymn of hate against human existence, an expression of sex without love, of life lived with fatalistic, violent despair without purpose or hope.

This brutal creation came about thus. Vigeland was struggling along as a free-lance sculptor and had already carried out some work for Nidaros Cathedral when someone persuaded the Oslo Town Council that they possessed in him an unrecognized genius of world stature who deserved encouragement. And so, in 1919, the Council made an agreement with him by which he should assign to the town all his future work in return for a studio, an income and somewhere to set up his work when it was finished—a remarkable contract of a magnitude enjoyed by no other sculptor who has ever lived. Whatever its results it was a contract which does at least show that Oslo's town councillors of the year 1919 did not lack a courage rare among officials.

Vigeland repaid this splendid patronage with twenty-three years of ferocious work which he carried out in the inviolable seclusion of his studio. The work, which was not revealed to the astonished gaze of the public until the early 'forties, has cost the town more than a million pounds and has burdened the Council with much abuse. It cannot be denied, however, that the Vigeland Plan is a powerful, if a frightening, thing, nor that Vigeland was a talented sculptor. Some of his busts, which can be seen in the Oslo National Gallery, are very good indeed. The Vigeland Plan, as Evelyn Waugh once wrote in an article in the *Daily Telegraph* after a visit to Scandinavia, "is a stupendous achievement". He goes on: ". . . in all that mass of writhing muscle there is no hint anywhere of any intellectual process or spiritual aspiration. I suppose it is the most depressing spectacle it is possible to encounter; something far more awful than the ruins of Hiroshima. And, standing in that sunny park with the children splashing delightedly in the fountains, I wondered what hope there was for the people who had made it." Devastating criticism, and not quite fair on the Norwegian people as a whole, who, after all, had this thing sprung on them without warning. Perhaps the best thing they could do with it now would be to transport it whole to some mountain fastness among the fir trees and snow, where its effects on the lonely traveller would be apocalyptic.

More of Vigeland's works can be seen near Frogner Park at the Vigeland Museum which was the artist's former studio. One of these works is a small piece representing a circle of Roman soldiers raising their spears to impale some poor wight with extreme neatness through the intestines. Other works seem to express the rage of a thwarted libido. One senses that if Vigeland had not found violent emotional release in his work, the Oslo citizens would have had to support him in any case—in the town's mental hospital.

Vigeland was apparently influenced by the morbid Superman philosophy of the nineteenth century, but he was influenced also by the ideas of his fellow countryman and contemporary, Edvard Munch (1863–1944). If Oslo had nothing more to offer the visitor than a sight of the paintings, drawings, lithographs, etchings and other works of Munch to be seen in the Oslo National Gallery and Munch's great frescoes in the University Festival Hall, a pilgrimage to the Norwegian capital would be worth while. Munch was a genius who has not yet received his due recognition in Europe, though Germany has appreciated him more than England. He has been well described as the most explosive force in Norwegian art. "In him we perceive something of a Norwegian synthesis," says a Norwegian writer, "the Viking with the whole high-tensioned soul of our age, a romanticist who cannot lie. He possesses a pathos and a heroism in vicissitude which, from our Norwegian winter and our brief summers, has attained a height of art in which the pain of the cold and dark, and jubilation over the eternal light, have become one. His delineation of human nature searches out the hidden secret powers which control our minds, which create the very drama of life. It is no accident that Henrik Ibsen is his poet, a kindred spirit who constantly fills his thoughts "* (p. 208).

* Dr. Harry Fett in *Norway* (Norway Travel Association).

Though clearly he learned from the Impressionists and from Gauguin and Toulouse-Lautrec, Munch cannot easily be placed in any fixed category, for he was utterly sincere and thus a supreme individualist. Perhaps for convenience sake one could call him a Symbolist in that he betrayed moods, especially moods of anxiety, of spiritual travail and those engendered by landscape. Illness, death and erotic problems were his constant themes. "Art is crystallization", he once said. But crystallization of what? To Munch it meant the external expression in brilliant, bold form, colour and line of his own neuroses. The work of Munch surely has something to teach those who are trying to unravel the great mystery of aesthetics. It is this: that provided the feelings and convictions of a creative being are sufficiently strong and are expressed with courage in an attempt to purge the inner conflicts by catharsis, works of art having meaning for other people will result—that is to say, patterns of perfect formal composition to which nothing can be added and from which nothing can be taken away without rendering the composition at once meaningless. What those works seek to express about the external world, whether a moral idea or merely some trivial scene from daily life, is material to those works as artistic expressions only to the extent that it is able to release the artist's emotions. In Munch's paintings, for example, it is not the idea that the enjoyment of sexual pleasure is the Great Sin which now appeals, for that idea seems to us a little ridiculous. What now appeals, and will always appeal, is the superbly composed forms which those ideas miraculously released in Munch's sensitive, tortured but life-loving mind. Because he was able to love, Munch succeeded as an artist. Because he could only hate, Vigeland failed.

Before leaving Oslo we must make the pleasant trip by ferry across the harbour to Bygdøy, the park peninsula lying to the south-west of the town. Here can be seen several symbols of Norway's maritime genius. First, the ship *Fram* in which Amundsen and Nansen journeyed to the North and South Poles. Secondly, the balsa-log raft on which Heyerdahl and his five companions drifted across the Pacific on their Kon-Tiki expedition of 1947, one of the most romantic and courageous adventures of all time. Thirdly, the three famous Viking ships which have been unearthed along the shores of the Oslo Fjord. Of these the Oseberg Ship found in 1903 is the most interesting. In it were found the skeletons of a young queen and her elderly bondswoman as well as a mass of grave-goods, including a cart, three beautifully carved sledges, three beds, a ribbon loom, a chair, a bar engraved with runic characters, chests containing domestic items, a wooden pail full of wild apples, fifteen horses, one ox and four dogs. It was a remarkable discovery, for most of the ship as it can now be seen is the original. Even most of the old rivets are there and part of the serpentine carving on the nobly curving prow. The rest of the prow is a careful replica and the joint between the new and the original work can be clearly seen. Boat enthusiasts will be interested in the construction. This is clinker and all of oak, the planking being held to the ribs by whalebone lashings. Caulking is of animal hair. In the upper row of planking on each side are fifteen holes for oars, though the ship, which is over 60 feet long, also had a mast and square sail. Being flat bottomed and lying low in the water, it was not built for heavy open seas but for the waters of the fjords or for those within the coastal skerries—a good, small chieftain's boat used for local voyages in fair weather round about the year A.D. 800.

The Viking ships lie on the edge of the Norsk Folkemuseum, which is Oslo's equivalent to Stockholm's Skansen. This collection of old peasant buildings and other works was begun several decades ago by an enthusiast, Hans Aall. The setting is a natural one of pine woods and is less sophisticated than that of Skansen, but it contains a good representative collection to explain and typify Norwegian culture through the centuries. The oldest buildings here are a chieftain's hall from the Saga Period of about 1200 and a fine twelfth-century stave church brought from Gol in Hallingdal. Of later date is the small eighteenth-century timber town, while in a permanent museum building are displayed articles such as furniture, costumes and works of fine and applied art from the Middle Ages down to modern times.

XVI

To Trondheim

TRONDHEIM, Norway's third city, with some 56,000 inhabitants, at one time the country's capital and the seat of kings and archbishops, is set back from the coast on the south side of the Trondheims Fjord, just where Norway begins to grow narrow. It can be reached from Oslo by fast train in about nine hours. The route is less spectacular than the Bergen–Oslo line, but grand enough, for it winds first along the fertile shore of Mjøsa, Norway's largest lake, to Lillehammer, well-known as a tourist centre for ski-ing and walking and for its open-air museum of Maihaugen, founded by a dentist named Anders Sandvig. Then on and over the wide, bleak Dovre plateau where we can see Snøhetta rising in the distance to nearly 8,000 feet, the highest peak in the Dovre range, to the junction at Dombås where we can stretch our legs and breathe fresh mountain air before re-entering the train to complete the last three hours of the journey northward.

* * * * *

Trondheim, called Nidaros until the sixteenth century, is a small, bright town set in the lovely country of Trøndelag and encircled by the waters of the fjord and the River Nid. It is an important distributing centre by virtue of both its railhead and its port. It is also an old-established tourist centre and the gateway to the mysterious Land of the Midnight Sun. With its wide, grid-iron main streets contrasting with narrow, twisting, cobbled alleys and cosy courtyards where the lilac blooms, with its white painted timber buildings (91), its old multi-coloured timber warehouses (some nearly 300 years old) set on piles along the semi-circle of the river (95), with its seventeenth-century fort high on a hill to the east (92) and with its great cathedral (88), Trondheim is, next to Bergen, the most interesting and picturesque town in Norway. A place rich in tradition and historical associations, it is as lively today as it ever was, for business here is brisk and ships, planes, cars and buses come and go; it has a Technical University, an airport, industries and several large hotels, one with a Victorian palm court complete with an orchestra and a head-waiter as large and impressive as a Berserk.

Culturally and historically Trondheim is far more important than either Oslo or Bergen, for until the Reformation it was the ecclesiastical, and therefore the intellectual, centre of the country, as well as the main residence of the kings during Norway's early period of greatness. The town was founded in the year A.D. 996 by the Viking adventurer Olav Tryggvasson, who became fired with the Christian faith and, having converted the people of the district, no doubt as much by force as by argument, built a castle and a church here. England knew this man only too well, for it is recorded in one of the most famous of the Anglo-Saxon songs how he destroyed the men of Essex at the Battle of Maldon, and, having plundered Ipswich, stayed on in England until he had exacted a large tribute from the inhabitants. His statue now stands on a column in the market square. Having been killed in battle by the Danes, he was succeeded on the throne by his cousin Olav Haraldsson, who died at the Battle of Stikelstad in 1030 in a conflict with his own people, as we have already recorded. The king's corpse, however, was saved by two peasants and buried secretly, and soon people began to talk of Olav as a holy man. The myth grew, miracles were said to have been performed through his sanctity, and a year after his death he was declared to be Olav the Saint and Martyr. St. Olav became greatly venerated in England and no less than four churches were dedicated to him in London, where Tooley Street in Bermondsey is a popularized version of the name Olav's Street. Olav's body was placed in the church which had been founded by Tryggvasson and in the sandy bank where he had first been buried a holy fountain sprang up whose water had healing powers. On this spot was built a wooden chapel which was the beginning of the great Cathedral of Nidaros.

St. Olav was succeeded by his son Magnus, who in turn was followed by Harald Haardraade, Olav's half-brother and the founder of Oslo. Harald built a new church in Trondheim in the middle of the eleventh century and this, the Church of Our Lady, still stands to the south of the market place. Here the Saint's relics were moved and from that time the worship of St. Olav made such progress that Trondheim became an important place of pilgrimage for the whole of Christendom. Haardraade's son, Olav Kyrre, a contemporary of William the Conqueror, pulled down the wooden chapel and erected on the same spot a Romanesque, round-arched, church of stone, whose foundations lie beneath the choir of the present cathedral. To this church St. Olav's shrine was moved once more and remained there for five centuries. His Holy Well can still be seen in the cathedral, though its waters dried up long ago. In 1152 the Englishman Breakspeare was sent by the Pope

to Nidaros as its first archbishop, the man who later became Pope
Hadrian IV. Then Kyrre's church began its transformation into
one of the great medieval cathedrals of Europe, largely through the
zeal of the third Archbishop, Eystein Erlendsson, who had visited
England and seen Canterbury Cathedral. Partly for this reason no
doubt Nidaros Cathedral has a distinctly English flavour. Eystein's
octagonal apse, with its screen and ambulatory, is perhaps the
finest part of the cathedral, being a beautifully carved piece of
Early English work; it is specially interesting to Englishmen for
another reason, however, in that its triforium has a peculiar form of
quatrefoil unknown anywhere else except at Canterbury and in
some of the nearby Kentish churches.

Apparently about the year 1320 the fane stood in its full splendour, 300 feet long with carved west front reminiscent of Wells,
and with a magnificent nave and choir reminiscent of Lincoln. Also
complete at last were the stately octagonal apse where lay the silver
coffin of Saint Olav; also the transepts, chapels, chapter house and
neighbouring bishop's palace. Disaster after disaster followed.
First came a fire in 1328 to destroy a large part of the building,
including the choir. Some years later the Black Death killed every
member of the Chapter except one cross-bearer. In 1432 and
1531 the cathedral suffered fire again and the repairs which followed each conflagration were only partial. In 1537 came the
Reformation; the cathedral was robbed of its treasures and the
silver shrine of the saint was taken to Denmark. In 1564 the town
and cathedral were plundered by the Swedes. In 1689 the spire of
the central tower was blown down in a gale, causing great damage.
In 1708 and 1719 the place suffered two more fires. By 1750 the
cathedral was in a state of ruin. The nave and west front hardly
existed and the damaged central tower was covered with an ugly,
provisional timber roof.

Then in 1869 the State took on the responsibility of raising this
greatest of Norwegian national monuments from its degradation.
Complete restoration was begun and in this year of 1951 is nearing
completion. It has been impossible to restore the cathedral to its
condition of 1320, for no one knows exactly how it then looked.
Controversy on how it may have looked has been considerable,
though it is conceded that the great nave and the west front may
never have been completed. The reconstruction has been carried
out with conscientiousness and intelligence and much has been
learned by piercing together the old stone fragments. A good deal
of the original building still stands—the transepts, the North
Porch with its zigzag ornament, the Transitional Chapter House

and the Early English Octagon of Archbishop Eystein. The nave is a complete reconstruction but is believed to be very like the original. Whether the West Front is near the original or not is any expert's guess. The lower part up to the top of the first row of figures is certainly correct for it tallies with a copper engraving of 1661. Some of the original figures are in fact being replaced or exactly copied where enough fragments remain to make this possible. Altogether thirty-two different proposals have been put forward for the restoration of the West Front, and French and English experts have been called in to give their opinions. The final proposal, with its central rose window and three tiers of arcaded figures, is now halfway to realization. Backed by two square towers at the south and north, it promises to be a splendid piece of semi-pastiche not unlike the West Front of Wells in appearance. The existing main spire is only temporary and is likely to be replaced by a great square tower with corner pinnacles, and the roof line of the choir will eventually line up with that of the nave.

The medievalist should be able to enjoy himself greatly in the Cathedral of Nidaros and he will linger there for many hours. But those who are less interested in distinguishing its original work from the reconstructed parts and seek only complete perfection should walk from the cathedral down Munke Street to enjoy the beautiful Stiftsgaarden, at one time the home of the County Governor but now the residence of the Royal family when its members visit Trondheim for coronation ceremonies in the cathedral and the like. Built to designs by General Frederik von Krogh in the 1770's of vertical external timbering painted white and embellished with Rococo ornamentation and a fine wrought-iron entrance balustrade, it is one of the largest and certainly the noblest timber building in Scandinavia (90, 93).

In Trondheim, finally, we shall visit the Museum of Applied Arts, which, though covering all European work, displays a first-rate collection excellently arranged of furniture and other objects of different periods from the seventeenth to the twentieth centuries. Norway is well represented, notably in eighteenth-century Nøstetangen glass, silverware from Trondheim and Bergen and various examples of beautiful embroidery. The Art Nouveau room of 1900 is interesting as containing furniture designed by Harry van de Velde and several fascinating coloured wood-cuts by Munch. Next to this room is one containing some tapestry designs and pieces of furniture by William Morris, who is rightly represented here, for he had considerable influence on the art and crafts movement in Scandinavia.

90 TRONDHEIM: The timber-rococo Stiftsgaarden (1774–78), formerly the County Governor's Residence, but now a royal residence

91 Traditional
Timber Houses

92 The nine-
teenth-century
timber draw-
bridge

TROND

93 Rococo
Entrance
to Stifts-
g a a r d e n

94 Eighteenth-cen-
tury entrance to a
Merchant's House

HEIM

95 TRONDHEIM: Old timber Warehouses, painted in variegated colours. Some date from the seventeenth century

XVII

To Bergen

ROM Trondheim we return along the line to the junction at
Dombås, a small village with a tourist hotel. Here we change
trains and proceed north-west down to Andalsnaes, which
lies on the shore of the Romsdals Fjord. For some miles the landscape is pleasant but unexciting, a broad, cultivated valley dotted
with traditional timber farmsteads and an occasional church. But at
Bjørli the curtain goes up. The valley begins to narrow and before
long we are enjoying one of the most spectacular landscapes in the
world, that of Romsdal, the ancient and famous pass from the west
into the heart of the country. The train runs along a ridge high up
the mountain-side and then twists suddenly down through a tunnel
to emerge facing in the other direction. Then along and round again
with violent vitality. All around the rocks tower up in grandeur to
the clouds, the river foams below among the fallen boulders, fed by
the many waterfalls which hurl themselves in white despair from
the heights, some never reaching the valley's floor but dispersing
ethereally in spray. As we descend the valley the scene grows ever
more splendid until we reach the grand climax where the pinnacles
of Vengetinder rise to 6,000 feet and the sky ahead is serrated by
the lovely Troltinder, both ranges giving power by contrast to the
great, lonely hump of the Romsdalshorn. At last we are released
from the giant gorge, the land spreads out with a sigh and the river
settles down to a gurgling contentment after its stormy life, until
at last it reaches the calm Nirvana of the glittering fjord.

An old legend, long favoured by poets and painters, is attached
to this valley. It tells how on a summer day in the year 1612, two
adventurous Scottish gentlemen, Colonel Ramsay and Captain
Sinclair, landed near Andalsnaes at the head of 1,500 mercenaries
with the object of marching up the Romsdal and across the mountains to Sweden to assist the young Gustav Vasa in his war against
Norway and Denmark. These levies were, according to the legend,
a rough lot and are said to have committed appalling barbarities,
raping, plundering and burning on their way. According to a translation from the Norwegian poet, Storm:

> They spared nor young nor aged then,
> But slew and burnt as on they went;
> The child they killed at mother's breast,
> Nor cared how sweet so e'er its smile.

With the backing of the authorities, the local peasants decided to avenge these atrocities. They ambushed the invaders in the steepest part of the valley and killed almost every man. There is a good deal more to the story. Mrs. Sinclair, for example, who had come on the expedition against her husband's orders as a stowaway, was slaughtered with her baby when a brave peasant attempted to save the mother and child from the affray. Misunderstanding his intentions, Mrs. Sinclair plunged a knife into his neck and was thereupon at once despatched with her infant.

The true story as painstakingly unearthed by Mr. Thomas Mitchell, a British Consul-General in Norway during Victoria's reign, differs somewhat from the legend. The band was no more than 600 strong and consisted mostly of a poorly armed and unenthusiastic group of men, who had been unwillingly impressed by Ramsay. As an official document describes them, they were "honest men's servants put on shipboard against their will to the universal grief of His Majesties subjects". An official report sent to Copenhagen later on in that year states that the invaders "neither burned, murdered, nor destroyed anything on their march through this country in Romsdal or elsewhere excepting one Danish man in Romsdal, who complained of the loss of a box containing a silver tankard, but the peasants will not acknowledge having got any such, but if found it should be returned to him." There is no evidence beyond tradition that Mrs. Sinclair ever existed, but should you ever hear the cry of a baby or the far-off wail of a bagpipe as you trudge up the Romsdal in the twilight and do not then sense a shiver down your spine, you will be either a very brave or a very unimaginative being.

Just above Andalsnaes, looking down on the fjord, stands a small, homely hotel with wide balconies where you can lie in the sun and admire the view. Let us stay a while here—a long while if we decide to try our skill at mountaineering. Otherwise let us depart by boat for Molde, which lies some miles west on the north shore of the Romsdals Fjord. This is an attractive small town, so protected and well warmed from the south by the sun that, in spite of being farther north than the top of Scotland, its vegetation is rich. The place is, indeed, famous for its gardens of roses and honeysuckle and for its beech trees and chestnuts which here reach the northern limit of their existence. This is a busy stopping place for coastal steamers and has a luxurious modern hotel. A large part of the town is quite modern, too, for during the war it was bombed to ruins by German aircraft and has since been rebuilt. From the hills behind the town can be gained a magnificent panorama of the mountains across the fjord.

At Molde we take to the water again and steam down through the skerries for twelve hours to Florø, stopping now and then at some small, fishing village of white houses huddling among the rocks. From Florø next day a bus takes us on a seven-hour journey through dramatic, mountainous landscape. We run for a while well above the timber line where the snow still lies in pockets, though it is past midsummer, and now and then we catch sight of the white edge of the great Jostedal glacier. At last we plunge recklessly down one of those remarkable zigzag mountain roads to the sea-level on the Vetle Fjord, which is a northern arm of the Sogne Fjord. A half-hour's journey by ferry then brings us to Balestrand and its white timber hotel, a well-known holiday resort from where the Jostedal Glacier can easily be visited. Thence by ferry and bus westward to Kaupanger to board another steamer which will carry us across the Sogne Fjord and down the sublime and awful Naero Fjord, its narrow water, where even ocean liners can penetrate, enclosed by walls of rock, high, dark, solemn and striped with white cascades.

At the hamlet of Gudvangen we can take a short bus journey up to Stalheim, which consists mostly of a large, red tourist hotel. But it is better to take a morning's walk to Stalheim along the valley and then up the zigzag road to rise a thousand feet or more to the heights, there to enjoy the grand view back down the valley and a long, long drink (78).

On by bus southward to Voss, another town devastated by German bombs and since rebuilt, whose notable medieval church has happily survived. There we can entrain either for Bergen on the last section of the Oslo-Bergen line or by a branch line for Granvin, thence by bus south-westward along the shore of the wide and spacious Hardanger Fjord to Nordheimsund, crossing on the way the suspension bridge of Fyksesund, a fine piece of engineering in steel and concrete built in 1937. Then due west up the Tokagjelet Gorge, another spectacle, where the road has been blasted out of the mountain-side and peers down several hundred feet to the valley floor and its tumbling torrent. So past a great waterfall and over the Kvamshaug plateau to come in the evening glow to the Town Between the Seven Hills.

* * * * *

We shall arrive feeling perhaps a trifle gloomy and overawed, not quite tough enough to take easily to this austere, remote, majestic land. But Bergen will cheer us up. It turns its back on the dark valleys towards the outer world and bustles about in an extroverted, maritime way. Though it suffers much rain and smells of fish it has an atmosphere all its own and a strong sense of independence. Even the people seem livelier, gayer and more emancipated from convention and prejudice than the rest of their countrymen. They possess a strong sense of local patriotism and, like the Gothenburgers, have their own university and a busy social and cultural life. This individual quality of the town and its people is the result of circumstance. Since the Middle Ages it has been one of the most important ports of the North Sea. Situated on a peninsula which is almost an island and isolated to a great extent by the mountains from the rest of the country, its people have enjoyed centuries of easy contact by sea with the rest of Europe. Before the railways came, it was, indeed, easier to reach any port of the Baltic or the North Sea than some town far off in the Norwegian interior. Moreover, for two centuries, from about 1350 until 1550, it was the centre from which the Hanseatic League controlled all trade along the Norwegian coast. Today it is as flourishing a port as it ever was, with a population of over 100,000.

Founded as long ago as 1070 by King Olav Kyrre, it has very ancient traditions and in spite of having suffered a number of devastating fires and other misfortunes, it still retains several medieval buildings. But it is the town as a whole, rather than the individual buildings, which charm the visitor, with its fish market, its miles of harbour and its intricate, narrow, cobbled lanes of white timber houses roofed with pantiles, which wander up and down the hills (98). Here and there this intricacy is broken clean through by wide ramps up which roadways zigzag between trees and worn stairways rise up to give one glimpses of the water below, alive with every sort of craft from small fishing vessels to dignified liners. This is a highly romantic and picturesque town of sailors, shipwrights and merchant adventurers, having that unity of form, texture and purpose, that homogeneity, which Le Corbusier has called Immutability.

In 1916 the centre of the city was destroyed by a terrible fire and that part has now been rebuilt with wide avenues and squares and modern buildings. But it is not the modern centre, where Ole Bull fiddles so quietly and persistently beneath his shower bath, which forms the focus of interest in the town so much as the old Hanseatic Quarter. Here the Hansa merchants carried on their own way of life and made their own laws in defiance of the citizens. The way in which these merchants lived can be understood very clearly by an inspection of the buildings which have been preserved

96   BERGEN : Eighteenth-century Warehouses, based on the medieval plan, in the Hanseatic Quarter

97   BERGEN: Looking across the Old Harbour to the Hanseatic Quarter

in the quarter as a Hanseatic Museum. Many of the old Hansa warehouses still stand along the quay-side (96, 97). Most of these remain warehouses to this day and one section of them has been monopolized for this museum. These timber buildings, with their gabled ends and façades of painted planks, appear now much as they did in the sixteenth century, for, although the whole quarter was burned down in 1702 it was at once rebuilt more or less as it had been before. The general planning and basic construction of jointed timbers is in fact in the medieval tradition. In the Middle Ages the buildings were probably dark and unpainted, but in the sixteenth and seventeenth centuries they were painted in reds and yellows and decorated with grape-vine ornament. Then in the Rococo period, as can be seen on the museum façade, the horizontal boarding was applied and painted red (99). Not until the nineteenth century did they follow the new fashion and receive coats of white paint.

The quarter was divided into thirty guilds, or *gaardar*. Each guild had its frontage to the quay and ran back with a side passage narrowly and deeply for about a hundred yards, and within each guild lived about six or eight merchants with their managers, apprentices, samples and stored merchandise. Thus the quarter must have contained at least 2,000 inhabitants at its most flourishing period. At the end of each *gaard* was the hall of the guild and an attached kitchen where the merchants could meet for discussion, to eat and drink or merely to warm their toes by the fire, for fires were permitted nowhere else in the quarter. The *gaard* ended with a small herb garden. A few of these halls and their kitchens have been preserved.

In the Hansa Museum facing the quay we can see the fully furnished and equipped rooms where a Hansa merchant once dwelt with his manager and apprentices. The rules under which they lived were strict, almost monastic, both for master and boys. No women were allowed in the Hansa Quarter, for instance, for the merchants were not permitted to marry outside their own kind. That may explain why a secret door was built between the merchant's living-room-cum-office and the stairs to his bedroom, for a local paramour could quickly slip behind the door on the appearance of some unexpected caller. Along the walls of the apprentices' room can be seen the short, built-in, cupboard-like beds into which the boys were locked by the manager each night to keep them warm and out of mischief. Perhaps the main interest of this Hansa Quarter, however, is that, though the buildings are mainly of the eighteenth century, they do, in fact, give a fairly accurate impression of timber town houses of the Middle Ages, and are thus architectural relics of a rare sort.

After the Thirty Years' War the power of the League declined, but it survived in a weakened form into the eighteenth century. When it finally died out in Bergen, some of the German merchants married local Norwegian women and set up in business on their own, becoming in time Norwegian citizens themselves. That is why Norwegian families bearing German names are not uncommon in Bergen today.

Behind the Hansa Quarter lies the Mariakirken, one of the oldest churches in Norway and still often called the German Church, for it was used by the Hanseatic community and right up to 1868 the service there was held in the German tongue. Though a good deal restored, it is one of the few medieval buildings left in Norway. It was founded in 1120 and much of the Romanesque, or Norman, part still stands. The two western towers with their pitched roofs, the vaulting and part of the choir are said to be of the thirteenth century, while the altar screen is fifteenth century and the pulpit is dated 1676. The best part of the church is the beautiful south porch.

Farther to the west of the town and closing the view along the Vaagen quay, where the Hansa warehouses stand, rises the Rosenkrantz Tower—part of the Bergenhus Fortress which guards the entrance to the old harbour. The Tower is another of the rare medieval buildings of Norway, for it originated in the reign of Haakon Haakonsson. Though its present symmetrical aspect was created in 1560 by the nobleman Erik Rosenkrantz, its effect from a distance, like the Hansa houses, remains medieval. The fortress was built to control the entrance to the harbour and to maintain some control by the Crown over the forceful activities of the Hanseatic League. Embedded in its walls are some English cannon balls, relics of our least happy association with the town. These were discharged by the ships of Lord Sandwich's ill-fated expedition of 1665 when twenty-four of our men-of-war chased a rich convoy of Dutch East Indiamen into this neutral harbour. As Pepys recorded, our fleet "began to play upon the enemy, and in three hours time (the town and castle without provocation playing on our ships) they did cut all our cables so as the wind being off the land did force us to go out and rendered our fire-ships useless; without doing anything, but what hurt of course our guns must have done them, and we having lost five commanders, and our fleet has come home in sad grief." Later, after receiving Sandwich's report, he added: ". . . nor, says he, could we expect more from the Dane than we did, it being impossible to set fire on the ships, but it must burn the town. But where the Dane did amiss is that he did assist them while he was treating with us while he should have been neutral to us both." Unfortunately for us, this neutrality was nominal only, for the King of Denmark at that time owed the Dutch some money.

Behind the Rosencrantz Tower, or Valkendorf's Tower as it is sometimes called, is King Haakon's Hall, a large Gothic festival hall, built during the middle of the thirteenth century. Though restored, like the Tower, during the nineteenth century, it is the most notable medieval secular building in Norway. Unluckily the whole of the fortress, including the Tower and the Hall, were severely damaged in 1944 when a German ammunition ship blew up in the harbour. The damage is now being repaired.

Of the other old buildings in Bergen we shall notice especially the monumental old Town Hall of 1558, one of the few buildings in the centre of the town which survived the fire of 1916, the arched "gate" on the east built in the time of Christian IV, the Cathedral which originated as a Franciscan church in the thirteenth century and the displaced twelfth-century stave church of Fantoft on the eastern outskirts of the town, still in an excellent state of preservation. We may also wish to see the open-air museum in the suburb of Sandviken, where a reconstruction of Old Bergen has been erected recently in the form of some sixty houses of the eighteenth and early nineteenth centuries.

Finally we shall, of course, ascend the 1,000 feet of Mount Fløyen by the funicular railway to feast in the restaurant at the top, and, unless the moisture from the west is condensing on the mountain-sides, to obtain a complete view of the town spread out below, of the fjord and of the countryside around, so typical of the North with its granite, its pine trees and its penetrating waters.

Our last view of Scandinavia, when we depart on the evening tide, will be romantic enough as the lights begin to twinkle up on the seven hills of this "droll city behind the vapoury sky". Then the night, the sea and soon the last rewards of travel—the grin of an English porter and the friendly smells of home.

XVIII

The Proper Study

THE purpose of travel, a modern writer has declared, is to obtain ecstasy. That is one of those wild, sweeping generalizations which are helpful, if not entirely true. Ecstasy is a rare state of mind and not one which can be accurately measured. It is a relative condition. It cannot be captured at will. It just comes or it does not come, and it is as likely to arrive at home unasked on a soft October evening when "the yellow smoke rubs its back upon the window-panes", as it is far off "on a cavernous waste shore cast in the unstilled Cyclades". It comes mysteriously and it is entirely personal.

What moments most nearly approached ecstasy for this writer on his travels in Scandinavia? In Norway it was to step on deck at the dawn of a bright day in the Oslo Fjord; the first sight of the great coloured warehouses by the water at Trondheim; the discovery of Edvard Munch. In Denmark it was the romantic approach to Frederiksborg Castle; the huge white womb of Odense Cathedral; the rush from the dunes across the flat sands and into the breakers on the shores of Fanø. In Sweden it was the inside of Södra Råda Church; the east ends of Lund Cathedral and the monastery church at Varnhem; a sail among the Stockholm skerries in the brilliant evening light of the North; the sweet scent of burning birch logs and the tinkle of a sleigh bell when the first snow had fallen on the woods of Dalecarlia and the skis were leaning expectantly against the wall; the early rising from a tent on the edge of Lake Vänern, the sun warming the flesh, the water as smooth as the granite, the fir trees dreaming in the haze across the water—very Sibelius, so that the Swan of Tuonela began to float around the brain, while Sweden's great gift to humanity, the Primus Stove, hissed swan-like at one's side in the stillness—

> The earth expanding right hand and left hand,
> The picture alive, every part in its best light,
> The music falling in where it is wanted, and
> stopping where it is not wanted . . .*

—stopping, that is to say, when the eggs and bacon were ready and

* Walt Whitman.

244

the steam from the coffee mugs rose straight up to vanish in the air of a quiet July morning.

* * * * *

The old cliché says that the purpose of travel is simply to broaden the mind—in other words, to increase one's mental store of comparisons. It remains a good definition, for in the end it is one's comparative study and understanding of human beings, both by direct personal contacts and through the observation of their works, which are most worthwhile broadening. By this study, one's personal philosophy moves towards wholeness, one's values are moulded into more harmonious proportions, one's enjoyment of living is increased and one's own contribution towards human development, however insignificant it may seem, is at least encouraged to grow.

Of course, no two human beings are ever exactly alike, nor can they ever be so, whatever the economic planners try to do. That is why, as André Gide spent his life in saying, the Each is always more important than the All. Nevertheless, individuals do tend to group together into types according to the conditions which mould them; the phrase National Character is by no means unreal, even if no single individual ever exactly reflects National Character. In concluding this work on Scandinavia, therefore, let us attempt to analyse the national characters of the three countries we have been visiting. Such analysis, and the odious comparisons to which it gives rise, is an interesting game for travellers, but it also has its didactic uses. For instance, what can Britain, now busily trying to establish the welfare state, learn from Sweden, which is running the longest established welfare state in the modern world? Can Sweden show by example how the colour of the personality of the Each need not be merged into the grey monotone of the All, in spite of central State control? Can nations with Protestant histories like those of Scandinavia survive happily with a nonconformist conscience but without a religious *mystique*? How have the national characters changed during the centuries for the better or the worse, and how have they remained the same? Such questions cannot be answered here but they can be suggestively posed as being important to the philosopher and the sociologist and so important in the end to the Each.

What are the Danes, the Norwegians and the Swedes really like and why are they like that? Let us start with the Danes and the Norwegians and end with the Swedes, who are the most neurotic and therefore the most sensitive, interesting and potentially creative of the Scandinavian peoples, in that, paradoxically, in a half-mad world only the slightly unbalanced, and not the normal, people can be mentally sound.

The Danes must be among the happier folk in the world. They are the least formal and the most relaxed of the Scandinavians. They enjoy living and do not feel guilty about that, in spite of the protestant reformers and the pietists of the past. Especially do they enjoy good eating and good drinking, which goes to show that they are highly civilized and would appreciate the words of our William Cobbett, as we so foolishly do not, "Good eating, good drinking, good lodging; without these, people do not really live; it is staying upon the earth." The Danes also love social intercourse, they laugh a great deal, they never stop talking and their curiosity about everything under the sun is insatiable. Like all the Scandinavians they have their feet firmly planted on the soil, they cope admirably with the practical side of life, they are excellent craftsmen and they possess a penetrating, sometimes cynical, sense of humour. The Danes are also, of course, splendid farmers, and it is perhaps because they live by agriculture rather than industry that they are in less spiritual travail than the rest of modern industrialized society. Growing food is, after all, the basic, stabilizing reality, and what shall it profit a man if he have all the motor cars, safety razors, bidets and explosives in the world if his belly be not filled with healthy, home-grown food?

The Danes are also the most tolerant of the northern peoples; that is to say, they accept the individual for what he is and do not frown if the superficial conventions are broken; one may still survive as an eccentric in Denmark without being ostracized. The Danes are the most friendly and "human" people in Europe, and the most genuinely democratic, even in personal relations. Denmark is, to use a specially Danish word, a *hyggelig* country. One can learn a good deal about a nation by seeking out such special national words which have no exact equivalent in any other language. Roughly *hyggelig* means a condition of contentment, good-will, of being at ease.

All things in *hyggelig* Denmark are on a human scale, openhearted and friendly—landscape, architecture and mental attitudes. The country's creative expressions are never marred by delusions of grandeur or vulgarity, and show few signs of that almost universal complaint of the modern world—paranoia. In Denmark one can be oneself. Just take one, two, three or four glasses of clear, golden Carlsberg lager, light a cigar (yes, even if you are a lady), smile benignly and relax.

Of course, this easy acceptance of life has its drawbacks. If one never descends to the depths, one is less likely to reach the heights. In Denmark one seeks vainly for drama, for exaggeration and, as Shaw Desmond wrote in *The Soul of Denmark*,* the Dane has a tendency "to call fresh air draught, to shun all shocks from cold baths to mental showers, to turn tragedy into comedy, and with the Preacher 'to have a little slumber, a little sleep, a little folding of the hands to sleep'; and this—the tragi-comedy of it!—in a world of quick changes, of revolutions, of war."

Yet somewhere in the Dane, buried deep down below that cheerful exterior, that naturalness and lack of affectation, that tolerance, that love of comfort, that common sense, that easy, undramatic temperament, lives a shy, romantic dreamer with ardent feelings, a strong national pride, a touch of melancholy, a touch of lyricism and a reforming zeal. After all, Denmark has produced Andersen, Kierkegaard, Thorvaldsen and Grundtvig. (She has also produced, curiously enough, that intense, beautiful but terrible film on witch-burning, "The Day of Wrath".) Moreover, the Danes are not mere plodding farmers or stay-at-home shopkeepers; they are adventurous seamen too. In the naval battles against Nelson and in the war with Prussia in the nineteenth century, the Danes proved themselves to be formidable and spirited fighters, and the underground movement during the Nazi occupation was by no means a schoolboys' affair.

In short, the Danes have come to terms with life. They have achieved a well-balanced community and a reasonably just economy. The people still fully enjoy living in a world which is elsewhere biting its fingernails. Unlike most other small nations (and several large ones also), she has accepted her limitations and hence does not suffer from a sense of inferiority. Denmark has heeded the sound advice of Grundtvig: "We were not born to grandeur and magnificence. To stick to the earth will serve us best."

To arrive at Oslo from Copenhagen is a revelation. The jolly, restless chatter gives place to a sense of quiet brooding. Tall, handsome, dignified people pad along like Indians on the trail or sit silently in rows below the lindens on Karl Johans Street, gazing into space. They speak rarely and then the soft, sing-song words are direct, simple and to the practical point. The Norwegians may also have come to terms with life, but the terms are more grim and more tense. Life in the bleak north, where nature is a ruthless enemy to be fought with courage and relentlessness, does not permit much frittering away of energy. Nature is not your friend, however noble, mysterious and beautiful she seems. Your friend is your own

* Published by T. Fisher Unwin, 1918.

247

sound, strong body; its training and its power is your pride and joy—your body which has learned to survive the rigours of a hard life, that can haul at the ropes untiringly till the storm is over, that can spend twenty hours of the summer day bringing in the fodder that must last through the long, bitter night of winter. The pride of the body that has survived and the courage of the spirit which helped it through—these make the dignity of the Norwegian temperament with its simplicity, its arrogance, its quiet, fatalistic stoicism, its heavy melancholy and controlled emotions.

The people have little time for the superficial things, the gay ribbons and subtleties of existence; they do not fuss like the Swedes in trying to perfect either broad organization or trivial detail; they will give you help if you ask for it, but not otherwise; they are kindly enough but undemonstrative. Less conventional than the Swedes, more so than the Danes, they reserve their feelings. Thus they do not stimulate or charm, as do the Danes. In Norway one's diaphragm is firm and controlled, but one's body is fully alive; the heart beats with slow, strong thuds and the lungs fill rhythmically with clean mountain air. It is difficult to love the Norwegian; he does not need love, for he stands firmly and independently on his own two feet ready to face the worst that life can bring. One does not love the Norwegian in that easy way one can love the Dane, for he does not "give out" as the Americans say. But one gives him full respect.

Yet, is this a true analysis? Is it not far too sweeping? The Norwegians can be lively and they enjoy gay company. They have produced highly emotional artists and writers like Munch and Ibsen. These views were obtained soon after the Second World War, and it is possible that the Occupation affected the proud Norwegians far more deeply than the easy-going Danes. That sense of cold self-containment, of withdrawal, may be the result not merely of the centuries-old fight against physical conditions but of a few fearful years of passive resistance against other human beings behaving at their Germanic worst. One remembers Norwegian friends who were not in the least like our generalization. One remembers that peasant deep in the mountains who invited one to breakfast—a magnificent old fellow, tall as a giant, upright, spare in limb, with clear blue eyes, a great beaked Viking nose, content with life, with his sturdy, smiling wife and his beloved possession—a flashing cornet on which to play the folk tunes of his valley. A lovable man, gentle and courteous, an aristocrat.

One meets the gentle, honest, free peasant in Sweden too. He is often despised by the middle-class townee and the industrial

98 (*above*) Typical houses
of about 1800

99 A rococo Doorway of a
Merchant's House (now the
Hanseatic Museum)

BERGEN

100   A mountain road north of Ulvestad

101   ROMSDAL : the Isfjord

NORWEGIAN LANDSCAPE

worker—wrongly so, for he is the backbone of his country. The Swedes also have the emotional reserve of the Norwegians but, perhaps because they are less pure as a race and have been in more frequent contact with the rest of Europe, their national characteristics are less clearly cut.

Sweden is a small country which has suddenly developed within little more than half a century from a poor agricultural nation to a wealthy industrial one, supported by a rich stock of raw materials. Thus she has done well materially, especially in being able to secure large export markets, within the framework of a world-wide financial system which refuses to equate consumption and production—a system which has had, and continues to have, such disastrous results elsewhere. Sweden has also managed to remain neutral through two world wars and has greatly benefited thereby. In Sweden life seems secure, no one is really poor and the State looks after its citizens, who now enjoy what has been described as Luxury Communism. Everything in the garden should be lovely, and yet the people do not seem to be as happy as they should be. A sense of anxiety and frustration, barely conscious, seems to hang in the air, together with a provincial smugness and an enslavement to petty conventions.

Sweden suffers, of course, from the same spiritual vacuum as do other industrialized nations with their drastic, impersonal division of labour; but industrialization may have affected her more than other countries in that the break from the age-old farming tradition has been so sudden. Clues to this half-conscious nostalgia for the land are the week-end rush for the country, the cult of the indoor plant in the cities and the universal nature worship. The urban Swede is a peasant who has lost his land and his old, deep, close contact with the soil. Adaptation to a completely new way of life may take more than two or three generations.

The Swede appears to be a practical, down-to-reality materialist, with a shallow hedonism as a basic philosophy. The purpose of life seems to end too often at the nearest *konditori*. But this is not really so, for he is not without a nagging, and may be divine, discontent, and is aware deep down, like the Dane, of a dreamy melancholia. *Stämning*, meaning more or less "atmosphere of time and place", is a popular and significant Swedish word.

The following extract from Kidder-Smith's monumental work, *Sweden Builds*,* may give a clue to the Swedish nature: "These inquisitive, inventive, athletic and healthy people . . . have as a consequence of their successes become a whiff stiff and a shade

* The Architectural Press, 1951.

staid. Their ability to run machines has convinced them that they can run themselves in their own ball bearings as so many controlled mechanical units. The State increasingly considers its citizens as so many children, and increasingly puts out controls on human activities. One cannot dance in Sweden after twelve o'clock; one cannot have a cocktail without buying something to eat; one cannot do this; one cannot do that. If this continues, the atmosphere (and this includes architecture) will become an unbearable norm of colourless mediocrity. Everyone might live to a ripe old age, but the reply might well be 'For what?' (As a not unexpected corollary of this legalistic and formal restraint, it might be added that 15 per cent of all Swedish children are illegitimate.)"

He goes on in another context: "The Swedes have accepted the revolution of the new architecture and the mechanized life more completely than any other people. . . . It is difficult to imagine their architecture in a non-socialist country. As a product of their own well-being and civilization which minimize extremes, the architecture itself shows fewer extremes (and excitement) than is found in less stabilized countries."

The designs which emerge from the large architectural office of K.F., the co-operative organization, reveals something about the Swede. It is clean, solid, earnest, worthy, practical, austere and utilitarian. One feels that everyone has done his best, driven by a remorseless pietist conscience, to make life orderly, hygienic, efficient, tidy and organized for everybody—including those who dislike being organized. It is all of sound craftsmanship carried out in excellent taste, and many of the buildings, especially the small country shops, have elegance. But it is all rather impersonal and lacks fantasy and humour. It is so *ordentligt* that one wonders how long it will be before some of its more individualistic creators will snap under the strain of this neurotic sanity and reel off to carouse with the trolls in the deep, wild forest whose verge is, after all, never far away.

Thereby, as a symbol, the K.F. architecture poses a problem of importance for the world—a problem of which the Swedes themselves are aware. The problem is this: Having attained a desirable, practical society in which all are well fed, well clothed and well housed (though, to be sure, even in Sweden the living space is still cramped); having also attained all the civic amenities, where do you go then? The welfare state has been consolidated, but still people are not happy. A kind of boredom is produced and there remains, to use a favourite Swedish word, a *längtan*—a kind of vague longing. But for what? One gropes for the answer.

Several random observations of life in Sweden today may act as pointers: (i) Education is good but highly standardized and the puberty rite of the Student Exam seems to have in it an element of cruelty. (ii) The eccentric character in Sweden is rare. (iii) In Stockholm bands of standard youths with round cheeks, immaculate mackintoshes and American hats have been reported to wander through the streets in their leisure time just breaking things up. (iv) Visitors to Sweden sense behind the polite, well-ordered provincial life a tense atmosphere of melancholy, and conversely Swedish visitors to England have experienced a great sense of relief here from this tension; they feel happier here after the first shock produced by our squalor, slackness and appalling food. (v) In spite of physical hedonism and a fair amount of sexual promiscuity, a deep, unquestioned puritanism hangs heavily in the air—of a kind which finds formal expression in the buildings of the K.F. (Of course, these criticisms are being deliberately exaggerated to make their point, and if any Swedish reader should take exception to them he must realize that the writer himself has Swedish blood and regards these searchings, to some extent, as a form of self-analysis.)

The Swedes perhaps burden themselves too heavily with an obsessional belief in perfection. The individual is given too little scope in which to exercise his personal foibles. Too much is expected of him from too early an age, especially in conformity of behaviour, and this acts against his deep sense of individualism fostered through generations on the ancient family smallholding. The Swedish temperament is, in fact, curiously paradoxical, as already stated, a mixture of Teutonic mechanical perfectionism and love of abstractions and of Anglo-Saxon individualism, earthy practicality and ability to improvize. It may be that the Swede under modern conditions cannot find enough outlet for the latter, Anglo-Saxonish, side of his nature or for his deep emotions. The violent Viking of old is in conflict with the cautious, tidy modern bourgeois (the term now includes the Worker) with his shyness, his restrictive puritanism and his, in many ways admirable, social conscience. That conflict poses a problem for the world—the problem of reconciling the deep emotional impulses, creative and destructive, of the individual with the demands and restrictions of organized society. The welfare state, whatever its physical advantages and its ethical justification, has hardly begun to try to solve that problem. For one thing, it tends to restrict the drama, the adventure and the power of the personal libido which give savour to life.

The tenseness of the Swedes may thus be the result of an ambivalent attitude towards the respective values of the community and the individual. The Swedish psychological conflict is becoming a world conflict and the basic question faces all of us : Is the individual more important than the State? Modern building is a matter of co-operation. Modern architecture, like all design, must be the result of personal expression if it is not to become boring and therefore in the end not architecture at all but merely utility building. The conflict can only be resolved in the end by a full acceptance of what mechanization and applied science can achieve in the near future— the release of the individual from enforced toil and from state regimentation to that life of leisure (i.e. freedom) in which his full personal potential can develop. We seek a condition, to use a well-known couplet of Pope on Windsor Park :

> Where order in variety we see
> And where, though all things differ, all agree.

In Sweden the suicide rate is too high, there is too much drunkenness in spite of the Bratt system of liquor rationing—surely symptoms of frustrated personal lives and inner conflicts. The divorce rate is also high, and sex relations often seem wrong. "The Orient begins at Malmö", a famous Swedish actor once remarked. By that he probably meant that the men behave towards their women like pashas. The women are too much a part of the convenient equipment of the home. Companionship between the sexes is not as easy and natural as one would suppose co-education would make it, and the cause must lie not in the immediate married relationships but further back in parental relationships. One is aware in the country of a certain pious Mother Image, a virtuous being who by the force of her character strives to keep her erring children from sin; a stern, forbidding one, who cleans and washes and sweeps without end, remorselessly instilling a sense of guilt in her offspring at an early age. She jabs her skirt down over her knees. The daughter in revolt pulls hers up, the son avenges himself on his wife, the Father (*pace* Strindberg) may sometimes go mad.

All this presents only the dark side of the Swedish character. It is counterbalanced by many splendid qualities. Sweden has borrowed much from other European countries which she has adapted to improve her own culture, especially in architecture, and she has given much to the world in her turn. The Swedish mind works slowly, deliberately and to good effect. Swedes, for instance, have discovered almost a quarter of all the known chemical elements—more than any other single nation; a significant fact. Sweden has produced, and goes on producing, great engineers and scientists, in spite of her small population. Thus she is giving more than her share to that human struggle towards the control of the economic environment, as yet only half-conscious, which, unless the moral adaptation to the new technological conditions proves to be too difficult, will soon bring about a new age of abundance, liberty and creative leisure.

Sweden has already given her people a relatively high standard of living. She leads the world in visual design. Though perhaps not the most cultured, she is the most civilized among nations. But she must not forget that we do not live by bread alone. She must realize also that something is wrong with a child who is always clean. She must never forget that the Each is always more important than the All.

SWEDISH TYPES OF THE PAST
From a drawing by Albert Engström

INDEX

Figures in heavy type indicate the most important entries; figures in italics refer to the *numbers* of the illustrations, except where the prefix *p.* shows that the page number is meant.

INDEX